THE BLURB!!

Okay, so your mate's Uncle used to be in the Navy. He has many variously coloured and differently logo'ed T-shirts from all around the world. He owns dozens of very strange 'souvenirs', and says he has been everywhere that appears on the TV or in the newspapers. He also claims to have done everything from mountain climbing to origami, and each time he opens his mouth, "When I went there", and "When I did that..." comes out.

But while he claims to have done it, you feel it may be just that he is winding you up – for he can never relate the same story in exactly the same way, no matter how many times he tells it, or how sober he is(n't) when he re-tells it.

But I did do it, and I did go there, and I can relate them too. So here are all the stories you caught half of, but didn't quite get the gist of, or missed completely, or didn't care about, following the career of a growing lad, caught between the ages of sixteen and twenty-seven, between leaving school and getting married, between a raw, green, spotty kid, and a very world-wise young man.

This book traces a fairly typical Naval career from start to finish, embracing all the activities of a life (of Riley) on the Ocean Wave. Oh yes, and some of the runs ashore, and the other extraneous activities too. You'll never wave back at warships again when the sailors wave to you as you sail past in the 'Saucy Sue' on your holiday trip round the harbour...

...And you'll always wonder why not – IF YOU DON'T READ THIS BOOK!!!

Published by Futures Publications, London
www.futurespublications.co.uk

ISBN: 1 87 1131 17 0

Printed and bound in England by Tandem Press – *www.tandempress.com*

When I was on the TARTAR

...And other Sea Stories.

An Autobiography

by

Michael Payne,

(Leading Seaman, R.N. (Retd.))

Contents

Foreword

In His Dedication, the author reminds us that it has been said "There is a book inside everyone...". For most of us that is where it stays – inside – but Michael Payne has fulfilled a desire to tell his story – the story of twelve years spent in the Senior Service : The Royal Navy. Enlisting at sixteen, the period covers his transition from boyhood to manhood, although it would seem the Navy makes no allowances for youth, and also disregards age in its demands and expectations.

The story is post-war, so there are no epic battles relived here. On the contrary, there is much about having a good time: visits to foreign places, much drinking, joking, teasing, and testing the limits of tolerance – sometimes of comrades, sometimes of those in command. Camaraderie was the essence of life ashore and no doubt an essential ingredient in the cramped conditions of a small metal ship subjected to the rigours of sailing in storm force conditions.

Some readers may find the language offensive – the slang terms, the swearing and the obscenities – but anyone who has served in the forces will know the author is portraying life as it really is in those spheres. An expurgated version would placate the sensitive mind, but would also be unreal.

For ex-matelots this book will revive memories of their own experiences and escapades. Others will find it enlightening and the racy style makes it an enjoyable read.

Admiral Sir (John) Jeremy Black GBE, KCB, DSO
Commander-In-Chief, Naval Home Command, 1989 – 1991

Introduction

I'll explain now – *my* TARTAR was a sleek, shiny, grey-painted, Type 81 frigate built in the early '60s, bristling with guns and missiles, radar's and matey-ness, two funnels, and a pennant number of F133. It was not her more famous predecessor of the line, which took part in that savage battle during the Second World War. Though, coincidentally, that one had Ludovic Kennedy as their 'gunner', and I met him when he came aboard us one fine day at sea. I was on watch in the gloom room, and he chatted with us for a while. Talking of television personalities; Richard Baker (the BBC newsreader) also came aboard us one day – he was an RNR (so would have otherwise been totally ignored by us) two-and-a-half-ringer, and I couldn't get over how short he was. He, however, didn't want to talk to us, preferring to stay in the wardrobe (wardroom). See – only the first paragraph of the introduction, and the first two sea-stories have made an appearance already.

Although I served on many other ships and several more shore bases, my Tartar was the best ship I was ever drafted to, and as you will see, it is where most of my better memories originate. I often wondered whether she ended up as a target, or if she had a more dignified end, serving out her own years having been sold on to some other navy, which – in fact – she fortunately was. Apparently, she is still going strong around Indonesia.

My story, then, is one of a young man growing up in the navy of the 1970s', and, as it is totally about my own experiences of sealife, everything is therefore very much first hand.

There was never a time when I stood and thought "In fuck's name, what am I doing this for?", although many was the time I thought "I don't want to be doing this". The difference being between wanting to be out of the Navy doing something else with my life right now, and wanting to be immediately in my bed, instead. Does that make sense to you? Most of the time I spent entirely committed to serving my country in the Navy was absolutely brilliant, a four thousand day adventure, with memories I will treasure, and with deeds being plotted and/or perpetrated and exploits being snatched in the moment, that I will remember forever, even if I would prefer to forget some of them…

The maxim of my day was "If you can't fuckin' take a fuckin' joke – you shouldn't have fuckin' well joined". That was so, so true. As was "Not so fuckin' jolly now – are we, Jack!!" in times of stress, guaranteed to get an instant reaction. Or a smacking if you didn't get away fast enough, or duck whatever sharp or heavy (or both) object was thrown at you.

The title is based on the Naval tradition of telling sea-stories, generally starting with "When I was on the…" or "When I was ashore in…". These stories would get wilder as they were told, finishing with the words "Black cat that then", with someone else coming in with an even better story being told, followed by others, all trying to outdo, or further 'Black-Cat' each other. The 'stopper' to all these was "Listen sonny, I was in Baghdad before you were in your Dad's bag". Or we would make sealike swishing noises whilst pretending to swing an oil lamp around to embarrass the storyteller into silence, which would normally be followed by indignant cries of "I'm tellin yer I did", or "Ask so-and-so, he saw/heard/felt/smelt it too". Every sailor past or present, any time, anywhere will have a large repertoire of 'black cats' or sea stories, most of which will be mostly true, though they must sometimes be taken with a pinch of salt as 'narrators licence' occasionally creeps in. Still, if you weren't there, then however it happened, you clearly cannot disagree or argue with it as it is retold, can you.

This book is full of perfectly true Black Cats, sorry – yarns, related exactly as I remember them, and even now when I meet 'ex' jack, and we find out that we were both 'mob', it is impossible to hold a sensible conversation for too long. You will always both know someone, or know of someone, or have heard about something – and then continue with these inevitable sea stories.

I was in the Royal Navy between 1969 and 1980, during a surprisingly peaceful era. We discovered we could always create our own trouble, without any help from thoughtless and interfering politicians, but I was nevertheless extremely proud to have been part of such a professional band of men. If you were there around then, I may have run into you, or across you, but I definitely didn't go through you, even though I may have GOT through to you.

They say 'Join the Navy and see the World'. Well, I did, and I did. And it really made a man of me. Well that's my opinion, and I should know – I did the time, I did the runs, I did it all, in ten and a half very short years. And yes, I do say "Been there" and "Seen that" and "Did that" – ask my wife and boys how many times I see an 'Atlantic 21' and say "I used to drive one of those…"!!!!!

It is hoped that at least some of the people referred to in the book will eventually read it, and will indeed recognise themselves. (In fact, several people have, and have contacted me, to my delight.) If you are one of those people who knew me, and are shown in a good light you are fortunate – I probably got on well with you, and I hope you have done well with your life. If on the other hand, I portray you in a bad light it is because you were, in my (and many other people's eyes), tossers – and I do NOT mean the 'bunting' type. You were tosser enough to attempt to, or even think you would attempt to make my life (and probably your own and others) a misery, but also tosser enough to think you could get on in the Navy, doing the tosser things you did, in the tosser way you did them. You therefore – unwittingly or otherwise – antagonized everybody else, you clearly enjoyed missing out on all those runs' ashore, you surely dipped out on all that camaraderie and friendship, and, above all you were oblivious of the total fun the rest of us were having while you watched from the scuppers. The Navy, you see, was all about teamwork, and if you weren't part of that team, you were left by yourself on the edge, looking in at everyone else having mostly very good fun. Together. You ask anyone who served – they will always tell you about the good times they had, and will rarely remember the bad days, much less remember and relate them. Unless they were those very same miserable shites still in those scuppers…

Nevertheless, however badly I regarded you, you only succeeded in reducing my good days to tolerable, and I probably disregarded your entire existence anyway, because I along with many others, worked like that. I still do – I cannot under any circumstances tolerate idiots or idiotic behaviour (or lateness, or slowness – if you found yourself behind someone dawdling up the Burma Road, you could at least curse roundly at them to their face, try that in a city street). It is something the Navy taught me. If you had to rely on fools, it could get extremely dangerous, so you saved a lot of time, and found you were better off to do it yourself. At least then you knew it would be done, properly, first time, even if it did mean doing it in your own time.

Even so, whoever you thought you were, and however much grief you thought you had given me – I always had the last laugh on you, and I always got my own back, and I still do. BELIEVE ME!! And if you fit this latter category, I hope you are still the, miserable, depressing, unpopular, objectionable, arrogant (pick your own adjective) arsehole I always had you down as. I'm positive you WILL know who you are, and you WILL be able to recognise yourself, won't you? I'll bet you're going red in the face even now. You DO know, don't you…

You may even recognise some of the events I describe – again, good for you – it would be nice to find someone who knows this isn't all made up.

The Royal Navy was, if anything, a 'quiet' service. After basic training there was none of this shouting and screaming of orders, nor that crabfat/squaddie '1-2-1-2getyourbleedinaircutsonny' business, just measured statements. Of course, if it was on the fo'c's'le in a force six, or in the middle of nowhere you'd have to shout, or while carrying out guard duties or something similar. But normally, you quietly asked/told someone to do something, and you got on and did it. You knew how long you'd be confined to the same small area of grey space together for, and knew how either side could make life more difficult, so orders were obeyed, immediately, and mostly instinctively. Unless you felt like annoying someone…

'Disobeying A Direct Order' was just about therefore the most serious crime you could commit, and one you could expect to get liberally lashed up for. So, while the book apparently describes the life of Riley we normally enjoyed, we were ALWAYS aware just how close to the wind we could sail, and still get away with it. Mind you, the threat of being "…down on your head like a ton of shit, Jack" was enough to forestall most direct conflicts between us and our 'superiors'. I nearly said 'betters' there, but that wouldn't be telling the truth, nor would it be doing anyone any favours. One thing that always left most ratings (including me) pissed off beyond all belief, was having to actually salute an officer we KNEW was a total waste of good oxygen, (and believe me, we met several) but knowing that we were duty bound to salute anyway, on threat of punishment if we didn't. We justified the 'salute' in this case by claiming we were recognising ONLY the uniform and therefore The Sovereign, but most DEFINITELY NOT the pigs-bastard inside it. As all lower-deck hated wardroom anyway, this justification was quite frequent, as was the epithet.

'Baiting', or 'winding-up' was a popular past-time, enjoyed by everyone in the mob. This is where you deliberately sit goading or needling someone, even if it's your bezzy run ashore oppo, by talking about various things you know annoy them. Like their crap footy team, or the ugliness or previous sexual experience you already had with his current party, or the fact that he still can't back-splice nylon, until you got him to flash up. You would then dance round shrieking "you bit, you bit", or be off running up the Burma Road with him behind you carrying a marling spike, or worse.

It was always more fun with civvies, as (unless we were 'trapping') half the time we considered them to be too dumb to realise what you were doing, especially if they were 'dockies', and dockies were definitely in a league of their own. We pondered and pondered as to how dockies managed keep their knuckles clear of the deck as they moved, or how they remembered to breathe unaided. Nevertheless, baiting was something we did easily – unthinkingly, and continuously. If nothing else, it passed the more monotonous off-watch times at sea. Clearly, the bigger and better the bite, the more we enjoyed it, the higher the authority of the person we targeted, again – the more we would enjoy the response. I wonder what trick-cyclists would have made of us – probably they'd have put it down to attention seeking.

Some days it would backfire, and we'd be getting the shitty end of the pineapple. We'd then look at the person baiting us, and snarl "You don't have the fuckin' brains to wind me up..." And continue what we were doing, absolutely seething inside, ready to tear his head off and shit down the hole in his neck. As we used to say. Or sometimes, (in pure stress, you understand), we'd knock the daylights out of him anyway. Nothing too severe, just enough to serve as a warning to others. Whoever started it would then ask "Got a shitty on then, Jack??" We just couldn't leave it alone...

So, you'll find that a lot of the escapades in here, were 'wind-ups'. Done to annoy someone. Done to get a reaction. Like doing a drunken Zulu warrior in a hotel full of naïve civvies, or singing filthy songs to them about lobsters, or steam-powered willies, or whatever else it required, to this totally unsuspecting 'audience'. I sincerely hope today's 'tars' are still permitted to continue with this tradition, as it would be a great shame to think this particular sociable and very matey aspect of naval life has evaporated.

To my mind – and indeed, to the mind of every matelot I have met since I left – one of the most stupid things 'The Admiralty' (and I'd much prefer to blame politicians anyway) have done in recent years, is to allow women to serve on front-line ships. Women, in the really old days, were considered to be bad luck aboard ships, and many of my erstwhile shipmates still feel that way. Two arbitrary, illogical reasons for this comment on the Admiralty's' wisdom immediately spring to mind :- one during 'drill' at Raleigh, the instructors would, on standing us 'at ease', scream "...getchyer legs further apart – nothin's gonna fall out". Well – will it? Secondly, if whilst 'plotting' radar contacts on the old LOP, you reached across the table to update a contact you were tracking, and you got in the way, you would be conversationally told to "...getchyer fuckin' tits off the table". Can this type of 'communication' still take place? I reckon not, which makes the Navy a sadder place, as this everyday banter has probably been reduced or eradicated. That banter helped to pass the time, and was always a key part of naval life, at all levels, at all times, without the fear of being 'trooped' on 'Conduct prejudice to good order and naval discipline'. That is to say "Can't get you on anything else in the book, so we'll do you on this one"

More logically, and more personally, I would NOT like to trust my life to a splitarse. For a start, they are not built or designed to go to sea. It was bad enough for me attempting to keep my balance in the middle of a Mid-Atlantic force ten, coming off watch after four hours scanning a radar screen, dog tired and irritable as hell, and hungrily struggling to carry my scran on a tray to a table, while using my other two hands to brace myself against anything available as the ship both pitched and yawed simultaneously whilst in passage with the swell off the bow. Or trying to remain coherent and report radar contacts to the bridge whilst three thousand tons of grey painted ship slammed into the next milestone, smashing me and my mates yet again into the unforgiving steel of the bulkheads or, on occasions – deckheads. Or when I (on countless occasions) physically strapped myself into my pit while the blunt end corkscrewed around, trying (and on occasions succeeding) to eject me from it, as – after yet another sleepless night – I waited for the 0345 'shake' for the morning watch. And these are just some of the easier bits. The sod was, that it was impossible to play uckers on a table pitched at 45 degrees – the 'blobs' wouldn't stay on!!

Of course, just to help me sleep better in these conditions I could be fortunate enough to sleep in the aft messdeck, and have the massive phosphor-bronze screws right beneath me, which would race and vibrate the entire ship whenever the arse end lifted out of the water, giving me another unnecessary awakening from my already light doze. Or if I slept amidships, the machinery powering the stabilisers (when they worked) below me would be fighting noisily to keep the ship on a (more) even keel. Or the gash-nasher could scream away above my head, trying to digest some dopey sod's knife. No wonder whenever we cleared a storm, we (from the skipper, right down to his steward, and down even further to the ship's cementhead) all slept at standeasy instead of continuing with our usual pratting around. Of course, we quickly recovered as soon as we heard the pipe "Secure – shore leave for port watch and first starboard will commence at…"…

In my day, as nobody ever fancied their oppo (contrary to popular belief we hated and detested fairies, and they were NEVER in evidence in my day), so we never needed to dress attractively, so we never worried about what we wore at sea, so we never found it necessary to overdress. Soooo, one of our 'rigs' for relaxing whilst off-watch after our scrobie, would be flip-flops, towel, and (if particularly cold) a well used and favourite T-shirt. It's doubtful if that is still allowed when splits are on the prowl. And I really cannot imagine Jennies (as were) stamping round frigates, themselves dressed in that same rig – I can imagine the comments from here. Or are they 'confined' to their own messdeck at sea? Come off it!

If 'Their Lordships' really imagine it is possible to keep sailors and splits apart, my answer to that is – cobblers. When I served, we would always, and easily find somewhere to slide off to and not be found until we emerged under our own volition, normally some considerable time later – it stands to reason those compartments are still available. The cable lockers' spring to mind, as does the deep radar office, and any switchboard room, and nobody EVER went into the 'tiller flat' voluntarily... But during the silent hours the ship would be your oyster, you would be able to go anywhere, even to the extent of sneaking a bath in the officers bathroom. Not an easy feat in a gale!! And when we had to 'shake' people to relieve us on watch, how exactly do you wake up a sleeping jenny without being accused of harassment? We used to prod our messmates in the ribs, or shine the torch right in their eyes to rouse them, do that to a split 'at the wrong time of the month', and you'd be on an attempted rape charge. Or worse – engaged to be married to it.

Ashore, where they were safe from harm, they were very competent at what they did – writing, cooking, stewarding etc – and most were petite, or attractive, but rarely both. Those that didn't fit either of the latter categories, would be accused of being 'Sea-King kick-starters', or 'Dumper-trucks'. Not only all that, but eventually they would suffer from 'fat ankle' syndrome (pregnancy), swelling up a lot, thereby using up more valuable space on board. If I come over as at all sexist – it is no accident. I – and many others – do NOT think it was a wise decision to let women on ships. I would also feel that now they allow these women on to Royal Navy ships, a lot of the tricks we used to get up to, and the stunts we used to pull are nowadays forbidden. Or heavily curtailed. If you fit into this repressed category, read on – you may resurrect some old ideas.

In any case, nearly every recent court-martial I have read about in the daily papers, has concerned 'Jack' (I use the term loosely, covering anything in the RN that is male) and a split. Whether or not Jack has touched, insulted, sworn at, had an affair with one (or two), or whatever, it is always Jack who invariably comes off second best in the eyes of the public. But whenever the split is described, it is then told that she has been discharged 'on grounds of temperamental unsuitability'. They also cite the fact that they sleep badly and suffer from emotional instability and seasickness. No Shit!! Why am I not surprised? I am also reliably informed, that when ships with splits get alongside, the splits go *back* to being just doggo...

Along with my shipmates, I visited well over a hundred different ports around the world, many of them more than once, and most of them were tremendously enjoyable and memorable, for one reason or another. I also went on numerous inland visits to see many more places clearly inaccessible by sea. I feel very fortunate to have done what I did, and to have been where I went, and to have seen what I saw, as since my days, the RN has been shrunk by faceless, spiritless politicians and bureaucrats to such an extent that it would be difficult for today's sailors to visit so many different places in such a relatively short period of time.

In between bouts of creating or receiving trouble, one thing most matelots did a vast amount of, while relaxing both at sea or if in harbour on duty, was read. If you were reading, it was generally assumed you did not want to talk to anyone. If you stuck your cassette player headphones on AND read, to disturb you could be like prodding a rattlesnake – the reaction would be instantaneous, vehement, and directed four-square at you. You would normally be given two choices – "Fuck off, or I'll fuck you off".

We had little lights on the 'buggery boards' that separated our adjacent pits, and many was the night someone's light would still be on while everyone else slept.

Personally, I could bang through a standard paperback in a little over an hour. Books on ships were like currency, we'd always be raiding other messdecks to swap books, and would never in any circumstances read the same book twice. Good books then, were at a premium, but we would wade through shitkickers to sci-fi, historic novels to 'Confessions of a...', Russian authors with unpronounceable names to Loius L'Amour to James Herbert, Mayfair to Commando comics, even Seamanship manuals took a beating – anything to pass the off-watch hours.

Occasionally, we'd find a really good read, but the rest used to be given 'the float test' down the gash chute which was permanently rigged off the blunt end of the ship as we steamed towards our next destination, whilst dreaming of the next nosh-up after the next beers during the next run ashore.

In one book – I don't remember where I read it, but it contained a 'Naval Curse'

"Oh Lord Above,
Send down a Dove,
With Wings as sharp as Razors
To cut the Throats,
Of them there Blokes,
Wot sells Bad Beer to Sailors."

I remember that even now and often, while ashore, wished it to be true. But most of the others I read made little immediate impact never mind a lasting impression.

Anyway, I hope all my hard work doesn't end up as a floater, but whatever your viewpoint – ENJOY THE BOOK!!

Acknowledgments

The acknowledgments for this book are made to many thousands of people – to those I went ashore with, and those I met while ashore, to those I drank with, ate with, swore at, played cards with, learned from, taught seamanlike skills to, taught antisocial things to, trained with, lent money to, borrowed money from, sang with, did favours for, swam with, saw things with, 'subbed' for, did rare, stupid and often dangerous things with, turned to with, did basin trials with, threatened, tied bends with, tied bends on, went on benders with, learned things from, taught un-seamanlike skills to, tied hitches with, tied hitches on, laughed at, laughed with, cried with, performed with, cursed at, got frustrated with, played uckers with and more often than not beat, threw uckers tables at if I should lose, threw wobblies at, threw spikes and chipping hammers at, did innumerable other, various, assorted, unmentionable, and best forgotten things with and, if I've omitted anyone above – all those who remember serving alongside me. I probably wouldn't recognize you nowadays if I ran over you, however, I still think about you, good or bad, and about the times we were forced to share.

I have, though, deliberately omitted you from the above list if you either accidentally or deliberately gave me the ache, as I also refused to accept you into my life at the time. I hope you have subsequently had a bad life, because on the form you had when I knew you – you very much deserve it. There is a simple rule – if I went ashore with you, or spoke to you ashore, you were probably classed as a 'good hand'. If I spoke to you onboard, voluntarily, you were probably a good hand, but I never got around to proving it. Otherwise...

However, and notwithstanding the previous disclaimer, I acknowledge, and above all happily wish well, all those people who gave me their friendship and trust, as I, in return, gave mine to, and I thank all those very same people who gave me that trust and friendship during my Naval Days. If you ever met me, you will know who you are.

I will remember you for the rest of my life, especially if you served between 1969 and 1980, on the Achilles, Active, Aisne, Ajax, Albion, Antrim, Apollo, Arethusa, Agronaut, Ark-Shark, Ashanti, Blake, Bristol, Bagshanty, Bellerophon, Bulwark, Cavalier, Cherry-B, Chichester, Beachampton, Brighton, 'The Britt', Bulwark, Cleo, Coventry, Dainty, Danae, Devonshire, Didlo, Dundas, Eagle, Eastbourne, Euryalus, Eskimo, Kent, Kepple, Euryalus, Exmouth, Grenville, Minerva, Falmouth, Fearless, Exmouth, Minerva, Mohawk, Glamorous-Organ, Tigger, Stinkin-Lincoln, Llandaff, Salisbury, Raving-J (Juno, you work it out!!), Gurkha, Grenville, Hardy, Hampshire, Herpes, Hermi-One, Naiad, Intrepid, Lowestoft, Penelope, Scarborough, Whitby, Yarmouth, Phoebe, Rothesay, Rhyl, Torquack, Scylla, Sirius, Triumph, Ulster, London, Kent, Nubian, Norfolk, Unwanted or Tenby, or anybody else I saw in the distance.

Also, those who RAS'd with me from Olmeda, Olna, Olwen, Tiddlypoo, Tidespring, Blue Rover, or any other RFA during that time.

Also, anyone who served ashore (remember shore drafts?) in Cochrane, Rooke, Dolphin, Osprey, Raleigh, Dryad, Drake, Excellent, Vernon, Sultan, Collingwood, Mercury, Malabar, Victory, President, Tamar, St Angelo, Terror or Nelson.

I mention all these ships and bases, as I either visited, exercised with, chatted to over VHF, tied up alongside, or got 'called round' during my 'career'.

I will also never forget you if you were on any of the ships sunk by those bastard Argies, just after I was discharged. I cried for days whenever I watched that on the tele. I had mates on the Sheffield, the Coventry and the Amazon, and I can't bear to watch it when they show it, Even now, even reading this let alone writing it, it still makes me cry.

But my thanks and memories go most especially those who were with me on the Zulu (1970-1972), Tartar (1973-1976), Plymouth (1977-1978), Londonderry (1979-1980), or Raleigh, Dryad, Victory (Nelson), Cochrane or Osprey while I was there. Good luck fellas!!

I would also like to thank the trustees and staff of the Royal Navy Museum who first printed my story, especially Chris Howard Bailey (who admitted that the original manuscript was the first she'd ever read 'in one hit'), also (ex-Commander, RN) Alastair Wilson who 'proofed' it for me, and lastly Admiral J J Black for his contribution. Also, thanks to Dr Jim Wallace who got involved with this first reprint when I started to work with him, and when we suddenly discovered we 'served' at the same time. Imagine the discussions!!

My final acknowledgement goes to my Uncle Cyril (my Mum's sister's husband)who did me the great honour of reading this book while it was in it's infancy. He was in the RN for a short period, but is one of the reasons I pressed on with this project. He – and my Aunt – are both quite religious you see, and it was with great trepidation that I asked him to read the rough (as in flowery, not jagged) copy of the manuscript. I had thought that if he didn't appreciate the stories and the swearing, then nobody would. When I next saw him, he laughed out loud, and pointed out that without the rawness, it wouldn't really portray 'life in a Blue Suit'. After some discussion we decided to keep that intentional, flowery' style.

Dedication

This is dedicated to my Wife & boys – Jan, Nick & Andrew, and my Mum and (now passed away) Dad. Without the fourth & fifth I would never have been in a position to write it – without the first I would never have bothered!

I further apologise to my wife, for all the Saturday afternoons, and other evenings I have spent writing this, when I could, according to her, have been helping her in the garden! Mind you, I do cook Sunday lunch…

I also dedicate it to the memory of a great inspiration to me – Mr. Alan Chalker who I met only briefly before he died, suddenly. He took great delight in showing me the book he was researching, on the Military careers' of his ancestors.

They say there is a book inside everyone, waiting to get out. I regard Alan as my catalyst. Perhaps he really was the trigger I had been waiting for, and I thank him (and his ancestors) for that.

Chapter 1

September, 1969: Baby Sailors: My First Few Days

It was a normal morning for the rest of the population of Northampton as I stood on the grey southbound platform of the Castle Station, and waved good-bye to my Dad. But the only thing signaled was the end of my childhood, and of my life up until that day, up until that time, when I used my free ticket sent by the Navy, boarded the Euston train, en route to a place called Torpoint, with instructions to call on the vicar who christened me all those years ago.

What had started as a choice I had to make, between the RAF as a pilot or the Navy as an anything, (but under NO circumstances did I ever consider being a common squaddie in the army) was made by me when I decided not to wait for my GCE results, but to go in the Navy anyway. An inspired decision as it turned out – I didn't pass enough exams at that time to get me flying in the RAF. Fortunate really, as I later found out that while everybody loathes squaddies, and while the RAF (as the most junior service) is also merely tolerated by all other servicemen, the Royal Navy was not only the Senior Service – as the oldest established armed force – but clearly, far and away: the best. This is not just my opinion – ask anyone who has ever taken the Queens shilling. We frequently met people who had transferred from the other services to us, but never met anyone deserting us for them. The other reason I really fancied the Royal, was – believe it or not – because of 'Yorks', the local Northampton coach company whose vehicles ran with the names of RN ships on them, so names like 'Matapan', and 'Cossack' had long been influencing me.

Eventually, that biggest day of my life was upon me. I had taken and passed all the entrance tests at the Royal Navy and Royal Marine recruiting centre in Derngate, Northampton, right opposite where I used to catch the bus home from school every day for five years. I was given an official, free travel warrant and subsequently gone by myself on the train to Derby (having first caught the bus to and changed at Kettering), for the entrance medical. It was there I had my hearing, and sight vigorously tested to determine my ability to distinguish between different sounds and pitches, and between ever so slightly different coloured pinpricks of light. It was apparent at this early stage, that applicants were already being screened. Those who passed these tests, but who didn't know what they wanted to do were being guided towards being sailors, especially radar or sonar operators, hence the emphasis on eyes and ears.

I had proved my ability to cough properly while someone put their hand down my Y-fronts and tampered with my goolies, had everything else tested, and finally been offered the role of Junior Seaman, which was odd, because up to then, I had actually thought I wanted to be a chef. Fortunately, after thinking how hot it would get cooking in a already hot galley, whilst sailing around hot, tropical climates : common sense prevailed, and I accepted the offer the Navy made me. I was possibly also swayed by the monochrome booklets I had been sent, showing 'sailors' having a good time, while chefs and things looked like they were working.

Soon after, I was sent this second free travel pass with detailed travelling instructions and times, with orders to join H.M.S. Raleigh, at Torpoint in Cornwall, and now finally, the day was upon me, here I was – the train doors slammed, off I went. Pastures New. All I had was what I wore, plus washing equipment as described in the official literature supplied by H.M.S. Raleigh. What was going to happen? Now I couldn't see familiar faces, great trepidation crept up on me, growing all the time.

I had previously been sent the booklet entitled 'Beginning to be a Sailor', which I had read, frequently, from cover to cover, though it was really more of a guide for worried parents. It still gave me no inkling of what was in store for the next decade and more of my life. Of where I would travel. Of what I would see when I got there. What I did know was 'that it would make a man of me'. All my relatives had told me that, especially my Uncle Cyril, who joined the navy centuries ago (it seemed), only to be pronounced colour-blind, and quickly discharged. However he wasn't a blood relative, nor was colour-blindness catching...

The first thing was to pass through Rothersthorpe tunnel, where I had just a few yeas before played, daring myself to run through the tunnel on foot, not knowing if there would be a train, not knowing whether to believe "those who had done it", who assured me there were small tunnels inside, where one could hide if the fiery steamies ever did hurtle through... I used to content myself with putting pennies on the track – like my Dad, and (apparently) his Dad used to do before me – watching the steamy make the copper coin even flatter as it sped over it, marvelling at the new resultant shape.

I never used to bother to tell Mum about these escapades – she had enough to worry about then. And anyway she was now behind me, probably already at work, where Dad was now on his way to, very likely via the Railway Canteen where he ate his dinner every day, then purchased large wedges of fruit cake, which he wrapped and took back for his afternoon break. Was my Mum as upset as Dad clearly was? I cannot remember now – my mind was on all manner of other things.

But here was the daylight at the end of that particular tunnel, and the first Monday of September 1969, and me travelling alone, on my way to Plymouth. Not that I had never travelled alone before – I was well equipped to do so. Hadn't I recently come back from a weeks' sailing holiday around the river Blackwater in Essex, covered in gnat bites and love bites, and with a badly gashed foot! That was all under the watchful eye of the local youth club. Before that, because I had relatives in Matlock, I had already become a seasoned traveller, being able to find my way from Northampton to Matlock, via Leicester (or was it Nottingham) and Derby on the bus, being collected and toured via the famous twisted spire of Chesterfields' church remembering the route my uncle drove, the JET garage he filled up at, then getting there and going walkabouts, from one end of Matlock up to Riber Castle the hard way, and back, and there again, and round the local mills, wondering at the varied stream colours – none of which were natural, due to the high concentration of woollen mills round those parts.

I had also been in the Scouts for years, caught (and severely punished) a kid from another part of town stealing from OUR scout hut, gone to scout camp for a week in the rain at Heythrop in Oxfordshire, pushed the trek-cart, made clanger, fought very popular wide games, been asked to leave for taking my bike on what should have been a hike – which we would surely have got away with had it not been for my puncture, and plaintive phone call for help long after we were due home. After all I had put in, shouldn't I have had a second chance? Still, all my mates quit in sympathy, so someone must have felt I was short-shrifted. I had done all the usual things like played 'tracking' in the local woods, blocked and unblocked every stream within miles, and had drunk Watneys IPA in a pub, at lunchtime in school uniform on Speech Day, scoffing Polos' all afternoon to cover the smell. A normal childhood really, with all the usual girlfriends, school, holidays and outings that made up our pre-adolescent little lives.

And then I was at Euston Station, and navigating my way across London to Paddington, finding and boarding the large, maroon but grubby diesel hauled train, travelling to Plymouth. So now here were more like me – nervous, spotty, beardless sixteen year olds, in a train which smelled like all the other trains, of cheap smoke and thousands of previous travellers, all of us on the verge of 'bin there', 'seen it', 'dun it'. We talked, the kids in my part of the carriage, and especially myself and a lad called Arthur, from a town in Essex I had never heard of (actually – Rainham), who talked excitedly about

Speedway racing. I was half torn between chatting to him, then, and gawping at the wonderful scenery on the South Devon coastal line – as that is where we now were, having left civilisation behind us long ago. I had never been to that part of the world before, and as with many things since – it did not seem relevant or possible that it would be weeks, months even, before we travelled it again. Nor how many times I'd travel the route after that. The changes that may be made to me between those future trips were not even a thought in the...

We would never have dreamed of attempting to buy alcohol from the buffet on THAT train – didn't even know we could get away with it, so it was with dry mouths' all round for more than one reason that we drew into Plymouth Station.

We were met by officious naval 'people' of unknown rank (to us at that time, so to be safe we addressed them all as 'Sir'), who ushered us into big blue coaches, with RN emblazoned on the side, for the trip to Torpoint. Nothing registered on that trip, except that as we got to the unexpected ferry, we all craned out of the windows to see the sea – like any tourists, really, the enormity of what we were about to do had still not yet sunk home. Not on that day at least.

Due to the appalling weather that day, we could not see the warships, but gossip assured us they were there, then suddenly we were across the Tamar, and driving off the ferry. I still do not understand why you only pay one way on that ferry – do they hate each other that much? I do not remember there was ever a war between them...

On reaching H.M.S. Raleigh, we debussed into a life and existence I never expected – but something I still experience dreams about even now.

I don't really know what I or my new-found oppos' expected to see, or what my first excited impressions would be as they are always difficult. Although I'd seen the field gunners and the Royal Tournament, and perhaps I expected them to be greeting us, and perhaps I also thought I would see frigates and destroyers gliding down the main road towards the vast parade ground, but anyway a naval base named after a great sea hero should have had more than a couple of silvery-looking cannons, and acres of grass, tarmac and wooden huts – shouldn't it? Okay, it had a sea view (when the tide was in the estuary we overlooked), and just a few sailors stamping about with round white hats on, but I was not impressed yet.

Maybe our bewildered reactions were transparent, for suddenly we were accosted by a short, black-uniformed (sleeves covered in red badges), red-faced shouting individual, demanding our attention, and perhaps that was the idea, him being there to distract us from our wool-gathering, forcing us to concentrate on our new lives. He indicated in fluent anglo-saxon, that we were here because we had chosen to be, that here we were to be for the next sixteen weeks in some cases, and that if we were not prepared for it, we could get back on the bus and go home to mummy now. Or at least that's what it should have come across as. He was rather more graphic and succinct, even to my previously trained ears.

Those of us who remained – for surprisingly few actually ran off there and then – were herded together, fallen in 'one behind the other twice' – i.e., three deep, and then 'marched' (gentle left wheel, right wheel…) to the New Entry Block, which lay out of bounds to the rest of the Raleigh personnel, and subsequently shown where we were to sleep later, what to do next, and when it would happen.

So, we were left then, with a person we were told to call Pee Oh. That was expanded by (there was always one, even then) the ex sea-scout. "That is a petty officer" he explained, tiresomely. "Known as a PO."

I got talking to the kid in the bed above mine – two things registered, one was that I was in a bunkbed, which I had got to make by myself with the supplied sheets, blankets etc, secondly I actually knew him! He had left my school some time before me, and had actually left the area – but now here was Glen in the bunk above me. We became good friends over the next few weeks, and beyond.

Later that evening, after we'd been fed, and while we were chattering – excitedly (still), and then again after 'lights out', and amidst people calling out "whatever you're doing now – don't", and the resulting sniggering, and among the muffled sobbings – I suppose we eventually fell asleep… …But then almost immediately – it seemed – we wondered what the hell was the noise, when milliseconds after, the messdeck door exploded inwards and all the lights were thrown on, followed by the Duty PO who stormed in, shouting at us to "get your hands off your cocks, and onto your socks", and, conversationally, – "get your fucking feet on the deck, two six". That was bearable, and made us giggle nervously, like schoolgirls. The next surprise was the large metal ashtray (known throughout the navy as a spitkin) being kicked down the mess ahead of the PO. This came to be accepted as the standard, though noisy, early morning alarm call, usually moments after 'Call The Hands' was bugled on the tannoy around the camp. Which we learned to ignore, gaining valuable extra seconds in a warm bed, knowing the Duty PO would be there, any second NOW"!!!

Our first job of that and every following day, was that of making these beds up Navy Fashion – nothing loose or saggy, no rough edges, taut counterpane, complete with right-way-up anchor design (that is – right way up, and not inside out either), smoothed out pillowcases. We washed and (some of us) shaved off the overnight gathering of bumfluff, which was why everyone called everyone else 'Skin', as we were to find out. We then gathered together (soon to be 'mustered') outside the Nissen hut we were to call 'home' for the next week, before being 'marched' to breakfast, where we queued around lengths of metal poles, as you would queue for a fairground ride. Due to the sheer numbers serving behind the counter, we quickly reached the front, chose and ate whatever we wanted, providing we could bolt it down in three minutes flat, a precedent set, and a resultant habit that I have tried unsuccessfully for years to break. I remember there being a vast spread all along this huge cafeteria type counter, with not only cereal, but fried acres of sausages, bacon, greasy eggs, fried bread, mushrooms, tomatoes, bread & butter, baked beans (for breakfast?), and vast tanks of tea. And milk. And toast. After several minutes luxuriating in this, we were 'marched' back, and told to make ourselves ready for the Joining Routine.

We started this Joining Routine later the same morning, with a talk by the Captain Weir R.N. of H.M.S. Raaahlly (not Rally as we all read it), during which – amongst other things – he explained what we had volunteered for, commended us on our commitment, warned us things would get tougher, smiled, and left. So, we drew our oilskins and had our teeth inspected – the cue for some painful dental work, and not just for me. I had spent most of my short life in a small village just outside Northampton (Hardingstone actually, now almost subsumed by Northampton) and it had not occurred to me up until that time, how many different types of people there were, all ostensibly British. There were short, fat, tall, thin, odd, quiet, noisy, chatty, sullen, ugly, normal, mouthy, too-clever, thick, absolutely bone kids there, all of my own age, but who – because none of us could at that time understand each other's accents – we all thought the others were foreign, from unlikely places like Scotland, Devon, Berwick, Hull, Chichester, Essex or Derby. As I said, up until then it had not even registered that other people lived in faraway places in the country, much less that they would all congregate on Torpoint with their peculiar accents and colloquialisms. I had hardly heard of some of their home towns, except to know some were North of me – they had perhaps previously been a note in a school geography exercise book, or a small flag on a map, or was it amongst the homework I skipped that time? I know, now, that we all lead fairly insular lives, but to be thrown in amongst all these faces, accents and attitudes at the tender age of sixteen, was like being smacked in the mouth with a brick. I wasn't particularly naive, but I could see I and my new mates had a lot of catching up and growing up to do in a short period of time. Having said that, once we got over the initial surprises, and began to settle down, we quickly formed (and surprisingly stuck to) small cliques within the classes we were immediately assigned to. We were introduced to Divisional POs', Divisional Chief Petty Officers, and then to our Divisional Officers (we had to stand up straight – they were Lieutenants (or Sub-Lieutenants), and consequently very, very important.).

'Colours' was probably the first thing stamped indelibly on us. Every morning, the Navy has colours, where the ensign is ceremonially raised up the mast on the quarterdeck. The quarterdeck exists, obviously, as the blunt end on ships, but is where the mainmast is on shore establishments. Colours (and 'Sunset', where the reverse happens) means that anyone on the upper deck (or in our case, out in the open) has to 'Face the mainmast and salute'. Then stand there at attention, saluting, until the flag is completely raised, at which time the 'carry-on' is sounded, and you continue about your business. God help you then, if you continue to amble around, gob-off, or do anything – except stand and salute. This, and walking (instead of doubling) over the parade ground, entitled you to be sworn at lengthily and loudly by anyone who happens to notice you breaking this first set of rules. And what a prat you feel, having someone, his face inches from yours, questioning your ability to hear/see/have a father. You only did it the once, even accidentally.

We were now marched everywhere, and on the next occasion, it was to the barbers, past other, obviously older, more experienced hands, who had arrived the previous week or month, and who jeered at our newness wherever we went in our segregation, and eventually we were shorn of our dead trendy hair. We went from there to the tailor to be measured for our suits – one blue serge, the other the very proper tar one – thence to the stores, where the only analogy is 'like Christmas'. We were given, YES GIVEN, three sets of Y-fronts (referred to as 'dung-hampers), vests, gloves, (both of which we pointedly refused to wear on the grounds that only little girls wore gloves, and only little boys wore vests) blue shirts and trousers, several pairs of woollen socks, a pair of shoes, two pairs of boots (one studded, one not), a gas-mask, sheets, pillowcases, gloves, striped pyjamas (worryingly referred to as 'brown hatters overalls' – but not explained, at that time), mugs, sports gear, including plimsolls, two gleamingly white hats (sorry – caps), a belt with a built in, buttonable, adjustable money-pouch, several white towels, a huge Macintosh – called a Burberry (very warm), two thick, blue (and extremely itchy) 'seamen's jerseys' (otherwise known as 'woolly-pullys'), a zippered, nylon anorak type thing said to keep out wind and rain, polish, soap, bits of white string called lanyards, mysterious sheets of silk, called silks, sheets and pillowcases, strange T-shirt things with very fetching bits of blue round the square neck called white-fronts, shoe/boot cleaning gear, a wooden scrubbing brush, and the most oddly shaped blue-jean things, know as collars. Oh yes, and a housewife (bag full of sewing kit, scissors, needles etc.), and a large offensive weapon, initially known as a clasp knife, subsequently called a 'pussers dirk'. ...With a large brown canvas kitbag, and a large, strong, green suitcase to carry it all in. All this was valued then, at around £50 – a fortune compared to the £7 we were to be paid per fortnight – the going rate in those days, when the MEN were made of steel, and SHIPS were made of wood... ...as the expression was relayed to us.

We were also given two 'cap-tallies' (black bands with the ships' name picked out in gold thread) to tie round our caps, so whilst ashore we could be identified to a ship. The bow to secure these 'tallies must be the hardest one ever devised by man – similar to that used to secure bow-ties, only ours had to be totally symmetrical before we finished it off with the scissors, or it was forcibly removed for another attempt. By the time it was secure, it was tatty – you had to buy a new one to replace it, or come up with some pretty creative ironing. Luckily (!) we had the ex sea-scout, so we got all ours done after only ten or so lessons.

We had a wooden 'block' made up – letters joined together to form our name on it, and told what would happen if we EVER lost this, or what would happen if we were EVER found with an item of someone else's gear (or kit), with their name 'blocked' on it. The block had to be dipped into paint, and the paint applied to the item of uniform. You obviously used black paint to mark light clothing, and white paint for dark clothing. Then told afterwards (or were we too excited to listen in the first place) to stamp ONLY where it would not be seen... You should have seen the gear ruined that day, with the name stamped on the OUTSIDE of brand new collars, on the outside of even caps, half-way up whitefronts, and clearly to be seen on trousers and shirts. The only cure was by way of replacement, so it was in all ways a very costly mistake to make. All these tasks were overseen by an old boy, dressed as an officer – I seem to recall – who was hated in much the same way as traffic wardens are. He was, as far as we were concerned, neither civvy nor jack, but seemed to exert enough influence and wield enough power for us to obey him. I think we referred to him as 'Cap'n Pugwash'. He was – to us – a little shit of a man, without patience or civility.

And that was that, we were now expected to wear all our new kit – which we did, self-consciously at first, but getting more used to it day by day, especially those funny little round caps, which accepted dirty fingermarks as easily as shit stuck on a blanket, but which refused to be removed, even though we scrubbed them with our little brushes, drenched in washing powder ('dhobey dust' to the older hands). We also discovered – the hard way

– that it was extremely silly to 'blanco' the hats clean, as the first drop of rain dumped diluted blanco all over your suit and collar, precipitating an expensive trip to the dry-cleaner to remove all the very fetching white tram-lines from your collar down to your shoes.

All our civvy gear was then rounded up, wrapped in brown paper, and sent home to Mum. Except that not everyone complied to the letter with this. I can still see "Spotty" (or was it "Kenomeat") now, in bell bottoms, highly charged black shoes, and a lemon coloured shirt, pretending to be a civvy in Plymouth, not knowing he a) looked a bigger plonker than all the rest of us, and b) had less chance of pulling in Plymouth anyway, than a broken tug.

In all the excitement then, our civvies went, never to be seen again, or until Christmas – whichever came first.

So we all got on with readying our gear, washing it, starching it, ironing it, and now here was our first uniform, the blue serge one. Straight on, god how that itched. "This, lads, is your number two uniform." Explained the resident PO. "Not to be worn on ceremonial occasions because it only has a red wool badge, but is to worn on duty. The blue shirt/trousers is Number eights, and when you get your best uniform, it is your Number Ones, complete with gold wire badge." And more. "Eights are worn during the day, unless you are on duty, in which case you wear twos. With or without collars. Or without a top – known as half-blues.". " To make life easy, ALL ships and establishments issue "DAILY ORDERS", telling you of such things as daily events, sunset/sunrise, duty personnel, duty part of the watch, special events, but especially – DRESS OF THE DAY. This takes away your decision of 'what to wear today'. It IS eights during daytime. You have two sets. If one set is in use the other set is in wash. You will change your eights either on a Thursday, or if they are grubby from use. You may buy further sets. Your silks must be folded EXACTLY like this. The strings are called lanyards and must NEVER be any colour but white, the collars must be folded like this, but, of course, the creases MUST be razor sharp. Your number two trousers MUST have either 7 or 9 completely parallel creases, but NOT 6 or 8, and they are to be ironed concertina fashion like this, to facilitate easy stowage, but NOT ironed 'fore and aft', as the RN irons their uniform trousers across the leg" (which made sense considering to size of our lockers). And so it went on. Interspersed with lectures, talks, discussions, meals, discussions, drill, talks, and lectures.

One of the downers was that we had to sew cotton name strips on our eights, and branch badges – little pictures of shackles – a fetching blue colour on a white background. These badges first had to be cut to shape to prevent them becoming unstitched, then folded round their edges before being sewed on the outside of the right sleeve of our shiny Number Eight shirts, NOT the inside, NOR the rear. 'Homeward bounders' (bloody big stitches) were NOT to be used, just small, neat stitching. We were sixteen years old, and here we were having to sew badges on. Mind you, we quickly learned not to mess the job up – as with everything else – if it was not Pusser fashion, it came off rather faster than it went on, helped by 'our' PO, and you did it again, and again, and again until you got it right.

The other major, major down, was that we now had to do what thousands of other trainees had done for countless generations and years before us – spit'n'polish our boots. Starting with the hot spoon to remove the dimples, then the laborious build up of polish and gob with the filthy rag moving monotonously round in small circles, until – suddenly – the glimmer of a reflection hits back at you. Followed by creating more reflective bits, until miraculously – the whole toe of the boot is now glimmering blackly, and what a sense of achievement that is. We used to spend hours bulling them back after we'd stuffed them up. Strangely, you either got it or you didn't. You are either one of those who CAN put a mirror on the toecap, or you sit there for more endless hours, getting nothing but a sore arm.

Did the tea really have bromide in it? What was bromide anyway – did it taste anything like iodine? Is that why the tea was always so brown? And anyway, before we could drink it, we had to get a china mug, which involved waiting in a queue until someone else had finished with one. Perhaps that was why the Naafi sold plastic mugs, with handles, either half-pint, or pint-sized, either in orange, or bright blue. We quickly invested in our new drinking utensils – preferring to invest then, than waste valuable 'off' time lining up for a china one. Once bought, we decorated our trophys with our name, in paint, or with indelible ink, or even with a bit of plaster with our names inked on. We could soon spot our mug from a distance, which made no difference whatsoever, as they quickly got nicked, or left behind, somewhere. There must be shops in Plymouth, Portsmouth and every other Navy town, selling used plastic mugs. Whichever ship or unit you then served on, there would always be the shop where you could buy mugs, or you'd buy your own from some foreign shore, and use it until it got smashed, float-tested, nicked, or – yet again – just plain lost. Occasionally, on future ships, we'd have an official issue of proper pusser's mugs, but they'd all get smashed in the first spot of rough weather, and back we'd always go to the plastic versions.

The food was good that first navy week – it had to be to sustain us through all the new things hitting us hourly, like being in an organised whirlwind really. The important thing was that we had hope. That following Monday we would move in as 'The New Intake'. No longer the new, new entries – we had moved up the heap. No-one could laugh at our shiny trousers and dull boots any more – we were here to stay, matey-bubbles – we were Jack!. We could now laugh at the new boys. We still had the alarm calls, complete with spitkin kicking, but now when told 'feet on the deck', we knew we could get a few extra, precious seconds in our beds, by swinging our legs out, whilst keeping our bodies in and under the warm covers. We could now call the new boys 'skin', and talk knowledgeably about things 'giving us the shits', tell them to "stop gobbing off while I'm talking" watching them return the same blank looks we gave last week. We could also call them 'heap' as in heap of shit, or – strangely – describe things we didn't agree with as a 'feed', short for 'feed of arse'. We never did get to the bottom (!!) of that particular epithet.

One of the major occurrences of these first few days, were when we all gathered (sorry, mustered – had to get used to this naval terminology) in the common-room at the top Nissen hut of the block, and were read the Official Secrets act. Which we then had to sign. And the contract of service between the Navy and me. As if any of us understood it at sixteen. We signed though, but not before a repetition of the 'if you have any misgivings, we will put you on the train home to mummy now' routine. Following the cryings we had heard from various beds in our messdeck over the preceding days, we were not surprised when several kids got up and left, obviously preferring their mummy's warm and tender company to ours.

Having got rid of those space-wasters, we had our photos' taken for our ID cards (something we would late overpaste with pictures of monkeys – nobody ever looked at the details, only at the card itself), with the lecture about how we would be instantly executed (or something) if it ever fell into enemy hands, and were presented with a paybook. This was a very pretty, green covered book, supposed to record all data about me, what I had been issued with, what else I could be issued with, brief rules and regulations about 'navy life', and now I had signed my life away, the bits in invisible ink. The bits that now became visible, and said that now they had my signature, they could stick needles in me to guard against various unheard of and undiscovered tropical diseases. Oh yes, and the bit that said everything anyone said to you from now on was definitely not preceded with "Please…", but with any shouted word/profanity/order! Fortunately, paybooks were exactly the same size widthways as the distance between the creases on our trousers. Imagine how helpful that was!

Plus I had my official number given to me. One I remember unconsciously even now.

We had more photos taken – this time for our passports. None of my new mates – myself included had ever seen a passport before, much less actually owned one, so we were indeed quite chuffed when we got these royal blue permits. Then we found that not only would we never need them in any port we entered, but that they were also a receptacle for more injections against the above mentioned diseases, and that every time we had one, the certificate (against for example – Yellow Fever) would be added to the already growing wad of others.

We had thus far been told about splitarses, with a snigger, and told we were to be interviewed by them. The splitarse – a traditional naval sobriquet – turned out to be a pretty WRENS officer, who attempted to get inside our heads with questions about our home-life, educational backgrounds, and inclinations. We also continued to learn more navy slang. Whenever we talked while supposed to be listening, we would immediately be told "Shi'ni", which we later got expanded to "Shit in it", (SHUT UP – NOW!!). Everyone said it, and for all I know they still do. Talking instead of listening was called 'transmitting instead of receiving', which could quickly get you slapped, or bollocked, depending on who you were doing it to. Something else we picked up, quickly, from bitter experience.

Chapter 2

The next few weeks

So we marched from the new entry block to another dull, black nissen hut on the other side of the camp, carrying everything we couldn't wear. One thing I remember from these months in Raleigh, was that weather did not exist. As in – if it rains, just get on with it. We had to muster every morning for diversions (divisions) EVERY day except for the days I remember it really being too foul to go ahead. In which case we used to hear it first from 'the beano man' The broadcast used to crackle into life, followed by "D'Y'Hear there – There will be no divisions this morning" But that was on exceptionally bad days. We otherwise had divisions in the shed at the far end (for us) of the parade ground, having first doubled across or around the parade-ground, so as to not get TOO wet.

We were assigned to PO Robinson, (who's favourite phrase was "I kid you not"), and were messed into Revenge Block, class Collingwood 37 for six weeks basic training, meaning our daily routine went something like breakfast 0610 'clean ship' until 0830, then divisions, prayers and instruction. Dinner was at 1210, training from 1330 to 1610, then tea, then sport until 1815, which was generally rugby, trying to beat the crap out of anyone stupid enough to play against us – normally the tiffies from the other training base right across the road from us. Supper was at 1835, with 'free periods' (mending, repairing, cleaning, washing, ironing, showering) until lights-out at 2200. On Saturdays, training finished at 1200. On Sundays no training, but divisions then church. Church was an oddity, with the 'irreligious' being advised to go anyway right from the off, as non-compliance resulted in extra duties!!! As a lapsed Methodist, I thought I might get away with it, but was lumped in with 'the rest' every Sunday. Except for the day I escaped, claiming I had been invited to attend a service with the minister who had christened me. I can only recall tea, and the evening service before hurrying to meet my mates later on in the pub.

During this time, except when on duty, leave could now be taken up until 2245, nightly. Aggie Westons and The Seamans Mission were the places recommended to us, they sounded as if they could be interesting, but having learned their true purpose, we rapidly swerved past them while heading for 'The Strip'. They were both explained away as being there for the more God-fearing of us. So despite all their best intentions, and the fact that they were there for our entertainment, we avoided them.

Or we were allowed to go into the Naafi (at stand-easys', or in the evening), which stood for "Navy, Army Air Force Institute", and most definitely NOT "No Ambition And Fuck-all Interest", as it was otherwise alleged. We grew up fast. The food in there was interesting, so was the milk, and the coca-cola, and pies and cakes and nutty, and the juke-box, and snooker table (if you got there early enough) but nowhere near as tantalising as the beer, served to older ratings. As a Junior Seaman though, aged 16 and a bit – the beer was definitely off limits while on-base. As were the WRENS quarters allegedly up the hill, patrolled by armed guards, accessible only over a wooden bridge, which rattled and shook, and over which we had to break step as we marched to the gym. Mind you, the bromide took care of thoughts of girls. And Wrens. Didn't it?

Stand-easy was a naval tradition. Where anyone else would have a break, a cuppa, or whatever – we'd have stand-easy. What happened at Raleigh, was that all standeasys were ushered in by a bugle (on a tape) playing the stand-easy tune. It came across as 'dee-da-didlediddledi-da-dee', which we always gleefully mocked as 'If ya wannoo have a shit, go now'. Which we'd do, unless we were near the Naafi, at which point we would slope off and have a blue-liner or three, or a very quick cuppa.

We did seamanship, involving absolutely every aspect of anything to do with the word sea, starting with tying bends and hitches, but not knots. Boy scouts could call them knots – we were much more sophisticated, and could (honestly) tie anything, within seconds, in front of us, or behind our backs, with or without our eyes shut. We had to – we were told that "one day your life could depend on it". We believed that – we therefore learned the bend thoroughly. Every time we entered the seamanship training room, we first had to go through these hitches and bends until the PO was satisfied, and that could take several attempts.

The first time we entered one particular room, containing the absolutely complete, scale models of ship fo'c'sle's was a wonderful experience. We were shown the principles of mooring, anchoring, replenishing, with all the miniaturised moving and working parts. We were allowed to play with these giant toys, and learned an enormous amount about blocks (not pulleys), derricks (not cranes) real life-jacket drills (in that cold pool again) and real life raft embarkation, having first learned how to jump off the top board, wearing a life-jacket, without breaking your neck as you hit the water. That was scary – we were told that is what COULD happen – if we didn't do it right. We did it right. We did PT, including how to ascend a rope. We did Naval General Knowledge – who fought who, and where, why the Russians had the hump after the Bay of Pigs, how the aircraft carrier had dominated recent naval battles etc, etc. And the fun bits. Doing damage control in a semi live environment, being aware that if you didn't stop the water coming in pretty handsomely (we soon picked these nautical phrases up!), you would get a belt off the live wires left dangling precariously near the rapidly rising floodwater.

Engaging in the practical boatwork at Jupiter Point was eagerly looked forward to, as it was terrific fun – it was a release valve as well as being educational. We had to get out of Raleigh, drive for a distance in the back of a real blue pussers lorry with its canvas roof, and then we were allowed to charge round the river Tamar in 27 foot whalers, either under power (or do I mean underpowered – engines which had to be convinced to start, then propelled us very slowly through the water), or pulling (under oars). This was a massive let-off of steam for us. I had (and since have) always loved boats. I was in my element. Even when we were literally thrown into Mirror class dinghies after minimal instruction, and drifted miles downtide after the wind dropped, totally, it was me that regarded this as an adventure. And when we got rounded up and towed back, all one behind the other, all fastened to the powered whaler, it was me that couldn't wait for the next visit. Well, I'd just spent a week sailing round the River Blackwater – hadn't I? So I knew what I was doing, didn't I?

The firefighting course was the most impressive, a large pan (several feet square) of oil was ignited, and left to catch, fiercely. Then the head fire-fighter showed us what NOT to do, which was NOT to hit the fire with water, When he did – the immediate and enormous eruption of fire and heat and smoke will stay in my memory for years. Having been shown how not to do it, we were given the foam extinguishers, and shown how to do it, properly, off the wall behind the fire, so the foam drifted back over it, smothering it. Piece of piss when you know how. We came back from that totally black from the 'fires' we put out. It took days to get the soot out of our skin and hair, those of us who had hair left – some had singed bits of eyebrows and hair remaining which took several weeks to grow back.

There was actually quite a bit of instruction based on the 'Don't do it like this, because this is what will happen if you do' principle. You tended to learn much more quickly, and it avoided expensive and time-wasting mistakes. Even the class (eventually to be 'back-classed') idiot didn't foul up when presented with 'not like this because…'.

We learned that bell-bottoms were like that, because it made them easy to roll up your legs, ready to scrub decks, and that our silks were originally to tie around your head to mop up the sweat, and that the lanyard was to fire the cannon, and that the three stripes on the collar represented three great naval battles, and the idea of the collar was to keep oiled pigtails off ones uniform.

One useful piece of information – if we fell overboard, we could remove our bells, tie the bottoms, and then trap air in the bags, to float with… Oh Yeah? Not that we cared – we looked brilliant in our bezzy (best) 'ones' when we dressed with silks, collars, white fronts and lanyards for the first time, and we all paraded excitedly in front of the mirrors for ages.

We did endless hours of parade training, "NOT-fucking-square-bashing-fucking-stupid-percy-fucking-pongoes-do-that" – the invective was showered upon us from all directions, and we greedily learned and absorbed it before we returned it amongst our peers and juniors. We practised among ourselves daily, inserting "fuck" at every opportunity and for every other word. We expanded that, using it as an adverb, an adjective, a noun or even a pronoun, just like everybody else did, as it was the Navy vernacular. Drill taught us how to throw around an SLR (drawn daily from the armoury after it had been checked 'clear') with easy familiarity, and how to about turn, and right turn, and move to the left in threes all became progressively easier, at least to us. Naval drill insists on "dwelling a pause of two marching paces" between each movement. We would therefore "move to the right in threes – Riiiight TUrn" at which point we would swivel on the heel of the right foot and ball of the left, count "two three", then complete the movement by bringing our left foot up 'smartly' against the right. Everything was done with a pause of "2-3". With us being made to shout it if we didn't immediately get it right. Which was quite frequent. Or having to 'hold' a movement like 'changing arms whilst at the attention', which involved changing the SLR from right arm to left. Pausing in the middle meant you now held several pounds of rifle at arms length, (very, very painful after several seconds) until the DI got bored, and shouted "TWO-THREE", at which point (if your arms hadn't locked up or fallen off) you would gratefully complete the drill. You tended not to prat about when doing that particular drill, just in case. Of course we were dragged out periodically and made to run round the parade ground with the SLR held above the head, or even worse at the aforementioned arms length, for the very slightest infraction, but we even got used to that. "Bags of swank" was the maxim we learned to good effect. Chests out, stomachs in, heads up, eyes front, shoulders back, push back the arms, bring them forward until parallel to the deck, fingers clenched at first and second knuckle, bang those feet down, thumbs in line with the seam of the trousers, feet at a 45 degree angle. And so on and on… …and the pride in ourselves, and what were doing, and what we were starting to accomplish grew by the minute. We were starting to become part of that team called the Royal Navy, starting to become men.

The "TWO-THREE" always gave us plenty of laughs – when inebriated, we would then do everything (and I MEAN everything) at the "2-3". It gave plenty of opportunities to let of more steam, which is what we needed to do – frequently.

We learned many things over those few first weeks – straight away we were told how to wriggle our toes while standing at attention to prevent fainting, rather than sway in the breeze for the inevitable earbending from the DI. Or worse – pass out. "Just you fucking leave him alone – don't you DARE touch him" ...we were told. "Fucking weaklings" – we used to think as they dropped to the unforgiving tarmac of the massive parade ground on the odd hot Sunday in full, gleamingly immaculate number ones, as the Marine band played whilst the armed guard was inspected by the captain, and as we stood motionless for hours (it seemed) at a time. Eventually, though, the 'first-aid' party who had been up until then on 'stand-by' by the side of the parade ground, would trot over, complete with stretcher onto which they'd load their human cargo, before trotting back to sick bay with the failure.

Personally, I used to hum along to the band to try to keep alert, though that was dangerous – if you got too involved in the humming, you would still be "at-ease", while everyone else was "Ho'd, then get a bollocking from the DIs' who constantly prowled the parade ground with their yardsticks or swagger canes during these most nautical, ceremonial divisions. Then you'd get a further one from the parade commander, who would want to see you after divisions.

However – as the tallest in the class, I was always 'marker', against whom everyone else fell in and dressed. I was consequently never out of position. If I moved – the others had to dress up against me. No-one ever caught on to me doing that...

The tunes the band played used to have me sniggering at times, especially when they played the Sousa March (Monty Pythons' theme tune). I will confess that "A Life On The Ocean Wave" is very stirring for a sixteen year old trying to stand still. Except for my toes – I would wiggle then non-stop, as told, whilst at the attention, to stave off the fainting. We were actually told, that if we felt faint, we were to go down on one knee. That seemed even more ignominious – attention seeking, we reckoned!!

We fell in, and fell out again, we put our caps on, took them off again, saluted (front, left and right and stand from under if you were stupid enough to salute to the left with your left arm), and had tick-tocking pointed out to us. This for the uneducated, is that normally, when marching, a coordinated person's right arm/left leg go forwards then backwards together. Except the ticktocker. He goes same leg same arm. and looks totally hilarious. Even now,

I can't watch people marching without scanning for the ticktocker. And when I do see one, I go into uncontrollable laughter. I also remember the short, bearded PO who 'took' us, with his immaculate turnout, highly polished black gaiters, and mirror-like boots. He was actually a DI (drill instructor), previously a chock-head, an airman, trained at 'waffoo' (Fleet Air Arm) land, and certainly not a GI (Gunnery Instructor) tamed (sorry – trained) at H.M.S. Excellent – Whale Island, at one time a feared and respected place.

We were taught nautical phrases, like 'Son of a Gun', and 'Between the devil and the deep blue sea', and were educated in their origins, plus many more like them.

We learned the hard way, that if we were caught ambling around with our hands in our pockets, that we would soon be sitting with our 'housewives', sewing up those same pockets, to prevent getting tempted next time. This would be most embarrassing to those who got caught.

We assembled, disassembled and fired the SLR (Self Loading Rifle). One day on the firing range we all looked forward to, I got 22 hits on my target, with only eighteen rounds, and got a well coveted 'divisional strip' for it. No-one ever questioned that one. At some point we were given bayonets to play with, and discovered they were not only sharp – they were also very pointed, and hurt if you accidentally stuck yourself with them.

We were given the SMG (Sub Machine Gun) to play with, and were told to put it on single not automatic. We all duly fired off round after round, and then put it on auto. We then discovered how just a quick squeeze of the trigger sent three rounds off, no matter how quick your squeeze was. You could, if you kept it pointed low enough, see the rounds driving into the ground, and as you adjusted your aim, the rounds gradually crept towards the desired aiming point. Once we mastered that, we were allowed to fire off the rest all at once, if we liked. There were many rules on the firing range – keep it pointed down range AT ALL TIMES was just one. But, when you squeezed the SMG trigger, the weapon jumped upwards and to starboard – and there was not a thing you could do to prevent it. Which was why you only squeezed three off at a time – you knew they'd get to whatever it was you aimed at. Of course, we were also told that if we DID use it in anger, just to point it, and hold the trigger until the weapon was empty, then change the magazine and repeat until all the mags were empty. Then you grabbed the hot end, and used the weapon as a club until there were too many in opposition, at which time you threw the empty weapon at whoever was coming towards you, and ran in the opposite direction, screaming loudly.

All these weapons were kept in the armoury, and we would queue for a weapon, check it was empty before accepting it, use it all day without ammunition, take it back where it would again be checked for emptiness – and all we did was swing them around on the parade ground, usually. The checks still had to be made. Just for added effect, we were shown the film about the squaddies playing with an unchecked weapon. The scene where the rifle discharges, and the round goes through the pongo holding the barrel, is unforgettable, and one which made us vow to always, always check our weapon. We didn't talk much on the way back from the cinema that day once we'd seen what a 7.62mm round does to a human. I know it was only pretend, but it still shocked.

We underwent the ritualised attempted drowning where we were forced to swim for several lengths, fully dressed, in order to prove we could do it. Or was it just for the fun of it. It was actually a 'back-classing' offence to not be able to swim. Fortunately, I swam well, and got another 'strip' for my abililty to do this, and rescue various irrelevant items from the bottom of the pool – I passed a couple of Lifesaving awards for doing this. What did surprise me however, was the number of entrants that could not swim, or who swam, badly. I would think that a prerequisite of joining the navy would be an innate desire to float under ones own power.

We did PT – we marched up the hill over THAT bridge, past the WRENS quarters, did our PT in the extremely and impressively well equipped gymnasium, and marched back down again. I don't remember seeing anything female. Or any WRENS.

We covered the assault course, where in any weather we descended into muddy and on occasions – water-filled holes, clambered across ropeways over ditches, climbed walls, got filthy, and enjoyed ourselves immensely. I was very pleased with myself the day I traversed a rope bridge on my stomach, one leg hooked – the other dangling. Even the people at the far end shaking the rope didn't manage to put me off, even when they threw the inevitable thunderflashes at me.

To be truthful, we all actually got extremely fit during our time at Raleigh, we doubled everywhere, we did PT, assault courses, swimming, rugby – you name it, we rarely stopped doing it. We were, therefore Fit (with a capital 'F'). We also learned teamwork, something which was to stay with us for very many years, and then some!

We had only been there three or four weeks when the First Sea Lord came especially to see me. ...And all my mates. Well, the whole of Raleigh I suppose. Admiral Sir Michael Le Fanu GCB DSC. I clearly remember all us baby sailors lining up and forming the word RALEIGH for him to see, standing to complete attention, in several inches of very sloppy mud off the bottom of the parade ground. Immensely proud we were that day, especially when he addressed us all. Until afterwards, when we had to scrape the mud and crud off our boots, then polish them again ready for the inevitable daily divisions in our immaculate eights the following morning. But we had at least seen a REAL admiral…

Oh yes, and kit inspections.

There was a magical a place called 'slops', wherein we could buy extras. Like kit which had gone walkabout all by itself from the communal drying rooms. Like kit which got ripped/wrecked on that brilliant assault course. Although on £7 per fortnight it was difficult enough to survive (on beer and extra food) let alone buy extra kit. So if you had extra cash, AND were sensible you bought extra gear, washed and ironed it to the highest standard, then kept it for kit inspections. The rest of us merely pissed it up against the walls and urinals of Guzz's pubs and Discos'. If the kit inspector found something annoying whilst your kit was laid out, he would take exception to the point of throwing all your gear round the room, for a rescrub later. This exception could be an unaligned collar, or uncoiled lanyard, or a skidder on your hampers, or the merest start of a spud in a sock. We learned that on the final week of part one training we would have not only kit musters, but full exams which if not passed would immediately entitle us to at least one further weeks training in part one, amongst those pointed out like lepers, as 'the backclassed'. These stupid people didn't feature in social lives, they were clearly lowlife – and we were scared witless in case we ended up like that. So we made sure our kit was good. The one very good thing about 'slops' was it was where you collected your ciggy ration in return for stamps. 300 a month at that time, costing around ten bob. For the three hundred. They made you cough after you'd smoked them all, but you got better when you ran out and went back to proper ones, like the 'Number 6' which was all we could afford. These 'Blue Liners' were allegedly sweepings up, along with the rat hairs and God knows what else. Still, at ten bob a month, who was going to complain. And you could always illegally scrounge or trade a few more stamps, especially from the non-smokers, to supplement your ration. It paid you to keep on their good side.

And then there was school, where we did what I thought was the most basic in maths and English, striving towards the NAMET (Naval Maths/English Test) where the highest attainment you could get was a zero-zero. On the first try I scored a 2/1, but then got my GCE result through which automatically gave me a zero-one (or was it one-zero), at which time, despite thinking I wouldn't need to do another test, found I had to anyway because all the rest of the class had to. Was I impressed.

All this and constant dental visits, plus the odd jab to keep you on (or off) your feet. Also a strange film showing us how to diagnose tertiary syphilis – said to turn the strongest stomach, and another about the dangers of drugtaking, especially LSD, where the anti-hero let down all his mates. We looked forward to the films, and took special interest in those showing damaged warships, or how to replenish, or how to…

Mind you, each afternoon we still had sport, usually rugby or cross-country – sometimes as a treat deck-hockey – which I remember kept our minds off most things really, which was fortunate. The food was still plentiful, but never that terrific. You generally needed to queue for many minutes in order to be at the front of the interminable (when at the back) queue, to guarantee first digs at a decent portion. If you left it too long, the best scran would go, you'd be left with the scratchings and scrapings, or even nothing but toast, and beans. If that happened, you were within your 'rights' to demand a decent meal. However, it was not in your interests to make that kind of a fuss – better to ask, please, for a couple of eggs to go on the toast, then scarper quickly to the Naafi to top up. Strangely, at each suppertime, an officer would cruise the dining hall, asking in a loud voice "Has anyone any complaints about the food tonight", to be met with stony silence. Already, we weren't that daft. No good deliberately going looking for trouble – we soon learned.

We had evening rounds daily, regardless, (and then Saturday morning rounds), where, on top of everything else we did, we had to clean up for the Officer of the day (OOD) to come and see how clean we could get the room. Or not, in the case of the ignominious rescrub, and cancellation of the snooker game on the real, full sized table. The weekly Saturday morning rounds were made by 'someone important' – the training commander for example, who (it was said) wore white gloves, and went over EVERY square inch. The mess considered to be the cleanest, or which clearly had the most effort put into it, or was the best improved since last time, won a cake, made of sponge, and iced all over, lovingly baked by the chefs,. I mock, but it was actually a terrific feeling to win it, it made you extremely proud to know that your efforts HAD been recognized.

One of the most degrading jobs, was that of 'skirmishing'. This entailed going round the outside of the mess and block, picking up anything unnatural. Grass, buildings and roads were considered 'natural', EVERYTHING else had to be picked up. Dog-ends, matches, nutty-wrappers everything. Skirmishing was the last resort – if you hadn't got anything better to do, or if you finished your previously allotted task early "Go and skirmish round the parade ground" was the order we all dreaded to hear. So we prolonged the chore. It didn't matter that it wasn't you who dropped it, or that you knew who did – someone, soon, would end up picking it up. We were even set targets "Pick up ten bits of garbage each, then report back to me". Where the hell where we expected to find ten bits of crud, each, in a class of thirty? Fortunately we knew how to raid rubbish bins, and we could always go back to the spitkin in the mess for a few dog-ends. Not that we ever learned to do things like that…

To get the messdeck up to the expected extremely high naval standard, the class leader would detail us off for various tasks, from the heads or bathrooms, or the beams (holding the roof up/on), or the buffer (the polishing machine – a large vacuum cleaner type beast, with a revolving head covered with a large soft pad) or whatever other jobs needed doing. All this gear was kept in a communal cleaning gear store, which was shared with all the other classes/messes within the block. Due to this shared option, it meant if you didn't get the gear out early, you had to wait until everyone else had finished with it before you got your crack. Oddly enough, you would spend hours hanging around the end of someone else's mess, so he didn't shit on you, and give the gear to another mess, ahead of your turn.

Smells are very evocative – for example, the smell of the first pub you ever went in, the smell of school dinners, but the all-prevailing smell from this entire building which I will forever recall, was that of the wax polish we dug out of a large tin, applied by hand, then buffed to a high gloss with that dammed machine. The polish came out of a large tin, was coloured orange, and stained your fingers as you applied it with a clean cloth. It was therefore in ones interest to make sure he (the class leader) was your mate, so you polished the ashtrays rather than the toilet seats. Our class leader was a fearsome chap of seventeen, who had come from H.M.S. Ganges – where they trained 'boy sailors' below sixteen years of age – who was to have 'leadership qualities', and knew all the wrinkles. Except the one which eventually got him backclassed. We would spend hours each getting the mess up to full brilliance in time for whoever did 'rounds' to find some minuscule fault. All cat and mouse, however, the week WE won the cake for the best one, we were absolutely over the moon, going ashore full of wind and piss. And cake.

After spending days and evenings putting it all together, we would unwind by raiding other messes and classes, which involved huge pillow fights, often degenerating into real fights as stakes were raised. Then we would run back in triumph, waiting to see if we would be raided in retaliation. Or we'd hold impromptu wrestling contests in the corridors. One thing, of course, that we were NOT allowed to do, was take out the crabby bastards who had lower personal hygiene standards than others. We were warned not to do this, and we therefore never took them to the bathroom for an enforced bath, and were told the rumours were not true about yardbrooms and hard soap, dressed or undressed. Finally, we were told, the large, open tanks of water scattered round the base were specifically NOT for throwing these crabby people into. They were deep and therefore dangerous, which is why they were fenced off. Their scratches soon healed though, as did the atmosphere. Not that WE ever did that...

We had class photos – tallest at the back, shortest at the front, intermediates in the middle, standing straight, eyes front, hint of a smile (that's all), with Robbo holding the board identifying the division and class we belonged to. We had two of these taken – first within a few days of getting our ones during those first weeks, with the second being snapped during the Part 2 Seamanship. I recognise and can put names to all of my classmates even now, and we were some collection of funny looking buggers too!

It wasn't all relaxation (!), we were divided into watches (naval long-standing tradition), either PORT or STARBOARD watch Then into First and Second Part of the Watch. Meaning that every fourth day we had extra duties to perform. Like staying in the mess and cleaning whilst our mates stuffed themselves with cakes and lemonade at the Naafi.

We learned about Naval traditions like watches, and that clearly The Last Dog ran from 1800-2000, and that the Middle ran from 2359 (NOT 0001) to 0400. A strange thing is that 0000 does not exist as a time in the RN. Only 2359, or 0001. Nor do you say 2330 hours like the rest of the idiots and Army and Air Force do – WE understood 2330, and didn't need to be told or reminded that time was measured in hours. It annoys me terribly even today, when people add the word 'hours' after saying a time. What is the point of saying "It is 22 hundred hours?"

We were taught one day, that the phrase 'No Red Port Left' contained all the ingredients we needed, to tell left from right – sorry – port from starboard, and what colour lights were on which side of the ship. Therefore – we were told – starboard was right, and had green lights! Absolutely mind-boggling...

We learned various 'calls' and 'pipes' on our bo's'n's calls – peculiarly shaped whistles which you held in a particular manner, and, depending whether you had your hand open, or cupped over the hole, the call could be made to issue a range of notes, therefore tunes. Again, either you could do this – or you couldn't. And plenty couldn't. Following this, a tradition at Raleigh, was to pipe (on the bo's'ns call) the tune for 'hands to dinner', and I remember being picked as one of the piping party when it was the turn of our class to do it. We proudly marched to the Quartermasters lobby, from where all tannoy broadcasts were made, stood in front of the open microphone, and blew a note perfect rendition. To no applause. Just an "off you go for lunch now lads". Very disappointed I was.

I made lots of mates in those very short six weeks, many of whom I never saw or heard of again. There was Arthur who I met on the train (Christened 'Oddbod' after the character in the then showing 'Carry on Screaming' film), on account of his gangliness, Bill the ex-trawlerman, very old, nearly in his late twenties, Geoff the nutty (chocolate) fiend, with more spots per square inch than was good for him, Stevie, the painfully shy Devonian, Pixie-Ears, Kenomeat, Spots, Topsy, and many, many more forgotten names, all sharing that part of the world for that period of time. I often wonder where they all ended up.

A strange description, but 'Catching the liberty boat' was a euphemism for going ashore. Not easy, you would think to catch a boat from the main gate to the bus stop. However – the Navy knew best. Catching the liberty boat, meant suffering first at the washer/iron, then getting into full blues, best hat & lanyard, then trying to get past the duty PO at the gate, who, it was said, would send you back to your mess, with no leave if your dress, bearing and demeanor didn't come up to his scratch. To get by him, you had to all fall in three deep, for him to inspect you, and boy – did you get hauled over. If you were caught with more than the 25 Blue Liners allowed per night, you'd be sent back, but not before being 'trooped' for the privilege. On the bright side, if you made it, you'd march nicely through the gate, then whoop and run to the bus stop, to get the duty bus to the ferry. Then would come the Torpoint ferry crossing looking always for warships tied-up (not berthed – liners berth, not warships), then another bus or the walk into Plymouth. This became standard. However what we didn't anticipated was the reception we got when I first took shore leave, splendidly turned out. Today we WERE ruffy-tuffy sailors on our first shore leave, we WERE smart cookies resplendent in our Number ones (with seven razor-like creases alternately facing front and back), best collar (with three razor like creases, one inverted one in the middle, one either side between the middle and the outside going the other way), best white front (with a crease starched so stiffly, you could cut steak with it), best silk (with NO burn marks from having the iron too hot), best hat (well nearly, we kept a special "going ashore" cap, with specially created "bow-waves" in it to show off with), high-gloss shoes – the absolute shining example, to be met by – well, nothing really – unless you include apathy. The people of Plymouth have not only seen it on countless thousands of occasions before, but also have it to come for many years yet, and they clearly weren't about to empty the town to come and look at a just another bunch of new recruits. Oh yes, and we stank (then) of cheap soap, and tins and tins of starch – we didn't wear aftershave – we couldn't afford to, and anyway only poofs wore that stuff. Apart from that – we didn't even shave properly (though it was coming along nicely), so aftershave would have been totally pointless. We settled for just a good deodorant!

You must understand though, that we were generally downhearted by the reaction of the population of Plymouth to our sudden emergence. Again, it wasn't that we expected the massed bands, and ticker-tape parades, and the local female population ripping their clothes off for us as we walked by (although we lived in hope), but thus far, we had been 'geed up', by trainers and to some extent by ourselves, and at that time we were full of the most incredible pride. Pride in ourselves for getting accepted and trained by the RN. Pride in the RN. But mostly, pride in our incredible new appearance. We had been transformed from scruffy, unfit, shambling, semi-upright, part-lucid teenagers with stoops, to board-backed, broad-shouldered, upright, forward facing, healthy, literate servicemen, dressed immaculately in the best uniforms Pusser could provide, all in a matter of weeks. And nobody really gave a flying shit. I was, to say the least, disappointed.

It obviously occurred to us later, that Plymouth (and Portsmouth and Chatham and Rosyth) WAS, after all, a naval base, and was therefore already full to the brim with sailors. Baby sailors, experienced sailors, old sailors, all dressed alike, and that actually, we were the only ones who knew we were fresh out of the factory, and therefore needed a welcoming committee. But it was too late – I still remember the feeling of apparent rejection. It hurt us all for a long while. Well actually, until the next day, when we were allowed ashore again, to gallivant round...

We soon got over most things, because we had just recently learned how to be extremely resilient, but above all we got over it – because WE WERE JACK!!!!!

So, it was good to get my first pint of Courage (so called, allegedly because you need courage to drink it), then to stamp around the Hoe and the town, feed greedily on burgers and milkshakes at the bowling alley, then repair to the Rooftop to finish off the job, sucking in large quantities of Courage Brown Ale, and Rum'n'Black. Bearing in mind we got paid £7 every second week, we used to make a large hole in it at that place at one shilling and eightpence for a pint of beer. It was then a game to see if we could time it right to get the bus, to connect with the ferry, to buy an Oggy at the greasy spoon, giving us enough time to catch the bus back to H.M.S. Raleigh before we were declared adrift at 2245. At this point, you collected your station card, a device to check whether you were on board. If you left the ship – you left your card behind. As you came back you collected it. If your card was still there past the allotted time – you were adrift. And believe me – if you weren't back by the correct time there were no excuses good enough nor were there any places to hide in front of the Captain at his table, again in your number ones, but much improved on the night out, to explain just how everyone in the camp got back in time except you, and how the navy would under no circumstances tolerate lateness in any fashion, and when we went to sea, and the liberty boat left us ashore because we were adrift for it – how would we get back to the ship? Therefore you WOULD be back on time next time, and to remind you of the importance of that – you would have your leave stopped for several weeks at a time, plus you would pay a large fine. This bit is definitely allegorical – I was never trooped in all my naval career for being late!! Sorry, adrift.

It did, though give me a phobia about being late at any time since – I hate being late myself, and regard it as a personal insult when others do not have the courtesy to be on time. I will always be on time, except in very extenuating circumstances (i.e., not my fault) – why won't others? That's the Naval upbringing for you…

One evening, I forget who it was, but he came back offshore a bit worse for wear (or 'shiters' as we used to say), then woke us all up barging about, and banging and smashing around. When he fell asleep, we held a hurried blacked-out messdeck meeting as a result, and when he awoke in the morning, he didn't realise his bed had been elevated one level up, above someone else's. He swung his legs out, passed his centre of gravity, and pitched onto our highly polished deck several feet further below. Not that we laughed. For very long. Or very loudly…

After that, everyone woke up cautiously, and first felt with their toes for the deck before swinging out, so we had to find a new game. Another night, somebody else did it, and was amazed to find someone had removed the roof from his mess during the night. Or was it that we'd carried him and his bed outside onto the roadway while he snored noisily in his drunken stupor…

Not that it was all hard times, we visited a ship in the dockyard one fine morning, passing the massive bulk of H.M.S. Ark Royal on our way, then in dry dock in the middle of a lengthy refit, and surrounded by scaffolding, canvas dodgers, and different shades of grey and red paint. Not what we had come to expect. Instant rumours spread subsequently, that it would be going back to sea fairly soon, and that it would require large numbers of junior ratings. Us, in other words. Until then, I had never seen so much metal in one place at the same time, and I marvelled at the organised chaos of men and 'dockyard mateys' as they were known, all apparently carrying different items from here to there, or wearing mysterious welding masks, or toting drums of paint, all travelling on small trucks dashing around the dockyard with their driver perched precariously at the front, on a minuscule seat. These seemed to be the official mode of transport, along with the official pussers bike, never left unguarded under any circumstances. Dockyard mateys' were bigger thieves than matelots.

The ship we finally reached was a 'Cat' class frigate, bristling with radar, funnels and guns, and it was with awe that I, at least, spent as long as I could clambering round it. My first footing on a real warship, even though the crew sneered at us as we squealed excitedly at each new bit of kit.

Robbo, our PO, was in the habit of requesting baby-sitters, so he and his wife could go out. We would have to wait our turn, but volunteering (Me & Glen) meant Robbo collected us from the main gate (still in our Noz Ones), and took us to his house on the married patch. Once there we could go to half blues, watch his telly, drink the bottles of brown ale and eat the sarnies – both extremely thoughtfully provided – and while away the hours until they returned. Then we'd have a ride back to the main gates. It didn't matter if we were late, in fact, I think we had special dispensation to be so. We all volunteered when we found out about this, not everyone got used, not everyone got a go, so we considered ourselves fortunate, and made full advantage of the extra night out.

We spent a weekend on Dartmoor, where we yomped for miles, reaching and signing off at various checkpoints until our boots became too tight. These were the boots which yesterday we polished to a high shine for divisions, and which were now caked in West-Country mud. This first 'exped' finished on the Sunday afternoon at an Inn on the moor, and the incentive to get back in time was that it would still be serving beer if we got there in time... I clearly remember me and my team running like bats out of hell down the hillside, reaching the Inn with seconds to spare, and gulping down more 'Courage' before bussing back to Torpoint. Even then there was no peace – we of course had to clean and repair all our gear ready for divisions the following morning.

One day we had the obligatory and much dreaded 'gas mask test', which consisted of waiting outside (in the cold and rain) a stone building, with just the one exit/entrance door. We then masked up, and entered the smoke filled room. After several circuits, we were told to remove the mask, and head for the door. Not me. I wasn't intending to be that stupid. I did not see why I should have to inhale tear gas deliberately. So I headed for the door hidden, I though, in amongst the rest. As I neared the door, and just as I thought I had got away with it, my mask was removed for me, in one swift yank, followed by a 'light' tap to the abdomen – just enough to make me breathe in sharply. If you ever get the chance to taste tear gas – DON'T. It tastes vile. The whole class stood (still in the cold and rain) but now made to feel much, much worse by this disgusting gas, coughing and retching while we got wetter. That was one 'test' everyone passed. It took hours for our eyes to stop smarting, and for our noses to stop running. That was actually the worst event in my entire naval career.

The last week exams came upon us quickly, I must have passed, because I then moved to my next class 'Frobisher 37'. But not without seeing the type of howlers that associated themselves with such exams. Nobody I knew, but to the question in the NBCD (Nuclear Bomb Coming Down) paper, "What is fallout" the response was "Come to attention, 2,3, turn right,2,3, then fall out. Not quite there yet. Still, get through we did, and the class split up all round the south of the country to various other bases, to take up different professions. Except us proper sailors. We stayed at Raleigh. For another nine weeks. Of the same routine, but this time pure seamanship.

The next nine weeks was, then, a blur of more training. Less parade training but more seamanship training. It got more involved and interesting to me anyway, as we learned how to climb safety nets, lower bo's'n's chairs, make up and lower paint stages, lower and raise seaboats (from the derricks, known as davits, with the ropes on them known as 'falls', on the parade ground in the full knowledge that if we fouled that one up, there would be a heap of highly painted, but very smashed up wood at the base of the falls). We learned how to distinguish between clinker built and carvel built boats, and how to repair them, and most importantly – how to preserve the metal the ship was made of, to 'prevent' it from decomposing in the middle of the ocean and subsequently sinking. This is achieved by a top secret method – something called 'painting'. But you have to know how to paint, properly – to MOD(N) standards. We therefore first had to learn how to prepare the surface to be painted. This overall procedure is known as 'ships-husbandry', and was to be how I would spend a large proportion of my time in the R.N., until I finally got promoted, at which point I could detail off and watch, while others 'did'. We learned how to use paint remover. Not just the chemicals which burned your fingers if you weren't careful, but chipping hammers, sandpaper – all sorts of interesting (!!) ways to legally deface paint and metal. Then how to paint it again, layer by layer. Primer, undercoat and topcoat. Holidays were explained, (otherwise known as 'you've missed a bit there – were you on holiday then?') as were sagging and other technical terms. I never realised painting in one colour could be so interesting. Honestly...

We also learned how to RAS or Replenish At Sea, where the movies were fascinating. Who would have thought two ships stamping along at many knots could transfer people and stores between them by using bits of rope. Not just any rope, mind you, but special manilla, of a certain thickness and predefined length, in accordance with the official Manual of Seamanship. Eighty fathoms of 4" to be precise. Plus twenty or so sailors to hold this jackstay taut as this took place. Plus learning to abseil down one side of the parade ground, a drop of almost ten feet. It was still all tremendous fun though.

Then, among other nautical lessons, we learned how to tie even more varied and technical bends and hitches, what colour various buoys were, how to perform lookout duties (more of which later), how to clean the gleaming paintwork once we'd applied it (still called ships husbandry) how to weigh anchors, accompanied by a thousand and one more, different nautical terms, all to be learned by heart ready for the final exams.

One weekend, we went on an 'exped' to a place called Pier Cellars – a small man-made harbour, once used to handle torpedoes, left over from the bygone age of war, we were told, around the coast from Raleigh. We 'stayed' in cold, brick, empty caves/rooms, where we slung hammocks. We practiced what we had been taught up until then, by undertaking various seamanship evolutions, such as jackstay transfers over and across the harbour, re-crossed the harbour via a rope bridge, and went on the death slide. That was an experience to have – one end was some hundred feet up the cliffside. Phase one meant climbing the cliff to reach the top. Phase two was the rules – Do NOT let go... Phase three was the stomach churning but euphoric plummet down the rope, attached by a wire strop around your wrists. Phase four was the frantic deceleration at the bottom, where several people held a rope to try to brake you. Phase five (if phase four didn't work) was the dip in the harbour as you overshot. Phase six was then trying to swim, and exit the harbour with three inch long legs.

In this very atmospheric setting (you could almost feel the previous occupants) the weekend there was fantastic. We were introduced to the delights of 'potmess'. Potmess is everything from everyone's survival rations which were issued to us individually, and which we ate every time we went on any kind of exped. Now, whether it was steak and kidney pud, bacon, sausage & beans, curry, peaches, soup, and/or biscuits, it was all thrown into one cooking pot tastefully named a 'fanny', heated, then eaten with more of the biscuits (tack) provided, washed down with several crates of 'Courage', thoughtfully provided by our PO. If you've never tried it – don't knock it, after a hard days' (!!) "exped'ing", nothing could have tasted any better than our variably flavoured, but nutritious and delicious potmess.

We did more evolutions, more games, clambered up and down the cliffs, explored every inch of the place, and finally returned to Raleigh on the Sunday afternoon. Exhausted, but elated.

A further 'exped' was up on the moors again, in early December as I recall. We really looked forward to going up there at that time of year! We ate more potmess, and tried to keep ourselves dry(ish) in the interminable, horizontal, driving rain. We attempted to sleep in the tents, but were too cold to, so we dozed fitfully during prolonged shivering bouts until being plunged back into the rain early the following morning. We again walked miles, and miles over the moors. One fortunate thing we found about eating those rations – they take away the necessity to use toilets. You went away on the Friday night, started on 'the compo', ate it all weekend' returned on the Sunday, then, finally, your bowels exploded on the Monday, if you were lucky. Oh yes, we got soaked, we got cold, it snowed like the North Pole for most of the weekend, and still we completed it.

We returned from that one suffering from 'Totally pissed off' syndrome, glad to get warm, even glad to be getting our kit ready, again, for the obligatory, and entirely predictable next mornings' divisions.

Throughout all the weeks at Raleigh, we were continually appraised and tested, whether by test papers, or by head-to-head with officers. We must have done well for ourselves, I cannot recall anyone being backclassed from the seamanship training.

Chapter 3

Our first days on the ocean, wave…

Towards the end of the year, we were taken for real sea training for a week, on H.M.S. Ulster, which had a bad reputation, not only because of her having had several accidents in her time. It was rumoured that she had to have her bows replaced from another ship, following an accident whilst alongside somewhere. Warmed by that, we were terrified as we boarded the first time, making sure we saluted the ensign on the quarterdeck as we did so. (something we were supposed to do each time we boarded or left a warship), but we had a wonderful week on her. She was then the fastest ship the RN had, and one day to prove it, we did a full power trial on her. I seem to recall 45 knots being the speed we attained – with a wake out of the blunt end you couldn't see over! Or was it that we had a race with the 'Cavalier', which turned out to be the swiftest. Whatever – it was still a bloody big wake we created, just astern of a very noisily vibrating grey metal box!!

We kipped in the after mess in hammocks during that week, and went to get our food in traps, or fannies (big metal lidded buckets) from the galley amidships. The smell downwind from her funnels was oily and vile, plus it took every bit of strength to hold on to that pitching, rolling ship and the food, enveloped by the exhaust fumes from the funnel. We did a mortar shoot one day, although me and Arthur weren't aware what or where the mortars were, nor that they were about to fire until someone screamed at us to "get out of the fucking way". As we moved away, and only seconds later the dull, triple thump made the ship recoil and vibrate as the huge depth charge mortars were fired – right through where we had just been standing. We had got out of the way sharpish, below decks, and expressed surprise when someone came looking for us. That was my first 'near death', and we steadfastly denied having any involvement in that one. We cruised Portland all week, stood deck watches, looked at the radar, lowered the seaboat, crewed the seaboat – in fact did everything we could. I even used a 'maul' (large sledgehammer) to knock the shackle of the cable to drop the anchor – although it took me two swings to do it!

It was related at the time, that the buffer of one ship had trouble slipping an anchor, and screamed at the inexperienced bo's'ns mate on the bridge, to "Fetch a maul up". The BM heard that as "Fetch 'em all up", and instead of providing the very large hammer as requested, actually piped "Clear lower deck – all hands muster on the fo'c's'le"… Apparently, the buffer was not best pleased about that, as wasn't the jimmy.

The seaboat one was scary – the Navy way of putting a seaboat out is to whack the ship through the sea as fast as necessary whilst lowering the seaboat halfway to the waterline, slow to around six knots, then drop the boat on the crest of a wave (to prevent its' back breaking in a trough). The seaboat coxswain then throws the tiller hard over towards the ship, the seaboat veers to starboard, and moves sharpishly away from the ship. At some point, the boatrope towing the whaler at this stage is slipped, and the seaboat makes off.

To recover it, there is a piece of equipment called the Robinsons Disengaging Gear. This is a complex bit of kit, which we had to play with until we could rebuild it, again with our eyes shut, and behind our backs. This gear is extremely critical for hoisting, and if it isn't made up correctly, the boat will be hauled half way up the falls, then crash back into the sea, probably drowning everyone who used to be in what was left of the boat. There is, therefore, enormous pressure to get it right first time. And some extremely tense, nervous junior seamen scrabbling with it. So when the boat comes back alongside, the bowrope is secured, then the front fall put on (hopefully correctly made up) then the after fall. Then the boat is raised – to a sigh of relief if it was made up correctly. In amongst all this chaotic activity, you had to make sure all the boats fenders were brought inboard as you were hauled up. Or the jimmy would be there, dancing around, and screaming at you "FENDERS,FUCKIN',FENDERS" as you got to deck level.

When we went alongside in Portland one day, Glen and me shot off into Weymouth, where we caught the next train to Poole (where he lived) for the day, swaggered into his old local pub in rig AND got served. That made a wonderful break while we were supposed to be watching some boring sporting event.

Of course, being (extremely) naive baby sailors, fresh out of our cardboard box, we still didn't have much idea about anything, other than what had been drummed into us, so it was left to Robbo, plus the Ulsters' crew, to teach us immediate rudimentary lessons and this one is THE most important lesson you can ever learn in the 'Mob'. If the sea state is 'bouncy', i.e. it is rough, and you feel a 'yak' coming on, you have two choices. First – get below, quickly, to the heads, where you can hide, and cuddle the bowl. This is nice and safe, and no-one can see you. You feel fine after a few minutes – until the next time. The alternative would be to find a spot on the upper deck where no-one can see you, and throw up over the leeward side. This is also quite safe, as long as you hold on to something. Except, as babies, we were not accomplished enough to tell the difference between the leeward (no wind) side, or the windward (very windy) side. If you chunder over the windward side, it falls several feet, gets caught in the strong wind, comes back, and redecorates you from head to toe, in your hair, clothes, boots, ears – everywhere. You can, therefore easily tell when this has happened to someone – and it is a long time before anyone allows you to forget it. People will stand behind you making retching noises, and sniggering. I stress I was only ever seasick the once, and it wasn't aboard the Ulster. But I took the piss out of plenty who were!! This was a fantastic lesson to not pass on to others later in ones career – especially Midshipmen for some reason.

Talking of which, the ultimate 'collapse laughing', is watching someone closed up in full anti flash and respirator, already feeling ill, trying to keep breakfast down and failing. The look of surprise in their eyes as their gas mask fills up from bottom to top, with fresh puke is something else. Panic is one word I'd use, as they try to rip the mask off before hurtling to a safe place to clean up, with the rest of the world's laughing ringing in their ears!!

Amazingly, we survived everything the Ulster and Portland could throw at our hairless chins that week, and could add a bit more swank when we got back to Raleigh, as WE had been to SEA, and we were JACK!!.

Eventually our final passing out divisions were held one fine day, where we were 'guard class'. We had rehearsed and trained for this, and were to be inspected in front of our families by the Captain. I looked forward to that, as did we all, and can still remember the bitter disappointment on finding my Mum and Dad hadn't come down to see my passing out parade. I scanned the onlookers, then scanned them again for a familiar face, but nothing. I (and my mates) had spent many hours getting our kit absolutely shining for those divisions, but I completed the parade with a heavy, heavy heart.

Actually, there was no reason for me to expect them, but I still lived with the hope... I can, though, remember every drill we did, stamping our feet down hard, to create maximum noise and impression. We even had pennies in the otherwise empty magazines of our SLRs' so they rattled noisily, emphasising each swing and drill maneuver.

We got to late December 1969, and were by then suffering from the traditional naval 'RDP' (Run Down Period), leading up to Christmas leave, until that day arrived and we now were to go 'home' for two weeks. We all got buses to the ferry, and to the station, thence on the fast train to London. We attempted to buy beer, but the buffet man demanded proof of age. So we slunk off, and stayed sober instead. We sat on our kitbags – there was no room on that train for seating.

Whilst on the journey, we whiled away our time looking for a lad classed as a 'nause', as in a person likely to 'cause nause'. He had a habit of poking his face into yours, and calling you 'sunshine'. We were out gunning for him, and you may rightly assume he was not a popular kiddy. I think the word went out, because we didn't find him until just before Waterloo station – by which time he had got himself locked in the guards compartment. I still don't know whether he or the guard had done it (or even if someone else had…).

We all split up, and headed for our own next stations, then home, and never saw 'sunshine' again, even when back at Raleigh. He really knew how and when to keep a low profile.

I forgot to mention – we travelled home in our Number One uniforms. Gold badges, lanyards – the works. Best hat too. And whilst all this went unnoticed in Plymouth and on that train, I felt the urge to (as our PO told us, repeatedly) 'give it stacks of swank and swagger'. So back went the shoulders as I virtually marched in my studded boots across the underground to Euston, stamped noisily down the platform to my train under the gaze of whoever would look in my direction, and thence on to Northampton.

I got a taxi to my home, which hadn't changed a bit in the fourteen weeks I had been away, but it was nice to be there for Christmas. In the weeks that had passed since I left to join way, way back in September – I was now sixteen, going on twenty.

That first leave passed in a blur, crossed examined by relatives, and friends from the village. I do, though, remember going to a photographers in the town, to sit for a portrait – in full uniform. I used to wear it a lot in those days. Northampton didn't see too many sailors – their main source of amusement was from the army barracks at Wootton.

Chapter 4

Farewell to Plymouth – Hello to Dryad

All too soon, that first leave was over, and once again I left Northampton station, this time to return to Plymouth. I completed my last week of baby sailor training, and was then drafted. As I was detailed now to be a radar operator – clearly the best job going, you NEVER, EVER met a stupid 'RP', – that meant moving to H.M.S. Dryad, just outside Pompey. This was reached after a long journey from Plymouth to Exeter, to Salisbury, eventually arriving at our destination of Portsmouth & Southsea station. We (still Arthur, Geoff, Stevie and me) then caught a navy 'tilly, or utilicon, (otherwise known as a minibus, blue with ROYAL NAVY emblazoned on either side) to the small village of Southwick, at the back of Portsdown Hill overlooking Portsmouth harbour. Except that Dryad was below and behind the hill, well away from any kind of civilised beings. We still hadn't seen any of the grey things called warships.

We immediately collected our bedding and cap tallies, having first dumped our gear off in the most tatty huts I have ever seen. These nissen huts, collectively known as Anson Block, apparently, was where we were to live for the next six weeks – I can remember the smell even now. Our training there began with the naval tradition of divisions, followed by the course PO (PRI) (Plot Radar Instructor) telling us of what we were to learn over the next six weeks of our basic radar operators course.

This introductory radar course consisted of learning all the technical specifications, bandwidths, pulse repetition frequencies, and operating frequencies of every radar in use by the Navy, and being word perfect on them. Every time you were tested, which was daily. We learned at what range we could expect to locate an aircraft on the air radar, or what range to spot the difference between a tin-can and a submarine periscope on the navigation set, and at what range we could locate other ships on the surface search. Also the principles of IFF (identification Friend or Foe) just so we could be sure we wouldn't necessarily engage friendly aircraft. We were given extensive training on how to talk to other ships, aircraft etc, over UHF radios, learned how to use HF radio which made your voice sound like you were on heavy helium, and how to annoy everyone else by repeatedly saying 'coco pops' into the 'radio' whenever you got bored. We were taught the CORRECT voice procedure for talking to someone over a radio, and thus I learned something else which annoys me on the telly. When someone says 'roger, over and out', and the person being talked to then also says, 'roger over and out'. Why? Roger only means 'I understand what you have just said, otherwise I would have asked you to "say again"'. If the first person said over and out, there is clearly no reason for the second person to also say it., as the first one has already said 'out', meaning I am bored with this conversation, and no longer wish to talk to you. We were then taught a little rhyme :-

'Mirror mirror on the wall – who's the fairest of them all?
'Why you are Jack, without a doubt'
'Thank you mirror. Roger. Out'.

We learned about attenuation and super refraction, both being meteorological effects on radar. We were also taken into 'models', where we learned how to put all the lessons into practice by doing as near to live situations as it was possible to get.

Dryad's 'models' are mockups of various ships' operation rooms, complete with fed radar from a control room. Any kind of situation can be modeled, any kind of war game could be developed. It was as much fun as you could have, without being seasick!! We were thrown into the models alongside older ratings, going either for their 'twos', 'ones', or 'I' (second class, first class, or Instructors) qualifications. That is, they were being trained as senior, more useful operators. Us? – we were firmly at the bottom of the heap, but still learning fast. It is amazing how quickly you do something once you've been smashed round the ears with the heavy metal rolling ruler normally used to plot 'dead-reckoning' lines.

On one of these sessions, I thought I recognized one of the WRNS being trained. It turned out she was one of triplets who came from my home village. They had all apparently joined up. We had a long chat after the models session, but she was a "two" and didn't really need to be seen talking to a "basic" like me, no matter what the background and circumstances.

We also learned that standing in front of live, transmitting radar aerials was not conducive to your health. In fact, we were told, it would cook you from the inside out. A great opportunity missed by someone there, in the light of microwave ovens!!

And still we had divisions, still in heavily starched, but slightly more faded (due to the innumerable washes) eights, but there was less emphasis now we'd got away from the basic training. Don't misunderstand – we were still jumped on, and treated like the lowlife we undoubtedly were – it's just that the shit had further to roll downhill each week, as new classes came along behind us. We were by now nearly five months into our naval careers.

We had the obligatory class photo – me, Stevie, Geoff, Arthur – it seemed we were becoming Siamese Quads, but more was to come yet.

And all those duty watches with us doing the crap jobs no-one elese needed. And a Naafi we could go into, but still not buy beer – we had to go into Portsmouth to do that. At that time, as Juniors, we still had to wear 'rig' to go ashore. Though as it was a thirty minute bus ride to Portsmouth, and as we weren't allowed (due to our tender ages) in 'the Beast', we contented ourselves with the shared TV rooms, the football tables, and the badminton. Apart from the time I spent all evening searching vainly for the girl who left her molar imprints on my neck all those weeks (months? years?) ago on the Blackwater, for she hailed from Pompey.

We actually kept our visits there to a minimum, and quietly got better on the football table. I got very good – enough to beat virtually anyone (I, or we if we played doubles) who challenged. The routine at the time was that you paid to go on the table, and play whoever was on there. If you won – you stayed on there, until either you got beaten, in which case you produced the 'reserve' money which was previously placed for such a rare occasion, or scarpered for a drink in the meantime, leaving another tanner there ready for your next challenge. Some nights I (or we) would be on there all night, taking on all comers – beating them all with the same disdainful flick from the back row, which would always beat everyone. Either that, or the right hand forward would move across slowly, then dribble the ball into the oppositions' wide open net – another successful dummy! We used to nearly get into fights about that one – it was just not possible to stop it deliberately, although you may have luckily got your man to it. It worked every time. The table was just inside the Dryad Club, right by the heads, so we always attracted a good audience. Footy tables were popular, in those days, and for just a tanner for an evenings entertainment – as far as we were concerned – we never complained!

There were, though, even more fascinating machines, in a special room just outside the Naafi, called 'the automat'. This, as we soon learned, was where everyone gathered after the Naafi shut, to feed up for the night. The automat consisted of three or four machines full of various foods, one hot, one cold, one nutty and cakes, one drinks, where you put money in the top, pressed the button on the visible selection, and hoped that the correct door opened to feed you. Except that when you were three sheets to the wind, they refused to work unless you kicked the shit out of the machine, which was why they always had a duty automat rating in there. But which was also why we used to gather there most evenings.

Apart from this very visible entertainment called 'getting the scran out of the machine', other events there were mostly initiated by a very old (it seemed, though he was probably no older than 25) Able Seaman, called Jed. Jed could play guitar and sing. And eat, and drink – all seemingly at the same time. Accompanied by a Wren called Blodwyn. That's what she was known as – being Welsh. I don't think they were 'together', but they may have been, it didn't occur to us to ask! Everybody at Dryad at that time knew (of) Blodders, even now, if I find someone who admits to being there at the time, I will ask "Do you remember Blodwyn?" If they say "No", then either they didn't 'mix' well, or they're fibbing to me about when they were there...

We learned lots more naval terms from sitting in that automat. The main lesson was that the six (or seven) storey building that housed the WRNS was a) TOTALLY off limits, and b) called Tampax Tower. It probably is still known by that name. It wasn't intended to be derogatory – it's just that that was what it was called.

We were introduced to 'TV Rooms' here – there were two rooms with tellys in, one showed BBC, the other ITV. Remember those days of only two channels? By consensus, the channel could be changed, unless someone wanted to watch something else. Fights broke out in TV rooms. They always stank of smoke, were normally full of cans and nutty wrappers, and always had the spitkins full. It was a 'duty watch' job to clean them out at 'lights out', – a job to be avoided, at all costs. All shore bases had these TV rooms. It was where you ended up, either after you'd pissed all your pay up against the wall, or were duty watch, but not detailed for anything special, or if you were just a git, who didn't mix with the rest of 'the lads'. For we were extremely "clique'y" then, and remained so for our entire Naval career.

Towards the end of the radar course, and after our final exams, we were given our 'drafts', and mindful of the fact that the Ark Royal was being stocked with boxes of new baby sailors, it was with extreme relief that I received my draft to join H.M.S. Zulu – once again along with Arthur, Geoff and Stevie. My relief was tempered though by two pieces of news. Firstly , it was in refit – whatever that meant. Secondly, it was in Rosyth – wherever on Earth that was!!

At the end of our course, and while we were waiting for our draft, I was assigned to the 'buffers party', which meant being attached to a group of real sailors, who walked around Dryad most of the day, doing cleaning-up type things. This meant you could go anywhere in the vast grounds of Dryad, virtually without restriction – provided you either carried a naval issue stiff broom, or pushed the (garbage) 'truck', at that time christened 'Thunderbird Three'. As the grounds were enormous, it was possible to disappear for hours on end without question, whilst exploring the estate. I found out one day, that what was the officers wardroom, was in fact Southwick House – where the D-

Day invasion had apparently been coordinated from. That there was also a commemorative D-Day tapestry there – this I never saw despite trying for then, and subsequently on other visits there.

The 'Buffer', so called because he was a buffer between the Jimmy (or First Lieutenant to give him his correct title), and 'the lads', was a seaman branch chief or petty officer, occasionally a leading seaman, but always knew more than was good for him. He commanded authority, was generally an expert on most things, and could usually be relied upon to organise anything, anywhere. If you were told to report to the buffer – you did so immediately, or later at your peril.

So there was a joke going round at the time, about a young sailor – Junior Seaman Smith – being assigned to the buffers party, and being detailed off by the buffer to go out and sweep up with the rest of the sweepers, but that most importantly, if anyone was to see the Admiral (who was going to arrive later that forenoon), that whoever saw him first, he was to tell the buffer immediately. The young sailor vanished with his broom, and was desultorily sweeping the gutters, when a large black car, complete with Admirals pennants pulled up alongside him. The Admiral leans out, and asks who he is addressing. "Junior Seaman Smith", comes the reply, "Why – who wants to know?". "I am the Admiral" says the Admiral. "Well I'd fuck off and make myself scarce if I were you…" says JS Smith, "…'cos the Buffers after you".

We'd also be walking round singing "Jesus loves me, this I know, 'cos the Buffer told me so".

To be assigned to the buffers party, was like getting a crash course in real naval life. I learned so much more whilst in the 'party', most importantly that at stand-easy, the buffers store became a sudden tea-shop, complete with strong cheese and thick onion in crusty rolls – something I still hugely enjoy – or ham if that was what you wanted. Provided you only wanted one of the two, and either without butter, or without butter (!). Amazingly, one member of the buffers party was permanently assigned to creating these rolls, and to wetting the tea for those stand-easys'. I recall this was all sold, very cheaply, presumably with the profits going to the welfare fund… It was also staggering, the amount of people who could cram in there amongst the brooms and buckets and mops and cleaning fluids and ropes at any one time. So too, was the number of people who would just 'drop in' for a cuppa, a fag and a chat. Also, the amount of knowledge I acquired based on gossip, and sea-stories, getting more wild as the standeasys' went on, a game forever played then – the "Black-Cat'ing". These 'Black Cats' (sea stories) would usually start with 'When I was…', and continue with someone else coming in with an even better story, saying "That's nothing, when I was in…", followed by others, all trying to outdo, or Black-Cat each other. Either that, or someone would push an imaginary ships lamp, then start swaying from side to side, making swishing, whooshing, 'sea' noises. At which point – the person talking would usually founder in his 'story', or start swearing "no shit, no shit" (honest, honest), at which point the swaying got more pronounced. Having killed that story – someone else would start after as short respectful pause. This game went on ashore, onboard, during work, out of work – every sailor past or present, any time, anywhere will have a large repertoire of 'black cats'. I did, though, learn how to sweep roads, on top of my other skills!!

The buffers store had a telephone, which would periodically ring if someone was looking for anyone, we wondered at the old hands who would answer the phone with "War Office – wanna fight?", or "Stonehenge – Duty Druid", or "Netley Hospital – duty loony", or any one of a number drawn from large repertoires of previous performances.

We also learned not to give our own name away when answering, so, when asked if 'so and so' was there – we could answer either "In the bathroom doing basin trials" or "Gone down the bakers for a loaf" or "He went mad, so we shot him", or "In the fridge, getting hard". They would guarantee instant crack-up locally, and a lot of yelling on the other end. We learned how to hang up quickly, and to make ourselves immediately scarce.

The Buffers Store was, as I said, somewhere to lurk, and thus had comfortable, handy, 'rabbited' (knocked off/someone blinked at the wrong time/superfluous somewhere else) tatty red leatherette armchairs scattered around – no mean feat considering the size of the place, but the best seats would always be taken by the same old faces, and if you happened to be reclining when you should have been (respectfully) leaving – heaven help you!

One thing literally burned into my memory, was the day we went to the fire training school, near Portsea, I seem to remember, where we spent a day learning how to put fires out. Again. In this 'simulator' (which was a mock up of a section of a ship), we were taken round it, up and down all the ladders, in, and out of the compartments, shown where the fires were to be lit, and again shown how to put them out. Again – these were oil fires, so they were to burn, fiercely. We were then shown how to get into 'Fearnought' suits (fire retarding) over our ovies, and shown how to don and switch on the ICBA (breathing apparatus) gear. That seemed easy enough. But as always we looked for the 'catch'.

We swiftly found it. The ICBA gear we had so carefully checked was swapped for facemasks which were blacked out. Totally. We were essentially blind. The fire pan was ignited, and in we went, dragging the hose with the spray-jet switched to spray, to form a protective water wall to shield us from the intense heat, and the other one linked back to the foam can, pumping foul smelling bubbles everywhere.

In we went, slowly, having ascended the external ladders. We entered the hatch at the top (doing all this by memory and by feel – no vision, remember?), and slowly worked our way through the simulator towards the seat of the fire, carefully slapping the back of our hand on the bulkheads. This, we were told, was the safest way to feel the heat. If we did it with our fingertips, there was an excellent chance they would weld onto the steel with the heat, whereas we would not miss the skin off the backs of our hand. We checked deck after deck, descending all the time, and compartment after compartment, eventually deciding this was where the fire was, as we could see a dim glow through the face-masks. It was also extremely hot, even with our water wall. We therefore called up the foam team, and then threw the foam everywhere, dousing the fire.

Scared? 'Course not, we couldn't see anything to be scared of. We were more worried about the PO Stoker who continually prodded us in the ribs with his spanner, insisting we keep going further and further into the unseen blaze.

Until it was the second teams' go. We sat back, drinking in the fresh (although somewhat smoky) air, whilst they went in. At that point, we could see what we had just dealt with. Believe me, if I had been in that second team, and had seen what really happened, instead of the dim glow, I would have been, in the vernacular, "shitting clump-blocks" when I went in. The flames and smoke leaping not only out of the top of the simulator, but also out of every opening, were frightening. And when the PO opened the ground floor door to check on progress, we felt the heat from many yards away.

All in all then, a brilliant course, more experience, more abilities learned and another good day for us.

A further skill learned rapidly was that of armed security guard. One weekday morning, me and a mate were detailed off to accompany the Pay Officer to the bank, in the minibus. I don't remember the bank we went to but we were heavily armed on that run. With helves (pickaxe handles), and boots and gaiters. I am not sure how much money we collected, but with several hundred sailors of all rates being paid the following day, there must have been a small fortune there, even for those dim, dark days.

Queuing up for your pay was traditional then, you had to fall in, get to the front of the queue, salute, announce – in a loud voice – who you were and your official number, and hold out your opened paybook in your upturned cap, with your station card also present, for the Pay Officer to give you your hard earned dosh. At that time then, the Regulators or Master -at-Arms (both of whom liked to think they were the RN equivalent of police, which made them not only hated personally, but made the 'reggy' branch THE most loathed in the mob) would deliver a swingeing attack on the length of your hair, and announce that you would have to report to them next day with your hair cut, and as a reminder, he would swiftly remove your station card, meaning you couldn't get ashore. As such, you dreaded going to get paid, and would find any, but any excuse to avoid pay parade. You thus rapidly got your ears lowered either ashore – where you'd stand a chance of getting a decent cut, or at the base barber – who'd shear most of your locks off, and reported back to the 'joss' to reclaim your station card. You also learned to 'lose' a station card, and apply for another one to use as a spare, though if you were caught doing that, you were in DEEP shit.

The other security guard aspect was that of 'security foot patrol', whereby you patrolled the whole grounds and perimeter of the vast Dryad estate, during non-working hours. This got you into all sorts of darkened corners, accompanied only by a 'stornophone' (short range two way radio) a helve, and a pussers torch, green. You did this, or the building patrols, where, even though all the 'secure' buildings – models, trainers etc – were locked, we still had to creep round making sure there was no-one there, or that they were in fact locked. We also checked all the safes, and God help the keeper of any safe found open. Or of any door open/unlocked when it should have been secured.

Although the security patrol had to sleep fully dressed in the same room, behind the QMs' lobby, ready to react and muster with helves, boots, gaiters, torches and windy-burbs within seconds, and even though they had to get up to do two two hour patrols during the course of their duty, at least that was preferable to being detailed for the fire cart. This cart contained fire fighting gear, hoses, hydrants, ladders, and was kept by the MT garage, at one end of Dryad. If there was a fire exercise, or indeed a real fire, the fire cart crew had to leg it from wherever they were to the cart, wait for everyone else, then high-tail it to wherever the fire (exercise) was, with the cart in tow. It was not a light cart. One person was responsible for the hydrant key, and as a matter of course, the stand-pipe would be fitted, the hydrant and hose connected, and the water turned on. Then it all had to be stowed away and returned to the garage. Absolutely knackering. Not for weak people, and at that time splitarses were not allowed to do it – they sat in Tampax Tower doing their own duties. It was therefore critical that the broadcast worked throughout the camp, and especially in the Naafi, where most of the duty watch seemed to muster after supper. As long as you were sober enough to do your job, no-one seemed to mind too much.

At that time, Dryad used to have an old, blue, single decker bus, converted into a greasy-spoon, known as Dots. Dots seemed to be open all day, every day, for what I still remember as the best SRE and BRE (Sausage, runny egg. Bacon, runny egg) sarnies ever made by human hand. Also for strong tea and coffee. Excellent for waking and sobering up from the previous evenings Naafi run. It was always a difficult decision between there or the buffers store for breakfast, always assuming you hadn't got up in time for your real breakfast, or were, indeed, still hungry anyway.

Chapter 5

H.M.S. Zulu, *in Rosyth, in dry-dock*

It was all too soon time to move on, so once again, we packed all our gear into the obligatory kitbag and suitcase, but by then we had also proudly acquired a pussers holdall, just like proper 'tars' owned. As its name implied – this carried everything and anything, and was made from heavy-duty brown canvas, with a ropey zip, usually replaced quickly with 'eyes' and rope. Ones name could be emblazoned on it, along with the ship(s) served on. Grips (as they were known) were the RN equivalent of the Ford Capri – customisable to you, unique to you. Recognisable instantly in a heap of dozens. Once correctly packed, they could, in emergencies, be used as pillows, seats, footballs – multi purpose bits of kit.

We boarded the train to Waterloo, then to Kings Cross and up to Edinburgh. We got off there (in our red-badged 'twos' as we were on official duty), and finally found the train for Inverkeithing where we were to be finally met by the standard 'tilly for transport to Rosyth Naval Base.

One feeling I remember, not only joining the Zulu, but joining any ship, shore base or unit, whether for a weeks course, two year draft, or any other reason – was the feeling of elation and expectation, coupled with those of unease, of fears of the unknown. What would it be like there? What would my new mates be like? Would there be anyone there I already knew? Where would we go? What would the runs ashore be like? What would the senior rates and officers look like? How long would it take to settle in? To find my way round? Would my 'pit' be comfortable? What would they think of me where I was going? These and hundreds more worries and fears would tumble through my head each time I approached new territory. I assume my comrades also felt them, and probably still do. It's a feeling that takes a lot of thought and summing up to put into words. The other problem was, of course, that unless an oppo was fortunate enough to get drafted with you, you were leaving the absolute comfort of somewhere you knew, throwing it all away to go and start anew. And that was pretty much the perks of that particular job.

Of course, you knew, deep down, that wherever you went, there would always be a good bunch of mates you would team up with, initially to go ashore with and suss out, but eventually to from absolute bonding friendships with people you would fight with and alongside of, to the complete exclusion of everything else. If you were matey with someone, you would always go ashore with them, play cards, uckers, doms and crib with them. Sometimes with others, but usually with them. You got to know their moods and behaviour patterns – and they knew yours. These were very much man-to-man relationships. From this bonding (if you like to call it that) you soon got to accept others into your group, until there would be a whole gang always doing everything together. This wasn't safety in numbers, as we didn't need gang mentality or behaviour – one of us would happily take on all comers, if necessary, but it was a gang of men doing what 'civvies' would love to do, but found it to be not really acceptable. We disregarded those conventions, and went round together anyway. So that took care of the question on mates. And we didn't entertain poofs.

If you met up with someone you knew from a previous draft, you'd clearly be matey with them, if that was what you were before, otherwise – you let the Navy take its course, and began building friendships again. After that, the rest of the worries eased and evaporated quickly. Once you'd settled in for that first sleepless night, and listened as that first 'Call The Hands' went, you knew the only way forward was to 'fit in'. If not – you'd have a very lonely future ahead of you. That first morning of any new draft, then, was the one to get past as it contained all the nause and surprises. After that – dead easy!!

So, I recall being absolutely and completely overawed by the first sight of the Forth Road Bridge, and nearly as much again at the sight of the Rail Bridge we found ourselves actually crossing, noisily. I remember also the first look at the dockyard at Rosyth, thinking we'd soon be boarding our first ship, wondering where it would be carrying us to. We hadn't been told much at that stage, just that it was a Type 81 Tribal Class, General Purpose Frigate, with loads of different radars', and well armed with missiles and guns and all sort of things. And obviously painted grey. I still get a thrill whenever I go across those bridges, and unconsciously look over to the dockyard for the 'Zulu'.

We boarded the 'tilly and sped off towards Rosyth dockyard, gabbling excitedly all the way, taking in all the scenery as we travelled. We were somewhat narked, then, to note that we turned off the road before the dockyard, into H.M.S. Cochrane. Surely some mistake, we thought, as we disembarked the bus. Not so, we were told, the 'Zulu is currently in dry-dock being refitted. She is over halfway through a two-year refit. She'll be afloat in summer, and… At which points our little Junior Seamen (Radar Plotter (Basic)) hearts plummeted. We had expected… well I don't exactly know, but we had at least expected to go on a real ship, and to sail off into the dawn. That was not to be. Not tonight anyway, as we unhappily unpacked our gear into the very smart (after the low standard we'd endured so far in our short

Naval career's) many-to-a-room accommodation block. We were in together, but had other Zulu ratings in with us. They gave us the run down, it WAS in refit, it WOULD be afloat in a couple of months, but as yet it was a mystery where we would be deployed to.

Throughout our time at Raleigh and Dryad, we had been exposed to lots of abbreviations, JS meant Junior Seaman, ME meant Marine Engineer, OEM was an electrician. We found a new one today, one that worried me. What was an MNE? A Bootneck, we were informed. What do they do? Not a great deal apart from what they are told. And weren't marines put on board in the old days to keep sailors in check? Yes, but not this lot – marines are very keen, and eager to please, and when not cleaning their weapons, they would be assigned to parts of ship with us. Oh yes, they were also riot squad, and landing party. More to worry about – what the hell were they? You'll soon find out if you get assigned to them, we were assured. Funny, even Marines hated the one musician in their detachment – even they regarded him as a waste of good oxygen. All he ever did was blow his silly little bugle, and do emergency first aid, if required. It follows that if we hated booties – booties hated their own bandsmen!

We got on with our first real joining routine, collect cap-tallies, collect bedding, and the anti-flash hoods and gloves we wore at action stations to protect us against explosions, fires – that sort of thing, get assigned to the watch and station bill, locate the Naafi. Return to the mess, unpack, go to supper. Go to the Naafi. In civvies. BUY A PINT!!!! YIPPEE – no-one cared how old we were – we got served. And then to the obligatory automat, as we didn't (then) go out off base unless we had to. The nearest 'town' was Inverkeithing – a taxi or bus ride away. Or Rosyth which was full of 'married patches', and consequently of no interest to us.

To explain 'Joining Routine' – this is a naval tradition whereby every time you join a ship, even if it is only for a few days – you have to go through the joining routine. Generally, it means registering your presence, usually it means being added to the watch and station bill (which records the watch, action station, defence station, day job, emergency station and liferaft station of everyone on board) all of which we took extremely seriously, and getting a new cap tally to tie. Sometimes it meant getting issued with blankets, pillows, mattress – all of which you would have to carefully carry to your bunk, along – of course, with all your other kit. If you put it down anywhere, it would have grown a set of legs by the time you got back, and would have walked off all by itself. That is one thing about sailors, if it wasn't nailed down, it would either would walk, or vanish into thin air, having never existed, or attempt to swim. If it was made of metal, someone with magnetic fingers would test its obviously magnetic properties. Theft from an oppo, or theft of personal property however, was not tolerated, as we were to find out.

The down side of the joining routine, was the leaving routine – the reverse, but this time you'd have to return everything you signed for when you joined. If you didn't have enough blankets, then officially, they would be stopped from your pay. So you ALWAYS made sure you had enough to take back exactly what you drew – even if you had to 'find' it elsewhere…

When we bedded down that night, in our Pjs', we suddenly discovered that nobody else EVER wore them. Now we found out why they were insultingly, but accurately called 'brown hatters overalls' – it was assumed only brown hatters wore them, in bed. They were therefore their overalls. Simple – but it ensured many laughs when 'new boys' joined the ship(s) and wore them. Nobody ever lasted above one night with them on (except Stevie who had also come to the Zulu), but we quickly swapped into the much more acceptable boxer shorts and T-shirt, as worn by the rest of the navy.

The next morning, we changed from green recruits into real dabtoes by virtue of the fact that we were now 'hands'. We were all mustered outside the 'block', and marched through the base, through the dockyard, round the dockyard, round the dry-docks, eventually coming to a halt against a red and grey blob sitting half covered with tarpaulins, at the bottom of an extremely large dry dock, all surrounded and dwarfed by huge grey cranes on railway lines, swinging seemingly impossible loads around with the greatest of ease. You will gather from this description that I was not in the least bit impressed – I had really expected more, at least a real grey thing. We scrambled down the gangway to the quarter-deck, saluted, and waited to be told what to do next. I will point out now it wasn't just us who had been marched down, it was the whole ships company, every day, twice a day. We used to march back to Cochrane for lunch (and a pint or two), and then march back afterwards. Unless you were 'cooks', in which case you cleaned up the accommodation until 0900, then walked down the ship unescorted, via 'Bernards' (Naval Jailors (tailors)) if it was open. Anyway, by the time we arrived on that first morning, it was within seconds of 0805, or BWH (Both Watches of the Hands) – in naval terms time to start work. We had already been assigned to our 'Parts Of Ship', and now we finally met and fell in with very much 'bin there' Able Seamen. Then we were checked over by the POS (Part Of Ship) Petty Officer. Having overcome that, the PO reported to the 'Buffer', who then reported to the Jimmy, who then told the Buffer to carry on, who then told the PO to carry on, who then ushered us away to start work. All very civilised, really. If the Jimmy wanted to say something special – he'd have his few words, as would the Buffer. We were also introduced to 'Father' Tribe.

Very old (compared to us), with three (long service/good conduct) 'badges', and a great deal of experience – he was the LHOM (Leading Hand of the Mess). He looked after us, and the rest of the radar plot department. We had our own PRI, but it was Father who virtually ran everything else. He quickly had us assigned to our daily work detail, which was either a) cleaning a part of the ship where a dockyard matey had just made a mess, or b) painting over where a dockyard matey had just finished with a welding torch, or c) removing paint from another expanse of metal, ready for it to be repainted. We used to get through gallons of red lead primer, and even more gallons of ships side grey. And through more paintbrushes than you could ever imagine, due to our indolence in cleaning them after we'd used them. Why should we? Pusser was rich, and could afford the new ones. We also had a 'painter' – unbelievably (!) a rating assigned to issue paint, of whatever colour, in 'kettles', with thick bristled brushes of a type determined by what you intended to use it for. No good issuing a varnish brush to paint with. Nor a paint brush to varnish with. He'd also recover the brushes just before 'secure' at 1600, at which point he'd clean all the brushes, hang them all up to dry, empty all the kettles back into the drums, then clean them, then run like hell to join the rest of the Ras in their dash to get ashore. However, it was not the done thing to wind the Ras' up, so the paint would HAVE to be returned by 1530 (or thereabouts, or earlier if possible, like before lunch).

One of the perks of being painter, was that he had to keep the 'crests' in good condition. Crests were shields, each with arms or heraldry on, representing the ship, or its battle honours. For the Zulu, we had a Zulu warrior's shield and assegai, on a blue/white wavy background, surrounded by a gold 'rope' design. So it was the job of the painter to not only keep all the crests gleaming, but to be able to make crests, from plaster, then paint them. We sailors would also be on the earwig for crests, as they were handy little souvenirs to get off the ship unnoticed, and could be traded for beer and other goodies while ashore. So the painter would normally be heavily leaned upon to make these. Unless you were the QM or BM, and had the keys to the paintshop at night, and were bored, and could paint with a steady hand, AND knew where the plaster of paris was, AND could find the right moulds…

RA stood for ration allowance, otherwise known as 'living ashore', quite rightly, with their families. They were allowed leave slightly before us, and would set records changing out of eights, and into civvies, before chucking all their 'gizzits' into their grip, and hurtling down the gangway to get home. It was not acceptable to get in the way of an RA under full power – you'd wish you hadn't . We knew of one who, after the afternoon standeasy, would put his civvies on, then put his eights over the top. He then only had to rip off trousers and shirt, and change into the old faithful elasticated boots (trendy!) before getting away ahead of the herd. How we respected him!

Gizzits were what they say. If someone was emptying out his locker, to tidy it up, or had superfluous gear, he would say "Anyone want any gizzits?", we would crowd round to see what he had. A bit like a car-boot, only no money changed hands. Or we would see someone doing this, and muster there, asking "Got any gizzits? Go on, Gizzit".

We had only then been with the ship for one day, when I was invited to go and find a particular stoker, one 'Nutty' Slack, a large, red-faced fender-bellied but happy chappy who, it was said, had a pair of overalls for me. I searched for him for hours, from one end of the ship to the other, and never did get my ovies – he later told me it was a wind up. Not that I ever, ever fell for any more, Once bitten – that was me. Though my mate spent quite a while in the buffers store, where he had been sent for a long weight (wait). He got well and truly bollocked for falling for that. Apparently the junior electricians would be sent all round the dockyard for red or green oil for the port or starboard navigation lights, or even for replacement filaments for light bulbs, and other people would be sent in gangs to find a ten-ton shackle, only to find you could actually put it round your finger. Oh it was fun. The really gormless ones actually went looking for the good old bucket of steam. More on gullibility later…

What we did get, though was an upgrade to our 'pussers dirk'. The dirk had been carried by us, tied to a lanyard, then secured around our waists, since day one at Raleigh, and God help you if your dirk was rusty, or your lanyard any other colour but pure white. So we marched down to the ship on that first day, and found no self respecting tar wore dirks. What they wore instead was a rigging set. This would be drawn from stores initially, and comprised a leather pouch, leather belt, marling spike (or 'fid'), and a large sharp knife with a wooden handle. This was our passport to instantly being able to free ourselves from unfortunate bits of rope, or at a push – splicing both rope and wires, with help from the fid to keep the strands apart. Well, that was the theory.

Splicing thus became dead easy, and I can still put a splice in any kind of rope, within minutes. Not that that helps me in any way – it is just one of those things you never forget. What we didn't bargain for, was that the 'older the hand' you were, the more personalised your rigging set became. For instance, while it was 'a good thing' wearing (for us) just a rigging knife and spike in a small pouch, we could extemporise the pouch, make our own from spare leather (or two unpicked then laboriously re-sewn together), then find (smaller) sailmaker's knives, small hand spikes and anything else to weigh the pouch down with. Essentially then, the longer you served, the more crap you would load into the ever growing pouch.

One chap I knew used to cart a hand-axe round with him, which he would throw in your direction if riled. Others would 'borrow' mole grips, pliers, small saws – anything to pad the pouch out. You would then need to zealously guard your pouch, in case any unscrupulous gits liked it (or it's contents) more than you. The original dirk, then, was never used again. I still have my original, still with my name stamped on it. We'd also sit for hours, with a whetstone, sharpening our dirks and knives until we were able to shave with them. Literally. We knew that – in all honesty – one day, our life could depend on our knives, and that if the time came when a piece of unruly rope wound itself round our foot, then we could instantly cut ourselves free, while we screamed and headed towards the ships side. Well, that was the intention at least. We just liked to show off how sharp they were, watching rope fray as we bounced the sharp side off it, without any sawing motions! Oh yes – we were intensely proud of our rigging sets, especially as the most common use of a 'fid', was to puncture goffa cans and beer cans in order to get at the contents!

Another thing most prized, was a green pussers torch. Peculiarly, these had a head at right angles to the body, with a clip on the back to allow it to be attached to your shirt pocket. These were highly prized and avidly guarded. You could even nick the batteries to go in them once they ran down, then throw the old spent ones at anything that moved. Shite-hawks, for example.

The other item now consigned to the bottom of the lockers, was our Seamanship Manual – our book of knowledge. Realistically, you would know it intimately, and be able to reel off any information from any page about any subject. I mock, but we really did know everything in there.

We discovered scranbags at this time. THE scranbag was where, if you lost any gear anywhere, it would ostensibly end up in the scranbag. The scranbag would be 'opened' several times a month, for people with lost gear to claim it back, at a price. Any money realised went into the ship's welfare fund. Oddly and eerily, gear would repose there for months and months and never be claimed. Conversely, if you lost anything useful or valuable the chances are it would never appear in the aforementioned scranbag. After months of non-movement, the scranbag would be consigned to the paintshop, and anything in it would be used as rags. Alternatively, 'scranbag' was what you were called if you looked a mess before you went ashore, or if your 'eights' looked like you'd slept in them. Scranbag, along with Shit-tip and Gro-bag were, then, terms of endearment. If though anyone hinted that you looked like a scranbag (otherwise known as a 'sack of shit tied round the middle with string'), it was a good cue to smarten yourself up. Pronto.

The welfare committee, responsible for the welfare fund, was a group of ratings, presided over by the jimmy, who would allocate outgoing funds against income, making sure the one never exceeded the other. Money went in there from varied sources, mostly external to the ship, and was allocated for, for example – ship's company dances, subsidising ship's crested lighters, ties etc. A very useful committee, and one everybody tried to get on.

Ship's company dances were organised infrequently during a commission, perhaps three or four times. Generally held in home port, they could be held abroad too. Unfortunately, I only ever got to one during my entire career, as I was 'duty' for every one ever held on every ship I ever served in. The one I went to was held at H.M.S. Victory (as the navy base in Pompey was named in the old days), and I was duty shore patrol for that too.

We were educated into 'dhobey bags', and 'dhobey dust'. The bags were where we would keep all our personal wash kit. We also hung large varied colour towels on our lockers to dry, as by now we'd got shut of our white pussers issue ones. Our bags held soap, shampoo, razor and shaving cream (if, by now, you could muster hair on your face) toothbrush, toothpaste, deodorant and foo-foo (talcum powder). If you grabbed your dhobey-bag and towel, it was a pretty good bet you'd be off to do your own basin trials – in the bathroom, for the traditional naval 'shit, shave, shampoo and shower'. The 'dust' was washing powder, for although we'd gladly give all our other gear to the laundry crew, we'd never dream about letting them have our 'nix and sox' – you'd never hear the end of it if you did!! We'd therefore carry that day's shorts and socks, and crash them out vigorously in the metal sink before rinsing them out, wringing them almost dry before we moved on to the shower. Incidentally, we would run with just two pairs of socks, and two pairs of shorts. We would wear one set, while the other was 'in the wash'. The height of luxury was to have three or more pairs of each!!

Shower over, we'd then drop our wet gear off in the drying room before proceeding back to the mess for the final rite – that of spreading the foo-foo about. Finally, we'd get re-dressed. All this would normally take place just after 'secure', and perhaps last fifteen minutes, perhaps up to half an hour, depending on how sociable you felt, or whether you were in a dash to get ashore. It would normally take place well before supper, except if you were duty watch in which case you'd do the fire exercise first, then eat supper, then get your daily dhobey.

It was, though, dangerous to leave your dhobey bag anywhere else but in your locked locker. It was recognised that if you came offshore and found a bag lurking, it wasn't unknown, that when you cleaned your teeth (religious at that we were), you would be sorely tempted to borrow someone else's toothbrush, to do things with it that it wasn't supposed to do, to put it in places they weren't designed to go. And then watch as the following day, you saw the owner putting it innocently into his mouth. We knew what had happened to it... We would though lend dhobey dust etc, if a mate had run out.

These 'basin trials' were a constant source of amusement, obviously, as the bathrooms were tiny and cramped, and would be full of many people, generally buck naked, sometimes wrapped in only a towel (for that was the accepted 'dress of the day' for basin trials), all trying to get ashore. Space was at a premium, with queues developing first for a basin, then for an available, free shower. The air was always full of water being thrown everywhere, but more usually full of ribald comments about other peoples anatomy, about the placement of various tattoos, whatever – the air was always vulgar, necessarily – we had to let off steam somehow, and it was accepted this was one of those places. Rank and seniority didn't exist. Comments like "I've dropped my soap – everyone stand still", or "If you wash it more than twice you must be wanking" would be the more repeatable... You can see, it didn't pay to be shy or retiring – you HAD to join in, or be thought of as... well, you decide.

If I make this sound like a 'brown hatters tea-party', that is most definitely not my intention – the Navy is NOT like that AT ALL. I will say now, that whatever anyone thinks about sailors, the incidence of queers aboard navy ships was non-existent. I only met one during my entire career, and he was very successfully working his ticket, so we were never one hundred percent sure about him. Nevertheless, it was common practice to pretend to be, to wind other people up, and phrases like "I joined the navy for rum, bum, and baccy, I've had me rum, I've had me baccy – come 'ere boy", or "Fetch I another cabin boy – I've split this'un", would be often repeated. Or you'd be in the heads (or a toilet ashore) in a pistil next to someone you may not know, look over into what he had in his hand, and innocently ask "New shoes Pal?"

On a daily basis, we learned new slang, new insults and new greetings. It was common to walk into the mess – at standeasy, say – and shout "Morning men" – the response would come back "Starboard Ten". Or we'd shriek "Morning chaps – oh, and you Poison" (or whoever), just for the response, which I'm sure you can guess.

As the ship was on shoreside power, and you were obviously not allowed to use the ships 'heads' or bathrooms, you had to climb up the gangway off the ship, across to the nearest shoreside ones in order to relieve or clean yourself. Bearing in mind we joined the Zulu in Scotland, in winter, we quickly learned to do everything in a hurry, just in order to keep warm. We used to dress in our Number eights, with a sweater, and our foul weather jackets, and put on the odd t-shirt (until that was banned). What we were issued with though, was foul-weather jackets and steaming bats (boots). The jackets were thick, waterproof (to a point), windproof, and extremely warm, with a padded bit that fitted round your face when the hood was put up. The bats were to be worn as dress of the day, to save wear and tear on our shiny boots and shoes. What a godsend they were – I don't think a day went past when you didn't spill paint or oil on them, or catch them against something – and the best bit was, when they wore out, you replaced them for a free new pair!

We found our way all round the ship in no time, and explored virtually every inch of it, from the magazines to the mast head, from the bridge to the radar office, from stem to stern, learning each compartment, its location, and anything else we were required to know. Each compartment, passage, and flat on a ship has its own identity. Normally, this identity corresponds to a generic marking, which (from memory) comprised the first number corresponding to the deck above or below the main deck, the next letter gave the compartment from 'A' the most forr'd then progressively aft, then which side of the centreline, then a final number. This made it easy for fire and emergency crews to locate the compartment holding the emergency. However, to make life even easier, some were individually named. For example, 'the bridge flat' was the one behind the bridge, the tiller flat, was the most aft place you could go below decks and was where the steering gear was. It got hot in there, and could be the scene of major panics if an emergency arose.

We were also assigned by then to our 'watches', taking as usual one duty every fourth day, with two long weekends per month. One snag with long weekends was the train fare south. At the time, we were paid still £7 per fortnight, having to queue up, and salute with our green paybooks open in our outstretched hands to claim it (plus fag-stamps), so that clearly wasn't enough to get us home. However, shortly after we joined the Zulu, we had a massive payrise to almost £25, which gave us money to burn. In those days we didn't even have to pay for food or accommodation whilst living ashore – that came later.

What we did get in amongst our pay, was two things. One was KUA, or Kit Upkeep Allowance. This was a set amount of money, paid directly to us, which was to go towards replacement kit – eights, shoes, socks and the like, except that it was such an insignificant amount, we just spent it along with all our other dosh, then bought replacement kit only as a last resort, and only when our current gear started to fall from our bodies.

The other item, was what some far-seeing Admiral included. This was what became known as the 'X factor'. This was an amount of money which was allocated into all future pay reviews and rises, and meant when the extremely mean fisted civil servants had finished haggling over our rises, the Admirals could then say "Ah yes – but what about the X factor…?", and get us a few more percent into our rise. Unsurprisingly, the X factor was highly popular, as was the person who introduced it, whoever he was.

By now, we had been 'exposed' to the rest of the ships company, especially to our own (radar) division, and therefore to the more able sailors who were to guide us over the coming months, and who took to letting us accompany them into the 'Central' in Inverkeithing. We felt we had 'arrived' then, sitting with the rest of the old hands in our radar division, getting pints of heavy down us like professionals, chasing it with 'wee ones'. Then calling at the chippy for a black mans dick (haggis) supper before returning by shared fast black (taxi) to Cochrane. We had a Leading Seaman – Mac he was, or 'Foul-Bowels' as he was known. He stank. We fell in for BWH one cold, crisp morning, with snow on the deck. I give him his due – he warned us he was going to, but we were not prepared for the result. I kid you not – he cleared the open quarter-deck. We hung over the guard-rails – gagging and gasping for breath. I have never inhaled anything so disgusting – not even the teargas. Mac? – he just cracked up laughing, and kept sniggering for the rest of the day.

Fast Blacks were always the preferred mode of travel, we would not usually walk through the dockyard to get ashore, relying instead on a quick shore call to the taxi rank outside the gate. They would nearly always be there in minutes, at which point we'd all scramble over the gangway to ensure we didn't have to ride shotgun. Shotgun was next to the driver, from which there was no escape from paying. We liked it in the back!!

The only time we ever fell over getting the fast black, was Friday secure (1600), when we started long weekend leave, or Saturday lunchtime (start of a short weekend). In most ports, it wasn't such a problem, having to wait for a taxi to get off on weekend, as the trains were at least twice hourly. But from Rosyth, we'd either have to get to Inverqueerthing for a connection for the 'every other hour' train, or get a taxi direct to Waverly in Edinburgh. This clearly cost more, but got you on to an earlier train.

Fortunately, I used to have a choice for Northampton, I'd either go West Coast, changing at Brum then straight to Northampton, or I'd go to Kings Cross, over to Euston, then back up. It depended on the availability of trains. And taxis, which is why we'd end up walking to Cochrane on a Friday, while we waited for the fleets of taxis to get back from Edinburgh, to eventually get us to Inverqueerthing for our final run prior to doing a duty weekend '48 on'!!

Sometimes on a Friday, we'd get adventurous, and cross the bridges to get to H.M.S. Lochinvar, on the opposite bank of the Firth of Forth. This was another base, but for H.M.S. Abdiel, and her squadron of attendant minesweepers. It was rumoured that there had recently been a mutiny on one of the sweepers over there, and – we were told – 'sweeper' ratings had hairier arses than us, and could drink more. So it was with trepidation we first went there, but we soon settled in – they were just like us after all.

As 'RPs', we used to muster in the Ops Room occasionally, for briefings, debriefings, and one day we were told we would be going for a weeks training at Dryad – called a PCT (Pre Commissioning Training). The plus side of this was that we would get a weekend leave at either end of it, the down side was that we would have to stay at H.M.S. Victory, commuting from there, up to Dryad daily.

Before this, we learned about the navy tradition of time, which was – everything was related to 'Zulu' time. Unfortunate, as it took us a while to figure out that 'Zulu' time was GMT. And not our own time zone, just for H.M.S. Zulu. More about 'Zulu' time later.

Chapter 6
Our first 'run' in Pompey

Yet again, we packed 'steaming kit', just the minimum required to get us to Portsmouth, do our course, and get back to Rosyth, with enough room for our civvies. At this time, 'going ashore rig', although civvies, had to be good, clean civvies. So you could tell 'jack' a mile off – sta-prest trousers, open necked shirt, and jacket. Plus maybe steaming bats. Or a 'thousand-miler' (similar to a 'polo' shirt), so called because of the distance between washes. So by the time they had been packed, there was precious little room left for the two sets of 'eights'. And, everyone always and only wore blue or black socks, either in uniform or out.

So we all met up at Waterloo on the Sunday evening, for the specific train (to ensure we all turned up together) to get to Portsmouth, and bundled into 'Victory', going through the joining routine, and on to the mess we were to use. This was on the second floor of an old building, heated by a stove in the centre of the room, surrounded by bunks and kit-lockers. Except that they didn't lock, and during that week things vanished mysteriously during the day while we weren't there. And we never did find out who or how.

On the first morning, we mustered, boarded the bus – all twenty or so of us, and went to Dryad, complete with 'attitude', as we were now Jack weren't we? We HAD been (limited) there, and almost seen it, but, importantly, we were proudly part of THE ships company of H.M.S. ZULU, and now here we were with our H.M.S. ZULU cap tallies, amongst all the Dryads. In amongst the trainees, who obviously envied us as we strutted and swaggered into the Naafi at lunchtime for our traditional beers with the rest of the lads. We actually enjoyed that week of training – we went back into the 'Tribal' model, professionally this time – not mere trainees, and took up the roles we had been given back in Rosyth, we operated the 'fed' radar, made all the correct reactions, didn't get sunk too frequently, and learned what the officers looked like who were to rule our lives over the coming months. We also noted how they reacted – who tended towards flat-out panic, and who didn't. Who would shout and scream, and who wouldn't. Models were now more fun (we knew more about what we were doing, and didn't make quite so many mistakes), and as they were to all intents and purposes life sized ops rooms, you could be forgiven occasionally for thinking you were actually on board the Zulu. Except that it still didn't rock, or bob up and down.

We cracked up one day – we always had very serious briefings before going in, so we would know of 'the threat' we were to expect from what force, from which direction, and if it was air, surface or sub-surface, or all three, or two – or whatever. One day, we were told the threat was whatever, which carried 'Kipper' missiles. Kipper being the Nato codeword for the thing in question. At this, Mac broke down into uncontrollable giggling. When asked to explain what was so funny about the word 'Kipper', he confessed he hadn't been listening properly, and had thought the briefing person had said 'Kirp' (a naval word for 'willie'). We all then fell off our own chairs.

We again learned much, much more, us four 'juniors' in that week, but it was the 'after hours' socialising that was the best bit, and moulded our 'crew'. Each evening we returned to Victory, checked to see what else had gone missing, changed, ate in the massive dining hall, and then vanished in amongst the hundreds and hundreds of like-minded matelots onto 'The Strip' in Portsmouth. We were taken round the old pubs, now gone – I don't even remember most of their names apart from the Albany – they have since been demolished, destroying a lot of the character and charisma of Portsmouth. But I can remember some of the inhabitants, and recall that at least some of the Inns we frequented had sawdust on the floor (to aid in the sweeping up of multi-flavoured, many textured psychedelic yawns). One of the more memorable characters was 'Landslide Face', so called because one side of his face had dropped, dragging his eye with it. This, and the resultant stalactites from his mouth, were alleged to have been caused by his habit of keeping the money from the newspapers he sold, in his mouth. Guess where we didn't buy newspapers. Plus the brown hatters, hair dyed and bouffanted – something I always found totally repulsive. Brown hatters – a term I have never heard since, originates from differently sexed people wearing brown hats, years ago.

Brown hatters could be wound up easily by ignoring them, or by showing them a traditional naval 'curse' – by putting ones thumb-tip between the index and second fingers, wiggling the said thumbtip, and going 'Ssssss' at them. This, for some strange and unknown reason, would irritate and annoy them intensely. As would trying out the well known pouf test, which comprises of asking them 'Can you whistle?', as it was a well known fact that brown hatters cannot whistle, especially with their thumb stuck up their bums!!!

A joke at the time was about a matelot and his parrot, who lived next door to the local queen, and every time the queen passed the parrot, the parrot would scream "Brownhatterbrownhatterbrownhatter", until the queen could stand it no longer, and asked the matelot to make the parrot stop doing it.

The next day, as the queen approached the parrot, he noticed it had its beak secured with tape, however as he passed the parrot, the parrot stood on one leg, tucked one free talon between the others, and went "Sssssssssssssssss"...

...and I know we drank 'blood' at one and nine a pint (scrumpy from the wooden barrel/blackcurrant top), and the local 'Courage', and more rum than we knew what to do with. All this was in the days, I'm sorry to say, when you could get out of your tree for a quid, including fish and chips on the way back. By the time we left after those few short days in Pompey, we could navigate our way not only through 'models', but also up and down the strip, back via the Chinese (or sometimes the chippie, or even the pie shop), back to Victory, knowing EXACTLY when to stop 'playing the OD' (when the patrol wagons hove into view), and how to behave toward our elders. We were, of course, still the lowlife as juniors, but we came to gradually be accepted by our elders and peers. I also clearly remember my first Chinese meal, in a sitdown, upstairs in the one almost next door to the 'Albany', washed down with large amounts of Mateus Rose. I even remember that I ate my prawn curry, and that it was extremely tasty. Whatever we ate, we'd always remember to bring back a pint of milk, ready to ease the hangover guaranteed to strike the next morning.

Oh yes, and eventually we were actually properly introduced to Dots – all RPs' knew of Dots, of what they served – it was a gathering point for us now, running up the steps shouting 'SRE and a tea please', then playing the one-armed-bandit at a tanner a go to try to recoup some of our spendings from the previous nights' run, while we attempted vainly to sober up from the previous nights' run ashore.

Chapter 7

Back to Reality in Rosyth

All too soon it was time to return to Rosyth, with the promised long weekend on route. We got back in time for job-changes, and I was moved from top part of ship, to bo's'ns mate. That meant being the gopher for the quartermaster, and standing on the gangway of the ship, In simple terms, the gangway was a piece of wood/metal, with sides, connecting the ship to the shore, providing a secondary way (after swinging across berthing wires) of getting between the two. Gangways came in all shapes and sizes, from rudimentary to elaborate and ornate. We even carried our own, which was pressed into service should it transpire that the port we were visiting didn't own such a thing. It was also there in case we went alongside another ship. Gangways were where the ship's routine was run from while alongside, by means of the quartermaster (QM) and bo's'n's mate (BM) making various 'pipes' over she ships main broadcast (tannoy system). Everyone would obey these pipes, or risk serious trouble. It was acutely embarrassing to make your first pipe which you knew everybody would hear, so you built up to it gradually. The worst was to pipe "D'You hear there", then add a message. But you had to do it eventually, so you practised quietly to yourself, then got on and did it.

Eventually, all aboard would have to cross the gangway, so we got to know the entire crew by sight within a short space of time. It also meant we could differentiate between miserable gits (for whom we had no spare time), and 'good hands' who we would make coffee/kye for, if pressed. Or if they bought us suppers back from ashore. Duty people would be mustered there, shore telephone calls would be received there – official ones, during the day (with us eavesdropping on the billing and cooing being done on OUR telephone, in OUR kaboosh (as it was called), then take the piss afterwards). And any duty person knew they could come and chew the fat there. From the duty clanky (who would always have hot water available), to the duty PO, who would come up for a natter, or the OOD who would relax there between his rounds, if he wanted to – everyone except the duty electrician, but greenies always were different to everyone else.

The QM and BM would, amongst everything else they had to do – run the ships' daily routine, by making various pipes (broadcasts) over the tannoy, or main broadcast, to inform the ships company of mundane things like 'turning to', 'stand -easy', and – best of all – 'secure'. We would fill in the ships log, recording weather conditions and current position. We also had the best supply of books, magazines of various subject matters, and pens, also torches, batteries, expertise – you name it, it all lived on the gangway.

If anyone wanted virtually anything on board, they would, nine times out of ten, ring up, or visit us to ask us. It was a thankless job, but it did have its benefits.

If anyone wanted to 'find' anyone, we would pipe "Able Seaman Smith – Gangway". If anyone better than the OOD wanted him, "At the rush" would be added. If the words "Lay Aft" were included, you were already in deep trouble, the only question was, how deep was it, and did you need a lifejacket!!!

Officers were "…requested to come to the gangway", unless the jimmy or the skipper wanted them, in which case they were (as before) already in the shit for not being available, but we'd pipe "Officer of the day (or Lieutenant So-and-So) Gangway -NOW". .And wait for them to bitch about missing the 'request' bit off. AT which time we'd indicate the jimmy/skipper standing round the corner, waiting, fuming…

Through all this we had to be on our guard (not that we'd ever skylark), for either people phoning internally (or externally) to the gangway, asking us to pipe various people to various places. So, if we were asked to pipe for (for example a radio operator (R.O.) – "R.O. BOTT, Computer room", we'd clearly smell a large brown thing with whiskers and tail. 'Specially if we didn't have an RO Bott aboard… Or PO(ME) Granite… We'd do the reverse of that – we'd wait until we knew who was indisposed, then pipe him to the gangway for a shore telephone call. He'd then appear, perhaps dripping wet, pick up the phone, say hello, then throw it down. We'd say "Must have been a wrong number/must have hung up", and watch them go back dripping (wet, and unhappily) back down below. We'd maybe then wait several more minutes before repeating the procedure.

Another trick, if someone was adrift at night, it was within our power to thoughtfully remove their station card from the box, hiding it from the duty PO and OOD who would check it nightly. The hapless rating would though have to stand where he could see, but not be seen, until the DPO/OOD went below, before they could hurtle up the gangway, unseen – except by us. They would then owe us big favours!! You see – it didn't pay to mess with, or be 'anti' towards the gangway crew. Ever.

Oh yes, and in foreign ports, it was also where there was always a copious supply of noddy hats, just in case the lads had enough stamina after the obligatory and sustained elbow bending.

We used to work Dogs, Middle and Forenoon one day, then 24 off, then

Afternoon, First and Morning. The dogs were fine, except that you were coming on, as everyone else was going home.

We stood there, day in, day out, for four hours on, four off for the twenty four hours, then getting '24 off', day after day, with a double shift at the weekend, unless you were weekend off. Ginge Harwood was my QM – a Leading Seaman, a gunnery expert, and very wise. The duty watch – who slept on board even though it was in dry dock, and of which we as QM and BM were part, had supper and nine-o-clock'ers brought down to us nightly, and it was usually still slightly warm by the time we got it. We could make up for it if we did the 'first', by sliding over to the dockyard canteen for a haggis supper. That used to hit the spot! Every dogs, though, the duty watch used to exercise fire and emergency, and muster wherever the OOD used to dream up to have a pretend incident. We would man the shore lines and ships tannoy, and when the OOD rang us to announce where the fire was to be, we would scream over the tannoy

'FOREXERCISEFOREXERCISEFOREXERCISEFIREFIREFIREFI REINTHETILLERFLAT'

or wherever we were told, then we'd sit back while everybody else on board ran round in a flat spin, or until the OOD was happy. If he was displeased, he would make everyone put all the gear away, then throw another exercise, much later. That used to pass thirty minutes.

When we came off the dogs, the 'watchkeepers' as we were known had their own mess. In every sense of the word. As the ship, and therefore the mess was still unheated except for small electric fires, we used to crash out on much used and shared mattresses, used pillows, still dressed, in our eights, with our watchcoats. To say it was fun would be a lie. Just as you dozed off, the BM doing the first would shake you for the middle. You then sat there for four hours, listening to the radio (if you had found enough batteries, and bearing in mind Radio One did NOT broadcast 'round the clock' in those distant days), and roaming the ship on 'rounds', making sure, presumably, that it was still there. We'd nose about and pry everywhere unlocked, until we knew every place to go on the ship. With luck, you could make rounds last anything up to half an hour, at which time you'd come back, and sign your name to confirm you'd completed them, and that nothing was amiss. Rounds were interspersed with endless cups of Kye (chocolate) or coffee made by me for Ginge, unless he felt extremely irritable, in which case he'd make it. On board all ships, in the engine room, is something called a 'steam-drench'. This was a tap, out of which would pour superheated steam – hot enough to heat to boiling point any sized jug of cold water, in seconds. You had to be very careful not to put your fingers anywhere near it... We'd drink the coffee with tinned milk, and scrounged sugar from wherever to sweeten up an otherwise foul brew.

Or we'd forage for what was left of the suppers, usually stale bread, then attempt to toast it on the portable heater in the kaboosh... Mostly, we would sit on or close to the heater, and talk. More accurately – he would talk, I would listen, as – being a junior, I clearly had nothing interesting to say. We used to raid various workshops for bolts and nuts, then attempt to shoot shite-hawks with a catapult we made. Or we'd put various delicacies on the quarter-deck for them. Things like yeast and curry sandwiches, or mustard rolls – enough to make them throw up shortly after they took off.

Most times, we'd nick nuts and bolts from the 'Engineers Workshop', or the MCR – the MCR being where the clankies run the engine and gearbox from whilst at sea, but where, also, the damage control state of the ship is handled. Usually, there'd be all kinds of armament for catties there!!

Towards the end of the watch, we'd fill in the ships log, with the ships position, and the weather conditions – gleaned from the bridge anemometer and barometer, or visually ('Snowing', 'Raining', 'Clear'), plus the 'sea-state', and the visiblity, then officially record everything in that most important document – the ships log. Actually, while at sea, every course, speed, position, BWH, Sunset, important event, whatever – was recorded in the log, for some boring fogey to read much later, back at 'The Admiralty'.

As gangway crew, we'd know the 'battle honours' – the board showing where previous ships of the name had fought, and when – and we'd be responsible for the ships bell, which doubled as a font for onboard christenings of crews' offspring. The bell and the battle honours were taken down whenever we sailed, and put back up IMMEDIATELY we got back alongside, as would the huge nameplates bearing the ships name which also had to be hung in position. It was also the job of the off watch gangway crew to adorn the gangway with canvas dodgers, also bearing the ships' name. This was great for us "H.M.S. ZULU" was only seven letters, and very light, whereas ships like "H.M.S. LONDONDERRY" meant you'd be there all day, carrying heavier nameplates.

We would also spread a cargo net beneath the gangway, between the jetty and the ships side, on the offchance that a lurching, legless matelot fell off the gangway – at least he would not get wet, even if it took him ages to sober up enough to make sense of and extricate himself from the cargo net. Not that anyone did that of course.

We also used to vaguely monitor the dockyard mateys as they 'worked' the night shift, lagging engine room pipes, spray painting etc. Only whenever we looked hard enough we'd always find them asleep in one of the unfinished messdecks. It was little wonder that refits in Rosyth always ran over budget and way over time.

Eventually, the middle used to end, and we'd head for our pits, get warm, doze off, in time to be re-awakened by our opposite number to get up and do the forenoon. That used to be a real soul-destroyer. Me as BM had to go and do 'colours' – that continued whether we were in refit or not. That continuation of the daily naval tradition consisted of the OOD, sometimes the Jimmy, the duty Radio Operator (or flag-wagger) to haul up the ensign, and me to pipe the still and carry-on with my bo's'ns call. Still mainly asleep, and hungry having had no breakfast. The QM would ring the ships bell vigorously, then broadcast "Attention on the upper deck – face aft and salute" – which everyone silly enough to on the upper scupper at the time had to do. After the ensign and jack had been hauled up, the QM would broadcast the 'carry on', followed by "Both Watches...". Occasionally, if he thought he could get away with it, the first broadcast could be "Attention on the upper deck, chase arse in a blue suit". Which sounded almost the same, unless you were completely listening for it, even then you'd need to think again. Once we got through that one, we were then twenty four off. Ginge, as a committed RA used to head home, I used to expire in my pit at Cochrane. Occasionally, I even managed to sleep for a couple of hours, before heading ashore with the gang later in the evening.

On the opposite watch, we'd do the afternoon, getting to the ship within minutes of midday . It was actually a point of honour in the Navy to 'relieve' each other at exactly five minutes to the hour, whatever watch you did, wherever you did it. If you were adrift, even by seconds you would not believe the repercussions. The afternoon usually passed quickly, then we'd relax off during the dogs, fill up with food, and do the first from 2000 to midnight. That would usually pass quickly too, and you'd generally be asleep shortly after midnight. Back up at 0400 for the morning, which would drag on, and on, and on. Nothing and nobody used to move in that yard until about 0700, then all hell got let loose. Though once we moved onboard, one of the perks was that when the milkman arrived, with his churns of ice-cold, fresh milk – you could always skim off several pints before the duty dining-hall ratings sleepily crossed the gangway, to return, manhandling the huge churns down below. Another perk was that of – if the 'paper man' or the 'sarnie man' arrived, you'd be able to get in first, before piping his arrival, thereby enabling the rest of the crew to get their turn.

The 'morning' was normally the better watch, it was traditional to write a short poem or verse, to be read out at 'Call The Hands', so at 0645, we'd 'pipe' Call the Hands on the bo's'u'ns call, then launch into the poem, which would either be followed by irate phone calls, or people climbing the ladder to the kaboosh to ask, blearily 'What the fuckin' 'ell was that all about'. Normally, if bored, it would be (in a loud voice)

'CALLTHEHANDSCALLTHEHANDSCALLTHEHANDSWAKEY WAKEYRISEANDSHINEYOUVEHADYOURSLEEPIWANTMINE'

or

'WAKEYWAKEYWAKEYWAKEYWAKEYWAKEYWAKEYWAKEY WAKEYWAKEYWAKEYWAKEYWAKEYHANDSOFFCOCKSHANDS ONSOCKS'

or

'EAVOEAVOLASHUPANDSTOWTHESUNSBRIGHTENOUGHT OBURNYERFUCKINEYESOUT'

or variations. We'd try to never do the same thing twice.

One of the jobs of the 'morning' watchmen, was to 'shake' the duty early risers – the chefs (more later) the greenies, the bunting-tossers, men under pun(ishment) – anyone who had to get up earlier than the norm. We would shake them gently, if we wanted to, or violently if they had previously given us grief, or with the lights on/torch in the eyes otherwise. We had a 'shake book', which anyone wanting the shake had to sign his name against. It was therefore in our power, that once we got the signature, to slope off quietly, to see if he went back to sleep again. He'd then be deep in the shit for not getting there, but we'd be clear – we had the signature after all. If though it was someone who needed to be up, and it would be in our (bacon sarnie) interests to ensure the duty chef got up, we'd go back several times, with coffee! Officers were also shaken by us – we'd go once, knock on the cabin door, await the grunt, whisper the time, and slink away again. We would NOT go back a second time, no matter who the officer was. We had enough to do to keep our own mates out of the rattle, without guarding the interests of the pigs in the wardroom as well.

If it was our own 'relief' we were shaking, we'd stand talking to them, to make sure they got up, and weren't adrift to take over. We'd always have a fresh brew ready for them, wherever we where, whatever the situation. As I said – we looked after our own (interests) over and above everything else!!

Sometimes, we'd wake someone else up (who hadn't asked for the shake) very gently, and whisper in his ear "wanna buy a battleship, Jack", before creeping off again. Oddly, if someone ever does this to you, you're immediately wide awake, thinking "What the fuck was that? Why would I want to buy a battleship?" ...and before you knew it, you'd be wide awake and unable to get off again. DON'T CROSS THE GANGWAY CREW!!!!

The not-so-good bit was entering a mess full of sleeping sailors at 0500, meant the atmosphere would be full of the varied scents of thirty or so sailors, generally after a night ashore. Ripe is the word I use, reservedly!!

One alleged thing, was that if when you were shaken, you hit out, it was one time you wouldn't get trooped for fighting... No matter who it was shook you. Apparently, you are not responsible for what happens while someone tries to wake you. We tried to train ourselves to bop the shaker, but... No-one ever tried that with me, but I always stood well back anyway!

If the captain went ashore, we'd have to keep an extremely good lookout for him coming back. If he ever got aboard without the OOD being on the gangway, he (OOD) would get his arse chewed off, followed by us getting ours bitten by him (OOD). To prevent this happening, we had a little code – whenever we saw the boss coming back, we'd immediately give two short pips on our bo's'u'ns call into the main broadcast, as used for making pipes, and sit back to see how long it took the OOD to get to the gangway, ready to salute the skipper. Occasionally, though, if the OOD was one of those who had previously wound us up, or one who was plain disliked, we'd leave it till the last possible second until doing the 'pips', to ensure the OOD just missed him – but, of course, we'd be admonished – we'd fulfilled our bit!

Otherwise, if either of us was on watch, and not actually standing on the gangway but was urgently required back at the gangway, the pressel switch on the microphone would be hit, twice, which would make a noise audible enough to be heard by someone keeping one ear out for it – wherever he may be on the ship, and whatever else he may be doing at the time. This would summon us back from late night drinks, the heads, illegal meals, chatting – whatever.

We also had the keys to the 'Buffers Store', which was where we kept all 'seamanshippy' things, like ropes, blocks, various string, marling spikes, sailmaker's knives – all the goodies you could possibly need. And because, by then, Ginge had taught me how to splice, properly, and tie decorative knots, I was well into making flattened out monkey's fists, which then looked like mats. These would be made from thin nylon, and looked terrific when completed and washed. These also were cash valuable ashore, in the same way as the crests were. We also created bell-ropes – highly ornate works of art, again worth plenty ashore.

The buffers store, was also where we would, later in the commission, make highly illegal marrow rum, by hollowing out a marrow, topping it up with water, sugar and yeast, then leaving it for several days to ferment, before drinking it.

Not that it was all work, the twenty-four-off used to consist of mostly sleeping and eating, with runs ashore in-between, back to Cochrane by midnight (all juniors leave expired then), with a lay-in the next morning, ready for the next batch of watches.

One weekend, we embarked on to a Pussers Coach, and disappeared up into the hills, alongside a Loch somewhere, into log cabins, where we spent a pleasant couple of days washing in a stream, drinking ourselves silly, and walking round the surrounding woods. We never did find out where the cabins were, but they were RN property, and gave us a break from the routine.

Eventually, after several mind-numbing months, it was job-change time again, and I went back part-of-ship. By this time we were nearly out of the refit, and came the day they mateys tentatively opened up the sluices of the dry dock, and the water rushed in and around the ship. Imperceptibly, amidst much running around with mateys hunting for leaks, and not finding any – we began to float. All too soon, we were actually high up in the dry dock, with the water level the same as the basin beyond the caisson. Without any more ado, the caisson slid back, the tug came in, and we were towed into the non-tidal basin. This meant more of the shore-heads routines, only this time we could (providing you didn't get caught) use the heads on board. At was about this time we had a 'coiler' strike, as in 'coil one down'. He used to use the showers as a toilet and we never did catch him.

As 'juniors', we always got the shit jobs. Literally. We would always be the first to be volunteered to clean the 'flats', bathrooms and heads for the first hour every morning, generally under the most detested Leading Seaman on board, as that would be his 'perks' for being what he was, and probably still is. He would make us clean the general areas thoroughly, and we yearned for the time when we weren't the shithouse sweepers any longer. Or we'd be volunteered for 'side party', sitting on a paint stage suspended over the ships side, either scrubbing or painting. The one which really got to us was cleaning and degreasing and regreasing the 'slips' on the guardrails all round the upper deck. That was a real pleasure on a cold day, when you weren't able to wear gloves.

After several weeks of continuous practice, it became possible to distinguish new-boys from old hands. The new boys would descend ladders between decks daintily, step by step – as you would when one over the eight. The real 'Herbert's' would even go down backwards, facing the steps. But the easiest way was to jump the first two/three steps, grab the rails, swing your legs forward, then slide down with all your weight on your hands, and with your back to the steps. You needed to slow, slightly towards the bottom or you would break your ankles with the shock of hitting the iron deckplate. I can still drop down a ladder like that now. Having said that, we had a lieutenant aboard – Gregory, nice chap, except that he had a metal leg. Apparently he left his real one on a Buccaneer when he baled out – or was that kidology? Whatever – he could descend stairs at an alarming rate, with a loud thump as he landed, but wasn't quite so good on the ascent. Which was a bit of a pain if you got stuck behind him whilst hurtling towards your action station. If he was on the ladder – you'd better find a different way. Mind you – at least you had an excuse for not being there when you should have been!! And he had a built in alarm system, so we knew when he was coming to do evening or even night rounds. We'd hear his leg locking as he threw it forwards with each stride, followed by the CLUMP as his 'foot' hit the deck.

Life, then, improved considerably. We started to warm up the ship, we did load trials, then we did a main engine test -known as a 'basin trial'. This meant doubling up on all the ropes and wires, then adding hurricane hawsers too (just in case), before engaging the engines, and then carefully adding just a few revs to check everything worked correctly. We gawped over the arse-end watching the invisible prop gently push water about, then ran round checking all the mooring ropes held secure as we gently inched forwards, then backwards... Everything was apparently successful. We tested the radar, we tracked aircraft. We moved out of the non-tidal basin to a jetty!! Now we floated up and down on the tide, and had to either climb the gangway up to the jetty, or down to the jetty, depending on the state of the tide, which varied enormously in Rosyth. We exercised the guns (stopping short of firing), and tried out all the primary and secondary weapon systems. We stored ship, which was another major evolution – every available hand is detailed to form long supply chains from the jetty to the designated store room, and every item to be stored is transferred from person to person, hand to hand, until it is all stowed. It is not only the only time the stores ratings ever do any work, but also the hardest work any 'tanky' or 'lockerman' does. Every item, from sides of beef and pig, to crates of beer, butter, brooms, batteries, sausages, eggs, fizzy drinks, nutty, soap, shaving foam, extremely large tins of fruit, bacon, tinned veg, fresh greens, sacks and sacks of spuds, – everything required to make the ship totally independent of shoreside support. It is amazing to watch, heavily laden lorries would lurch along the jetty one after another and be stripped of their entire cargo within moments, with empty lorries slinking away, with absolutely no trace of their ever having been there. Just a lot of very tired sailors with aching arms and backs, and dry throats, all ready to be lubricated with 'heavy'.

So, we continued to visit the Central in Inverkeithing, punctuated by visits to Dunfermline, to see the Dunfermline Debs' dancing to the current hit – 'Yellow River'. A never to be forgotten experience you could hear several streets away as you approached the place – "yell(left foot clump)ow(right foot clump)Ri(left foot clump)ver(right foot clump)..." went the song, as up and down moved the dance-floor, and the building shook. The best night I ever had there was when one of my then favourite band's – 'Family' were on live.

I distinctly remember going ashore one day, after coming off watch, and going shopping in Dumfs, for a pair of Adidas trainers, to wear with my Sta-prest trousers (at that time, jeans were not permitted to be worn ashore), and I eventually spotted and did the deed. I then proceeded to the pub, met some oppos, and there we sat for the rest of the lunchtime, imbibing. I can remember that I'd changed out of my old tatty shoes into the trainers, but had carefully put the shoes into the box, and the box back into the carrier. So, as I was walking towards the bus station, I felt the urge to sit down in a doorway. The next memory is of someone tugging at the carrier bag, of me letting go, and of someone running off. By the time I came to my senses, and realised what had happened, the only thing I could do was laugh. Image the startled look when my mugger feverishly opened the box to discover a pair of discarded old shoes!! Serves him right, thieving bastard, hope he got bunions wearing them.

Late in the spring, we moved, excitedly, and as a ships company, on board, into our very own RPs' mess, with our own locker, our own pit, and with the rest of 'the lads'. As we were still lowlife, our pits reflected that lowness – we were all put on the bottom bunks. I'll explain. In those days, pits were three high, in several rows. Our mess was sort a of reversed 'L' shaped, with the top being a quiet area, with the whole of the side of the 'L' being right on the ships' side, and with the bottom being the 'mess square'. In this area we drank tea, beer, played card games – and did our socialising and entertaining. Bearing in mind there were probably 24 or more RPs in that mess, you can get a feel for how cramped it was. So the 'three high' pits were probably five deep. In each row of three pits, the top one tilted upwards out of the way, the bottom one was therefore now where everyone sat, and the middle on, once secured properly, dropped backwards, so the sleeping part was now pressed against the ships' side, with a cushion now there as a back-rest. If that makes sense so far, between the pits and the ships side proper, would be stowage space. As there would also be boot lockers and blanket stowages beneath the bottom pit. So, if you were a junior, on the bottom bunk, you'd have to ensure your bed was made up properly, before sheathing it in its own casing, before putting the seat cover on, so everyone could finally sit down. Now, if you wanted to go to bed early – tuff – if someone else in the mess square wanted to party, you'd have to wait 'till they were good and ready, before you could finally get your head down.

Each pit had its own small light, a punkah louvre for some air, and – importantly – a roll-bar, to 'prevent' you falling out of bed in rough weather. Each person also had his own kit locker on the front of which was a bar, to hang your wet towels and dhobey bag, with all uniforms being stowed in a communal stowage – a large wardrobe, really. In this small amount of space you'd have to keep your uniforms, Burberrys, civvies, going ashore gear. And anything else that could be crammed in.

There was also a tea locker, table stowages, chair stowages, ironing-board holder, cubbyholes, and glory holes, all of which could hold gear of whatever description. It was in these stowages, that all gear had to be secured, and sometimes lashed in, ready for going to sea in any more rough weather.

Our mess (7 Mess) was amidships and starboard, right over the stabiliser compartment, and below the dining hall. Food was plentiful, and remarkably good, especially if you were up early, and could bribe a 'chef' to knock you up a bacon sarnie. The exchange on this was a cup of NATO-standard (white, two sugars) coffee when you shook him at five a.m. for him to start cooking breakfast, while you did the morning.

As the Zulu was a relatively modern ship, being then only five or six years old, we uncommonly at that time, messed in some style in the dining room, having queued up for our scran. We would then sit and eat it cafeteria fashion from metal plates. These plates were some fourteen inches by perhaps nine, and had three spaces. One was for a soup bowl. We could have soup every lunchtime, if we wanted, and if it was on the menu... The second space was ostensibly for pudding. The last and biggest was for your main meal. The idea was then to cram as much grub into each compartment as you could, then scoff the lot as fast as you could, so someone else could move in on your bench to eat his own. Having eaten, we'd take the empty plates to the scullery, for the dining hall party to wash up. Total luxury. Especially the toaster!! This was an enormous device hanging from the scullery wall, and was essentially a box containing racks on chains, onto which you put your bread, if you could find any. The chain revolved taking the rack and toast, disappearing for several minutes into the depths of the obviously hot machine. Eventually, it would drop out of the bottom onto a large tray, but if you didn't get there fast enough, some bastard else would RAS it, and you'd still be left waiting for yours. If, however, you got caught having it away with someone else's' toast – stand from under! Toast was also our name for anyone who looked good, but was actually useless at anything. As, indeed, toast is. Another derogatory name was 'Floater', as in what floats in the heads.

This was all very civilised and pleasant, unless you were detailed off to be 'dining hall party', and thus had to clean everyone's plates and gobbling rods as they finished with them. They, to be fair, had a dishwasher to do it, and a 'gash gnasher' to 'eat' the leftovers – that is smash them up before chucking it out of the side of the ship. However, it wasn't unknown for the less observant/intelligent to mistake 'food' for 'rods', and throw the lot into the whirling 'gnasher'. Very shortly there would be a terrible graunching noise as the choppers hit the knife or fork – and the whole thing would literally grind to a halt. The thing would then be switched off while the duty stoker/duty greenie would, cursing violently all the time, stick his arm in to remove the rod, replace the fuse, and start it up again. Of course, we would loudly jeer the idiot who caused this to happen. Further, if the DHP didn't have any clean rods, and you had to wait for someone to finish eating before you could get a set, then the abuse really used to fly about. Comments like 'fuck all else to do but wash me a clean knife and fork, and still they fuck it up'.

We RPs, at around 1200 every day, would knock off for eats. As of course would everyone else. But the 'pipe' made would be "Seeeecure. Hands to Dinner" followed by the massed chorus from below decks, of "RPs to lunch". We radar merchants clearly had the piss taken out of us. That never stopped us being amongst the first in line for anything and everything being handed out at any time. As RPs it was a point of honour to get to the bathroom early, get washed – using soap lumps squirreled away underneath sinks, between rounds – and be amongst the first in the queue for all mealtimes. Nevertheless, we'd occasionally be beaten by the clankies, who we used to think had been there since the end of breakfast.

We'd then gobble away, and be out of the dining hall rapidly, to get back to the mess either for a lie down, or a sociable game of uckers, or crib (both games I was always good at) or just to listen to the sea stories. Whatever, the "Out pipes – Hands carry on with your work" would always interrupt us, even if we did always query why it was that this German matelot called Hans was the only one on board who had to turn to again in the afternoons… Well, actually, him and his French submariner 'oppo – Pierre E'Scope. It got to be a game, being the last one back after lunch, to get 'Father' after us, to see if he could find us, whilst pretending to have been turned to elsewhere. There was always 'cooks' to fall back on. Cooks-of-the-mess still had to clear up the living accommodation every day (but different people), after both watches, by emptying the bins, sweeping and scrubbing through before drying it all off. At Stand-easy they'd have to wet the tea and coffee (if available), then clear up after that. After lunch they'd clean up again, and wet the tea for the afternoon stand-easy. Then the duty watch would take over, and do it all again ready for evening rounds. So, you see, the accommodation was always clean. Cooks was the ideal excuse to slide off early, and be back late. We took

FULL advantage of this situation. At least if you did cooks, you wouldn't then have to be shithouse sweepers. There was also a small 'perk' of being cooks – if you found anything, like money, tins, ciggies – you could claim it as 'sweepers perks', and refuse to give it back. Unless you were physically threatened. Or smaller than the original owner. It was still worth a try...

On the subject of us RPs' we also got the stick about standing with hands on hips, which you do, but other ratings would be told 'thumbs rearward, you don't want people to think you're an RP'.

We were given the 'promulgation' at one point – to tell us where we would go during the commission, and when. It was relayed to us that we were going to the Fez (Far East Station). For a year!!! We were going to sail in January, returning in December. That was better than I had ever hoped for. All the messdecks were suddenly abuzz and alive with chatter about who'd been there before, that we would be going to 'Singers (Singapore) for a mini refit, then to 'The Fid (Honky Fid – Hong Kong) for several weeks. On route via Beira patrol, Mombasa, four months in Bahrein as Gulf Guard Ship, then The Seychelles, South Africa – more than I could bear. Except that we were to keep it amongst family at this stage and no further. All the married men griped and whined, all the single men could be heard cheering clear across Scotland, I should think. We (single men) couldn't wait. But first we had to get through weapon training, work-up and other nautical pre-requisites before sailing around the world.

One of these neccessities was to muster at slops in Cochrane, for tropical kit issue – as if we didn't have enough gear to worry about already. This kit was only issued to ratings going to hot places, and you only got one issue, which had to stay with you whether you went there again or not. So we 'gratefully' accepted and signed for two ice-cream suits, two pairs of cream shorts, two pairs of blue shorts, some white socks, thick, uncomfortable leather sandals, and white canvas shoes. We then had several more injections.

I said the shorts were cream – they were, so were the suits. Unfortunately they should have been white, so off they went to the dhobey wallahs for instant refits and colour changes, until they were deemed by the older hands to be white, at which point we were allowed to sew the blue badges on. Strangely, even though we dressed in these white suits, we still had to wear the black silks, blue collars, and lanyards.

Chapter 8
A Farewell to a Part of Admiral Nelson

An extremely sad event happened that year, one which depressed the entire navy for quite some time – some nameless shitbag decided it was a 'good idea' to abandon Nelsons Blood, which had been served daily to all serving men 'of age' for decades. I had never before, and certainly never since tasted anything quite like the tot. We juniors used to do anything for 'sippers', something bestowed by the owner only on special occasions. Or 'gulpers', which really deserved something different, or 'halfers' which required even more favours, right up to 'have the lot', which meant you got his tot. Since even swapping a duty only earned sippers, you can guess that the lot was only in extreme circumstances. Juniors were therefore classed as 'rumrats', which meant we'd lurk about at tot time, on the off chance someone was too hung over to drink (or illegally bottle for a rainy day) his tot, in which case we stood a chance of a drop.

The certificate provided at that time, to mark that sad passing, had a poem on it :-

A MATELOTS FAREWELL TO HIS TOT

You soothed my nerves and warmed my limbs
And cheered my dismal heart
Procured my wants, obliged my whims-
And now it's time to part.
'Mid endless perils of the deep
And miseries untold
You summoned sweet forgetful sleep
Cocooned me from the cold

Ten years ago the "pound 'o leaf"
That cast its fragrant smell
About the ship, expired in grief
And sadness of farewell
Though guests might find the pantry bare
When e'er they choose to come
Your hospitality was there
A tot of Pussers rum

Two hundred years and more you filled
The storm tossed sailors need
Now you've been killed by spite distilled
From jealousy and greed
And petty clerks with scrawny necks
Who never saw a wave
Nor felt the spray nor heaving decks
Consign you to your grave

Alas! However I protest
To save myself from hurt
They tell me that it's for the best-
To keep us all alert
And so the time has come, old friend
To take the final sup
Our tears are shed. This is the end
Goodbye, and bottoms up!

Although the beer allowance then went up from two cans a day to three – it was never any kind of consolation. There was a lot of bitterness and tears that day and onwards, I kid you not.

We had, as all ships do, many characters in our mess – Dolly Gray, who's excuse for being adrift one day was that he had been run over by a train, Sid Saywell, know as PD (Poison Dwarf on account of his lack of height, and the smell from his rear end after a night ashore), Jock Arthur who HAD been there and seen it, and done it. He had more 'black cats' than anyone else I have ever met. He was my adopted 'sea-daddy' – everyone has one, someone who teaches you 'the ropes'. 'Sugar' Kane, who eventually moved into submarines, 'April' Ashley – who knew more than was good for him, Jock Norrie, who had the biggest nose I have ever seen on just one human, MacNosh (from MacIntosh) who's' run-ashore boots I used to borrow, and 'Charlie' Howe, who's party piece was to sing a ridiculous song about a frog – to name but a few. We gradually got to know each other well enough to throw abuse at the drop of a hat. We knew we could all trust each other.

We soon learned lots of other tricks designed to get your own back. There was always someone, usually a poor 'RA', who could never afford his own fags, and would ponce yours. This we could get round by doing the 'Irish Fag Dance' – standing there patting all your own pockets to demonstrate their emptiness. Or we'd carry a dog end stuffed in our cap, and offer that. You learned to be more fly than they were. Or there were those who, every time you opened unwrapped nutty, or cracked a can of goffa, would say "Giz a bit" or "Giz a wet", and drain half the can. The antidote to this one – and remember, this was in the days when you had to make your own hole in the top to drink from, usually with a can spanner, more often than not with your marling spike – was that you normally poked a second hole in the opposite side, to let air in as you drank. But if the 'RA' was around, you'd then make a third one, in the side of the can, just below the one you drank from. The 'RA', would say his piece, you'd hand over the can, and leg it away, as he drank thirstily from the can, only to find it all poured out of the third hole, and dribbled down his chin, his eights, his jacket...

The other trick, was that at 'stand-easy', when you'd have the tea wet, you'd industriously stir the cuppa with the shared teaspoon, 'borrowed' from the dining hall, whilst watching everyone else's concentration lapse. When they were distracted, you'd take the spoon out, and only for a fraction of a second, you'd press the hot spoon onto the back of someone's hand. This would normally cause them sudden and great pain, which actually only lasted for a few seconds before going away. Meanwhile, we'd all be on the deck, laughing – especially when the one you'd done it to would usually throw his tea down himself as well, giving us even more to giggle about. You were, then, always on the lookout for 'revenge' attacks!

It was one night, when Charlie and me were detailed to be QM and BM – I forget why., but, it was the one night that the lads decided to throw a hooly in the mess. As it befell Charlie and me to stand the first on the gangway, we decided to take it in turns to visit the mess, for a can (or two) at a time. By the time 'pipe down' came, I was totally legless, and can remember being kicked awake by Charlie, me having fallen asleep sitting on a locker on the opposite side of the ship to the gangway, while I was supposed to be doing my turn! Good job it was him who found me and not the OOD or Duty PO, or I'd have been automatically given a ninety day break for being not only asleep on duty, but drunk on duty to boot!

We soon learned how to further stretch out the grand 'staying in bed until the last possible moment' game. Call the hands was at 0645, and the duty PO would be round shortly after, to ensure everyone was up. But if he wasn't too sharp, you'd stay there, listening to the hubbub of your mates as they shaved, farted, lit up, then clattered and chattered into life, listening to the ship coming to life, daily routine getting started, the 'hands to breakfast' pipe, before finally getting up, doing the dhobey, coming back and making you bed up, before putting the seat covers back on it, before drifting greedily past the galley, seeing if you could swipe anything on the way past, before finally emerging onto the upper deck five seconds before the pipe 'Both watches of the hands muster on the quarterdeck'.

Chapter 9

…and Off to Sea We Go…

Eventually, we got to June 19th 1970, and Commissioning day was upon us. We had worked hard for this – we cleaned, painted, repainted, painted over rust and dust, scrubbed, swept, polished – you name it we did it. We had the ship dedicated by Commander W Jenks R.N., held divisions in our number ones, cleared lower deck of all hands onto the gleaming quarterdeck for the reading of the commissioning warrant, ate the best meal I had ever seen, then went ashore once more, to get pissed. Once more…

By this time, we had discovered that as RPs' we didn't stand 'deck' watches like the rest of the seaman branches, but instead stayed snug in a warm ops room. Not for us the boredom of doing lifebouy ghost, or the cold of being bridge lookout – Oh no, we stared, and stared at the ever spinning trace on the varied displays hoping to spot the new contact first, or at least – before the OOW saw it, demanding to know why we'd missed it. So, soon after the commissioning, we sailed for sea trials and shakedowns, which consisted of leaving Rosyth, sailing under the Forth Bridges (which showed up as slightly diverging bars on the radar), then haring up and down the Forth at various speeds, doing various drills.

We discovered a new pastime -but this was always one of 'Jack's' favourites – goofing. This means aimlessly watching anything, or nothing, usually whilst illegally leaning over the guardrails. These are pvc covered wires which run mostly all around the edge of the ship to stop the more stupid from (accidentally) falling over the side. Us 'upper deck technicians' kept them in good condition by greasing the slips used to keep them taught, and were usually affronted when stokers etc decided to 'test' them with their body weight. Nevertheless, leaning on them was what everybody without exception did, until interrupted by someone screaming 'DON'T LEAN ON THE FUCKIN GUARDRAILS'. The best vantage points to lean, were around the quarterdeck, which gave a great viewing area to watch the sea build up astern of you as we increased speed to around 28 knots, at which point the following crest of water was far higher than the guardrails we goofed over. The bridge in roughers was another good goofing area, as was anywhere (permitted) on the upper-scupper during flying stations or RASing, or generally just aimlessly passing the time, whether alongside watching other ships or the local life, or at sea in the middle of nowhere, especially socialising after supper with a cup of tea and a fag when you'd catch up with any buzzes going around.

We fired the mortars one day, then dropped the seaboat which came back loaded to the gunwales with fresh fish brought up by the deepwater explosions. They tasted good when we had them for supper that very evening.

Previously, we had always lowered and raised seaboats (at Raleigh and on the Ulster), by hand, with long lengths of ropes, called 'falls', and a complicated series of blocks stretching right down both the ships waists, using the whole complement of seamen to raise it, but just two or three very cautious ones to lower it. Consequently, everyone looked forward to seaboat drills with great trepidation. However, the Zulu had electric hoists, and wire falls. The operator merely released the gravity brake slowly, or engaged the drive later to recover it. Much, much easier.

We scampered past Bass Rock & all it's gannets, then down the coast to Holy Island and back, and stayed out all night for the first time, which in itself was THE big adventure, so far. We conducted seamanship evolutions, and fired the guns which had taken so long to tune. We did full power trials, steering gear breakdowns, exercised fire, everywhere, but most importantly, we were let loose among the radar. That was the most exciting thing we'd done yet in our short naval careers – excitedly waiting to go on-watch for the first time, then sitting up all night in the ops room, actually reporting 'contacts' as they appeared on the radar – being told to 'disregard' (too far away to worry about), 'watch' (if it does anything silly, report it again), or 'report' (keep telling me every 2-3 miles/2-3 minutes until I tell you otherwise). We learned that the reason the Naafi (onboard all naval vessels) opened at around 1930 (and at lunchtime, secure, and stand-easy), was so that the first and middle watchmen could not only purchase soap and dhobey dust, but could also stock up with nutty and goffas, ready to take on watch with them. The nutty was pretty standard wherever you went, although the goffas could be coke, orangeade or lemonade (remember – this was the 70s'), or if abroad we could get repulsive types of alleged flavoured soda waters fit only to give a float test to. Whatever we bought before going on watch, and this could also include several tins of sausages in baked beans, it was really a point of honour to have eaten all of it before you were relieved by the next watchkeepers, even if you had eaten both supper and nine o'clockers AND scratched late suppers off the chefs. Having the nutty feast was traditional – as was not going for more than half an hour without having a (now duty free, as we were at sea) fag. We would often take it in turns to 'get the nutty in'.

We also launched and recovered the seaboat, countless times. A dummy was kept on the quarter-deck, and occasionally, the 'jimmy' would stamp down the arse-end, throw it over, and see how long it took the 'lifebuoy spook' (stern lookout) to suss it, and react. We reckoned to be able to recover 'a body' within minutes. The pipe would be 'Man overboard, prepare to recover by seaboat', followed by 'Away seaboats crew', which we would (being Scottish based) change to "Away the noo the seaboats crew, Och, wait a minute – there's no fucker in it", and collapse giggling.

To relieve the tension, and get out some of our cooped up energy, we were given a new game to play. This was called 'scrubbing down' (the decks). This consisted of starting at the front end, throwing soapy water or even neat detergent everywhere, then following down with stiff brooms, scrubbing as we went. If we had wooden decking over the main metal, as 'Tribals' had down both 'waists', we'd sometimes use a buffer similar to these used at Raleigh all those years ago (!), but these would be outdoor, waterproof versions, able to take much more stick. They also survived being hosed down, but still were unable to float, once worn out or rusty, or even in the way at the wrong place at the wrong time. This was followed by the hosers, with the upper deck fire hydrants and hoses being rigged to blast away all the resultant crud. This is why we started 'fore' and ended up 'aft' – so we didn't finish, then have to clear up someone else's crap half an hour later. The 'hosers' were usually the older ABs', whereas us 'juniors' manned the brooms. We'd gladly prolong this as much as we could, reasoning we could at least have a laugh doing this – and (again) it beat the hell out of being shit-house sweeper. The older hands, though, would occasionally be not to accurate with the hoses, and we'd all end up soaked. Not a barrel of laughs on a cold day, but great fun whilst in sunnier climes.

We quickly learned to that the detergent we used was mixable with salt water, quite necessarily really, as we'd otherwise use all the fresh water the clanks lovingly pushed through the small on-board desalination plant. We also noted the best way to get water into the bucket, was to turn on the hydrant, slowly, and fill it from there. The alternative (only tried the once), was to believe the ABs, and to tie a length of rope round the bucket handle, chuck it over the side, and retrieve the full bucket. Easy when alongside and stationary, but now try doing it at twenty knots. One of three things happens. One – you immediately get a sharp burning sensation on the palms of your hands as the rope rips through them. Done that. Two – you try to hold on, and get dragged towards the stern of the ship until CDF (common dog fuck) prevails, and you move into the previous one. Seen that. Three, tie the other end of the rope to a handy stanchion or guardrail, and watch as the stanchion bends, or the guardrail breaks under the pressure of the entire North Sea being forced into that small bucket. Or if you are lucky, someone with more

CDF than you uses his extremely sharp rigging knife, and cuts the rope before this happens. Seen that too!! Surprisingly, options two and three cause you to stand mesmerised, and in total disbelief. Time stands still for you. As I said – we used to need to have some fun, and NOT get the new boys to 'dip' the buckets whilst at sea. Unless we were bored…

Each part-of-ship (POS) had its own gang of seamen assigned to look after it, and we had three parts of ship. 'Fo'c's'le' (FX) ratings obviously did the sharp end, 'quarterdeck' (QD) did the blunt end, and 'top' did everything in-between, including the radar masts and funnels. Each POS also had several 'below decks' compartments (heads, bathrooms, flats etc) to also clean twice daily. Considerable rivalry therefore existed between each POS. Coincidentally, each POS had its own cleaning gear stowage containing the buffer, brooms, scrubbing brushes, detergent, ropes, heaving lines, bluebell (metal polish), squeegees (rubber blades mounted on broom handles, designed to sweep water in front of you – a quick way to get rid of surplus liquid), cloths and everything else necessary to keep the ship sparklingly clean and, well shipshape and in Bristol fashion. Each POS had a 'lockerman' responsible for keeping our own gear safe. The lockers were unsurprisingly kept padlocked while not in use, just in case. The lockers then were places to go for a quick skive, or for a quiet smoke. Lockerman was a valued job, as it meant not only could you legitimately draw new gear from stores, but you could also slide round the ship RAS'ing (stealing) gear from wherever it was left laying about, in order to build up your own stock. However you came across the gear, it was swiftly daubed with the paint coloured according to the POS you worked – in our case orange for top, green for QD, red for FX – thereby authorising only the relevant members the use of the equipment. Woe betide if you were found with someone else's gear. There was no excuse, not even "I was just bringing it back". You would thenceforth be known as a "…another fucking JUST rating". There were plenty of them – "I was just about to do that…" would normally result in a sudden pain in the backside, from a well directed, heavy, steel toecapped steaming bat.

When you had a good supply of brushes, polish, spanners and everything else essential (along with other 'may be useful one day') to cope with every possible contingency, other cleaners and sweepers would then come and borrow gear from you, and you could charge them sippers or tinnies in return for the favour, regardless of the fact you might have nicked it from them in the first place. Ownership – especially colour coded ownership – was the last argument.

One of the jobs of lockerman was to ensure a good supply of heaving lines, and other useful lengths of rope which you never knew would come in handy. Heaving lines were lengths (twenty yards or so) of special, thin rope, used to get the mooring wires and ropes across to the jetty. The idea was, the ship got maneuvered to within throwing range, we banged out the heaving lines, and once a dockie had made contact, we'd tie the line to a wire rope, the dockie would haul that across and secure it, the ship could then be winched on to the jetty and made fast. So it was a point of honour to get the first heaving line across. The lockerman, on finding a spare coil of this rope, would then spend the next several days (although in truth it could be done in minutes) forming a complex, decorative knot called a 'monkey's fist' at one end of the rope, with an eye splice at the other end. However, the monkey's fist would not be considered heavy enough, so large nuts or lumps of heavy scrap metal would be found to tie the 'fist' around. Once that was completed, several layers of varnish would be soaked in, at which point a final topcoat of (POS coloured) paint could be applied and left to further soak in order to make up the final weight. Eventually, the whole thing would be christened with several POS members taking it in turns to get the whole length of the rope out in a line. I used to do well at that, and could always be relied upon to get the first line over.

The problem lay in Rosyth and Portsmouth, where the dockies took exception to our lovingly crafted lines, and took pleasure in immediately cutting off the 'fist' before throwing it off the edge of the jetty. That would incense us, and the matey (to remind you, we always hated mateys – they were without exception idle gits) would be verbally abused over his parentage, or accused of having sex with himself. Or was it that we'd wait until he wasn't looking, and was offguard, before throwing the spare, bigger fist at him instead of near him. We always got our revenge, and we could always tie an even bigger 'fist' on (from the emergency supply!!), to get him the next time.

If the weather prevented us from throwing heaving lines – and it was clearly absolutely essential that we got the lines across to the jetty – we had a backup in the form of a highly illegal bolas. This was really a heaving line with TWO monkey's fists on, which we would whirl round our heads, then let go. These were nearly always successful, but the third backup was to throw a lighter line with a heavy fist, which in turn was tied to a heaving line, which in turn was tied to the mooring ropes. We always got there eventually.

The mooring lines were stowed on each relevant POS, the headropes, (man made ropes) and foresprings were kept on the fo'c'sle, the stern rope (man made again) were stowed on the QD, and the breasts (made of wire, as were the springs) were kept on TOP. At sea, they were all stored on various drums or reels, amd it was a git of a job to put them on. Some poor sod had to rotate the drums to gradually get the ropes on. Once stowed, we had special covers made to fit the reel. Getting them off was a little easier – just keep pulling and laying them down until all off.

Another naval tradition, is that of 'piping' other ships. Generally, as you sail past another warship, whether it is tied up, or floating, the junior ship (that is to say, the one with the most junior skipper) pipes (the still) to the senior. The senior then pipes the still, waits a few seconds, then pipes the carry on. The junior then pipes the carry on, obscenities are exchanged, and both units proceed. While the stills are there, anyone (caught foolishly) on the upper scupper, has to face the other ship. So we became practiced at spotting approaching ships, and legging it to cover, or to the far side, so we wouldn't have to comply. Sometimes it was fun, like seeing another ship miles away from anywhere, sometimes it was poignant, like piping the war memorial on the beach at Southsea, other times it was a pain in the arse, like piping FOSNI (Flag Office Scotland/Northern Ireland) in his house by the Forth Bridge, every time you went past it/him.

Each time we went to sea, as soon as the last mooring rope was undone, we'd strike the jack and ensign, running up a second ensign on the main mast. We'd then lower the jackstaff, right in the bows, and the ensign, right aft, securing them tightly with heaving lines, until they were required again. The jack would remain stowed, but the second ensign would remain at the mast head until we returned to harbour, for all to see and recognise.

We also carried out 'Dipping the ensign'. If we went past a merchant ship, it was common practice for the merchantman to dip his ensign slightly, as a mark of respect. We would then dip ours, re-raise it, the merchantman then raised his. We'd both then continue on our respective journeys. Obviously this didn't happen at night, only when we had ours raised, but we used to giggle, and watch intently through powerful binoculars, as the merchantman suddenly remembered what he had to do. You'd then see his bridge door fly open, and a figure would scuttle aft to his Red Duster (Red Ensign) , hurdling and dodging everything in his way, getting there just in time to dip it before we steamed past.

If he wasn't flying the red duster, the OOW would have to identify from his flag, what nationality he was. And we quickly learned which ones to, literally, steer clear of. For example, anything registered under a 'flag of convenience', such as Libya. We learned these flags and therefore identities as bridge lookouts. It all helped.

Whilst 'on watch', if we happened across a 'friendly' warship, or noticed aircraft 'squawking' on the IFF, we would be able to tell the type, country and exact unit. The aircraft were more difficult, but we could say what it was and where it was from. We would also track airliners just for fun, and watch their squawks. We could interrogate them on our IFF to make their transponder automatically tell us who they were. It was all very good fun, for us baby RPs', playing with all this technical stuff FOR REAL.

The contacts we tracked were all called 'skunks', that meant we didn't know what or who it was. It was therefore a 'skunk' And we named them, from alpha to zulu, so we reported 'skunk alpha' – our first real radar contact to play with. We tracked that first contact until it disappeared off the edge of the table! If we ever got to handling more than twenty-six, we'd have been stuffed – it didn't occur to us to use numbers on the Zulu!! It also didn't matter that the contact was identified, and that there was no real possibility of anything other than friendly ships or aircraft anywhere inside the twelve mile territorial waters – they were still called 'skunks'.

We also monitored the worldwide 'Guard' (Mayday) frequency of 243mhz. A speaker would be permanently live, and if we heard anything we'd have to alert the RO's. We only monitored, never, ever transmitted. Apparently, if you responded, that made you responsible for locating and rescuing the person screaming for help.

We did see the very occasional AGI (Russian 'fishing boats'), they were still skunks, but although we never took any official notice of them, we always stopped transmitting on all radars and sonars whenever we recognised what they were – probably too late. We'd also never transmit on the fire control radar, nor would we ever under any circumstances train the guns on them, even for a laugh. We'd skirt them, they'd skirt us, when we'd all finished filming and recording, we'd steam away from each other, and get back on with what we were doing, before we were interrupted.

If, therefore, we came upon a non-Nato ship, we'd frantically search through 'Janes' (Fighting Ships) to find something that matched the profile of the ship we could see. No matter that the ship would probably be at a strange angle, making all the silhouettes useless...

The Zulu actually had four radar 'sets' for us to play with, the old 965 long range air-search, the 293 surface search, 978 navigation, and the 944/954 IFF. All of which we were technically word perfect on – our PRI Ray Antell had seen to that. It was still a wonderful experience though, to be actually standing behind the Local Plot, tracking real ships, working out real courses and speeds for real ships, and then calculating their closest point of approach, before telling the watch boss. He would then relay this data to the OOW on the bridge, who would then tell us either 'report' or 'watch'. Eventually, the OOW would tell us what kind of target or ship we were tracking, at which point we would scan the radar with great earnest, looking for more echoes to report.

The reporting procedure on the intercom went 'Bridge – Plot', the OOW on the bridge would say 'Bridge', at which point we would report the contact. Unless you had never spoken on an intercom before, in which case you would be told to speak clearly, or not to gabble, or whatever. I didn't have any such problems, and I took to it like a duck to water. Except when I attempted to copy the older hands who would, in the middle of the night, call 'BEE BOP', or 'PLIP PLOP' and the OOW would answer 'Bridge', as he would assume HE had misheard. Anyway, I got caught out doing it didn't I. And a right earwigging I got on the bridge that night. Mac, our leading hand of the watch thought it hugely entertaining, I learned a lesson, and was never caught again. No, I didn't say I didn't do it again, I said I never got CAUGHT again.

As the contacts were tracked, we used to record their progress on the plotting tables with chinagraph, a greasy pencil really, which shone highly when exposed to UV light. We also used small widgets, which were colour coded shapes, green for friendly, red for hostile, orange for 'dunno', which we placed on the contact, so anyone looking at the table would see us, and everything around us. These also glowed under UV. Which is what the Ops room was continuously bathed in. Paradoxically, it also showed up our eights – if they were clean, the UV would make them glow, but any grubby patches would not 'shine'. White fronts or whit T-shirts were to be avoided, as they'd be completely dazzling to an onlooker. Otherwise, the room was in pitch dark, and known as the 'gloom room'. Gloomy or not, we always had an audience – from clanks (stokers) to greenies (electricians) to stewards – they would all come to see the radar! Or was it to see what proper sailors did? Or was even it to scrounge a wet of coffee, which was always in plentiful supply for us official watchkeepers, even if we did have to descend two decks then walk half a ship length to get some hot water. Maybe it was purely because we were sociable people, or perhaps it was just warm in there with all that electrical apparatus running.

One of the jobs I learned, and another thing I can still do (another useless attribute) is that we had to either write upside down (because we were round the back of the plotting table, and the people at the front needed to see), or back to front (on a large sheet of Perspex) so it could be read from the front. We would stand for ages, tongues out with the concentration, trying to get it right first time, knowing if we came round the front and it was wrong, we'd be back there 'doing it properly', with plenty of stick for being wrong previously…

We would, whilst offwatch, and just for the mindless relief it offered, steer the ship. We had been trained to do this in the simulator at Raleigh, but now we could do it for real. We would go to the wheelhouse, and ask if we could have a go. Whoever was on the wheel would say "Bridge – Wheelhouse" (or "Fridge – Greenhouse" on occasions), and when answered, he would ask for "Permission for Junior Seaman So and So to take the wheel". If it was "Yes Please", you would have to announce who you were, what course you were steering, and what the telegraph and rev indicators were set at. Woe betide you if you got that bit wrong. Then you had to steer the ship, following the compass. On the compass was a thing called the 'Lubbers Line' which was what you steered to, and God help you if you started to 'chase it', that is to say drift off course and apply the wrong and opposite 'wheel' to get it back on course. You'd normally be instantly thrown off the wheel, and banished from the wheelhouse. It was though a point of honour to be able to steer the ship, continuously to within just one degree, especially if the weather was bouncy and the ship wanted to veer about. If you did well, the OOW would always praise your spell. Apparently, and allegedly, (according to the black cats) someone on another ship, unspecified, had actually taken the ship round in a full 360 degree turn one night, without the OOW noticing. Could this be true…? Whatever – the first time you plucked up the courage to steer was scary, after that, after steering it for several thousand miles – it got much easier, and you learned how easy it was to predict which way it would try to drift next, and by how much, and thus how to move the wheel gently to stop it and to regain the original course. All on board eventually succumbed to driving the ship, even bone-idle greenies would come and steer it, though chefs seemed to prefer it to making biscuits!

We held exercises with aircraft, using the giant bedstead array (965) atop the main mast to locate aircraft at extreme range, tracking them in, reporting on them on a live UHF radio to the shore station we would play with at the time. Slowly but surely – we were shaken down and worked up gently to the big one. We sailed to Portland – an inhospitable area in summertime, but a nightmare to us whatever the time of year, whatever the weather conditions (normally a full gale as far as we were concerned). One day, while we were setting up the gunnery/fire control radar, we had the use of a Canberra, which flew off in various directions, at various heights, then came back in again. I actually had a go at controlling him – there I was, stood on the bridge roof like Ahab, telling this bomber where to go, at what speed, and looking for his extremely bright light in his nose as he hurtled back at us. He eventually told me he was getting low on fuel, and went home. That was a very enjoyable afternoon for me

As armament on that – and all the other Tribals , we had a four point five inch gun fore and aft, Seacats port and starboard, Oerlikons port and starboard, A/S mortars aft, and a helicopter. Plus many small arms, assorted maching guns – light and heavy, in the magazines. All or some of these would be exercised at various times, sometimes all at once at action stations.

While we were closed up at action stations, we'd have closed the Damage Control state up to One Zulu Alpha, that is – everyone closed up at their action station, every watertight door and hatch shut and clipped, gastight and airtight. Officially. We'd have previously proved the gastight bit, by creating a positive pressure below decks, then by trying to find anywhere the air was getting out. This 'state' also made it painful if any dickhead were to open any door once the pressure was up. The resulting de-pressurisation could not only blow the door dangerously open once cracked, it also made your ears hurt!!

Once at this state, we'd sometimes pretend there was a chemical or biological or nuclear threat, and rig 'pre-wetting' on the upper deck. This meant rigging hoses all round the ship, spraying water all over the superstructure, the theory being that if anything dangerous or radioactive or mind-altering wafted down onto us, the nice water would wash the nasty bits away, and that would clearly leave us quite, quite safe from harm, wouldn't it... So anyone going out on to the upper scupper, would have to come back in through a specially rigged decontamination shelter (actually the QMs' kaboosh), where a special shower would be rigged. In this showere, the person would need to be scrubbed by his mates to get rid of all contamination. Not that we gave a shit – we were in our nice cosy ops room.

Action stations meant everyone was closed up. Whether that meant the stewards manned the hoists in the mags, or the chefs manned the gun turret, passing the bricks and the cordite, or the stokers on the throttles, or the greenies... Sorry, nearly lost the thread there – greenies were still asleep that time of day. Or night. Maybe they painted eyes on their anti-flash, and pretended. Like we did when we got bored, putting our anti-flash on back to front to annoy someone.

Everyone was actually on full alert during action stations, and we were – most literally – ready for anything anyone could throw at us in the coming weeks. We'd had the practice, now we sailed from Pompey, to Portland to exercise properly!

Chapter 10

And Now Portland

Portland, otherwise known as 'work-up', or 'shake-down', generally lasted in the region of six weeks. During these weeks, we sometimes got evening shore leave (if we needed to store, without RAS'ing), but never got weekend leave, unless it was a short one, from Saturday lunchtime until Monday morning. We did, however, get grief, exercises, grief, more grief, and more work. On top of that, we got more exercises.

'Working up' (getting the ship's company ready for every eventuality) comprised anchoring out most nights, going alongside rarely. And carrying out seamanship evolutions like RAS'ing, towing, mooring, anchoring, you name it – we did it. Coupled with exercise fires, damage control, and pretend NBCD attacks. And being closed up at Action Stations before the rest of the world was awake, and sailing out of the harbour line astern with all the other ships down there, knowing quite well it would be you who first saw the telltale echo of the Buccaneer from not more than ten miles away as it came in at sea-level to 'bounce' you, as it was you on the radar. By the time you reported it – it was upon you with a roar you could hear below decks. Or you would see just one trace, which could either be a tin-can, or a submarine periscope. It was not in your interest to keep quiet – so you would scream now, rather than be screamed at for missing it. What would annoy us more, was that particular Portland this visit was during peak holiday season, with all the tourists, all with their daughters – and here we were, sitting in a grey steel shitheap, doing things we didn't want to do, while they were laying in their caravans snoring, and dreaming about the sailor they met last night!

It was now we really found out about keeping everything to 'Zulu' time. All exercises started at 0730Z, or 1000Z, or 2030Z, and if we happened to get there at 0730A(lpha), or 1000A – we would therefore be an hour late. Or was it an hour early. So Zulu time it was.

Portland was famous for 'FOST Funnies'. FOST was Flag Officer Sea Training, and his staff officers used to find it amusing to drop an exercise on you, any time day or night. Like waking you up at 0300 to say there was a SUBMISS or SUBSMASH (Submarine missing/Submarine Smashed), gearing everyone up to sail, as far as singling up all the lines, then saying "...just an exercise". Bastards. Or calling a fire on you just as you were about to go ashore, so the whole ships company were either involved in it, or caught up in it.

At sea, even though we in the ops room would be conducting a CASEX (Combined Anti Sub Exercise), or ARREX (Air Raid Reporting ex) or Gun Firing Exercise, or whatever, and whilst our job was clearly the most important on the ship – well it was obvious really, if we didn't see 'the threat' coming in, we'd soon have large holes to repair- the rest of the ships company would be rehearsing Damage Control exercises, power failures, chemical attacks – everything to keep themselves amused, and us pissed off. What would start as an 0600 'weekly war' sail out from the harbour having first got everyone up at 0500 to weigh anchor, would then degenerate rapidly, as the ops room crew closed up before passing through the breakwater, then we'd be hit, then we'd have the 'DC ex', then the NBCD attack, by which time we'd be sitting there in the gloom room, in eights, trousers tucked in non-nylon socks, anti-flash gear, gas masks – looking like a bunch of ultra-violet lit pervies, all gazing at various displays, and shouting various attack threats at the person who needed to know. Occasionally, the staffies used to either 'kill' the ops room officer, or the Captain, or some of us. Or they'd cut all the power. They used to think that was a brilliant move. So did we, we never let on. It was always much more peaceful without radar to play with, except that it got hot without the fans going, and we'd lose pounds waiting for the FOST prats to get bored and allow us to go in peace.

Occasionally, when everyone from the skipper down to us, started to get a bit ratty, 'the proceedings' would come to a natural break, and 'one-all-round' would be announced. Everyone would then gratefully light up, drawing the ciggy smoke deep down, to ease the tension. Well it felt like that anyway. Pretty soon you wouldn't be able to see across the gloom room, although the air conditioning would soon clear it away, ready for the next load of grief. It wasn't as if you could sneak off for a sly drag by asking to go to the heads – it didn't work like that, and anyway the heads were two decks down, and probably blocked by a DC exercise, and if you went near it, you'd more than likely be co-opted into helping some moronic greenie or spanner-wanking stoker to 'shore up' a pretend hole. As the prospect of doing that involved physical labour, and thus filled us with more dread than being in the ops-room – we stayed put, and suffered. Once 'closed up' at action stations – you bloody well STAYED closed up at action stations, either until stood down, or until you were reduced to defence watches, (either the whole of the port watch, or the whole of the starboard watch) meaning half of you could stand down (and get turned to) while your mates remained closed up (and sat down)., and in the warm.

Some exercises required running silent, we'd trudge about at four knots, listening on the passive sonar for the 'enemy' submarine. God help anyone who decided to smash around or bang anything aboard whilst doing this. Or we'd stamp around with the active sonar pinging, searching for the elusive black pig. Active sonar is like you hear on the telly, except that when you are encased in a metal-hulled ship, the transmitted pulse reverberates through the entire hull, and you will also hear the returning pulse as it bounces off the contact. There is an album by Pink Floyd, called 'MEDDLE', which I used to play occasionally, which has several minutes of apparent 'sonar' transmissions. I fooled my messmates with this for ages until I finally owned up to what I was doing. One bloke would normally shoot up to the SCR (sonar control room, situated on a room off the ops room) each time I played it, until someone wised him up. Was he narked or what!

Talking of weighing anchor – we sailors would muster on the sharp end, complete with stiff brooms and hoses coupled up and ready. In Portland, the harbour bottom was thick gooey mud, and as the cable was worked, more mud and filth would be raised, which we would energetically hose and scrub off as soon as the cable came through the hawse pipes, with the cable on it's way to the cable locker, round the capstans, with the occasional pre-marked link being painted in transit, so everyone would know how much cable was left out. Occasionally, sea creatures would survive the ascent, and we'd be hosing not only prehistoric mud, but also the crabs and starfishes off the cable. Unless it went a'cock bill (meaning it came up & got stuck the wrong way round, or wouldn't fit into the hawse pipe), eventually, the anchor would get clear of the water, and we'd slowly move ahead with the hook dragging through the sea, being cleaned off nicely. We had to bear in mind though, that as we revved up, the hook could start to wobble about in the increasing flow, so the trick was to get it out of the water half way between being 'automatically' cleaned, and having it smashing embarrassingly through the ship's side. We often had almighty bangs as it hit us, but no holes. Eventually, we'd raise it out of the water, nearer to the 'home' position, at which point we'd blast the remaining mud off it by leaving it hanging over the side, and increasing the hydrant/hose pressure to full pelt. Once we were satisfied it was clean (and remember those FOST goonies were always out to criticise something, even if it was only mud on the anchor), we'd haul it all the way home, fasten on all the shackles, including the bottle slip to drag it home that last few inches, before hosing down the whole fo'c's'le whilst still getting under way a bit faster. Anyone who has never done this at 0500, in full foul weather gear, in the teeth of a gale, complete with driving, persistent rain has never lived. Lucky them. We'd then have to wait some hours till breakfast, or close up in the ops room for the first exercise. Still – we always had that day's exercises to look forward to… Or the tourist's daughters that night – if we were allowed alongside.

Something else we would always have to do before it got picked up – we had an exhaust from one of our generators (known as 'donks' or donkeys) half way down the ship's side just around the bridge wings, i.e. the highest point on the ship's deck), and every time we flashed that up to give us totally shore-free power, it would gob out filthy black and blue smoke, leaving a huge black trail round and downwind from it. And every time we stopped, out would go the bo's'n's chair with the duty hands, with his duty ship's side grey in a pot, covering up the crap. Again. You would think that was all sailors were there for, painting the side, cleaning everywhere for everyone else to live, polishing everything not already covered in paint. Or was it just to keep everything important going…

Now, gunnery exercises were always fun. One such exercise would involve doing a pretend shore bombardment. We'd steam up and down the coast in Lulworth (I think), ensuring stray targets, such as grockle boats, fishing boats etc. didn't get between us and our real target. Once we were absolutely sure – we'd open fire. It never sounds much – a 4.5" gun throwing a fifty-something pound projectile up to ten miles, but the racket as it fired was enough to wake up long dead people. Every molecule on, in and round the ship would immediately be thrown ten left in reaction to the shell being hurled through and out the muzzle. Dust would fall from undusted places, unsecured glasses would jump from tables, and unwary people who hadn't heard the warnings that "'A' turret is about to open fiBBBAAANNNGGG" would literally shit themselves. The first time I heard it, I jumped out of my new steaming boots – and I was ready for it!

On occasions, we'd fire just a few rounds, but on the shore support exercise, we'd fire, and fire, and fire shell after shell after shell, for minutes at a time, up to ten rounds per minute – which is an awful lot of hard work – until your heard above the din 'Guns' screaming …

"STOPLOADINGSTOPLOADINGSTOPLOADING-CHECKCHECKCHECK"

and when the cry came back "ALL GUNS EMPTY", you'd close your open mouth (previously opened to reduce the effect of the cordite blast), shake your head, and get on with what you were doing. If you were on the upper deck when they started, it could literally be deafening.

Then there was that unforgettable and unmistakable smell – a mate on a future ship would describe it as 'cordite and sweaty sailors'. The stench from the exploded cordite as it forced the projjy out of the barrel was completely gross. If the air-conditioning was still switched on, within seconds, the whole of the interior of the ship would be filled with that stink – comparable to rotten eggs but worse. Choking, acrid, and once in your lungs it took hours to get back out.

Shot Mats were normally placed around the turret during firing. These were thick cord mats placed to protect the metal decks from impact damage from dropped casings, and after the exercise (once they'd cooled) we'd try to steal these empty cordite casings – they made terrific ashtrays onboard, but were highly prized by naval type 'inn-keepers' in shore hostelries, and were thus cash-valuable. Unfortunately though, they were either given the old float test, or returned to the mags for later removal.

If we were on watch in the ops room during gunnery exercises, we used to physically track the projjy out on the radar until it vanished or hit the target. That used to be something to watch out for, as you'd only see it for three or four sweeps. It was said, that if you stood behind the barrel, and watched, you could actually see the projectile out for some distance before your eyes failed. In my view, it would take a brave, or foolish person to stand behind a gun that size as it exploded, blowing shit and derision in all directions, plus the large ever-generated smoke ring, which always hung in the air, drifting slowly aft, as the thunderous detonation eased off your eardrums. Imagine the guys on the old battleships with 15" jobs?!!

The other good one, was when we'd either have an old RAF Canberra or similar towing a drogue, or we'd launch a PTA (pilotless target aircraft), both of which we'd acquire on radar, line up both guns, and again commence firing, until we'd hit it. Which we did with monotonous regularity. One day we cleared the aircraft out of all his drogues, shooting either through the tow wire, or zapping the drogue. And hitting the PTA was even less popular – it meant the crew (who came aboard with it – nothing to do with us) had to rig a second one before firing it off our quarterdeck. Which all took them much grumbling time to set up.

Eventually, you'd hear the broadcast "SPONGE OUT", at which time you'd know the racket was really over. The gun captain would then make his crew clean up the gun, put the tampon back in the end of the barrel (to prevent seawater invading the inside of the gun), put all the covers back on it, and there it would stand, deserted, but menacing. Until the next time.

Our favourite exercise, was actually the Z-Ex, which was always the last one, and entailed legging it back to your pit, laying on it fully dressed, shutting your eyes, and snoring, loudly.

"ZZZZZZZZZzzzzzzzzzzzzzzzzzzzzzzz...Ex".

Of course, it was easy to whack the shells out, but we'd suffer later – 'ammunition ship' was the most loathed task in the RN. No smoking,

ANYWHERE, until it was over, no fags on you, no matches on you, no nylon on you. Then you'd sit in the 'mags' unloading shells (and the cordite) from the lifts, swinging them nonchalantly around, and into the racks, trying to forget that one dropped could ruin your (and everyone else within a several mile radius) marriage and career prospects! They were heavy too – a normal projectile could weigh 50 to 60 pounds, and the casing could be about twenty, both of which we'd throw at each other to stow, quite happily. If nothing else – we were fit!

When we did NBCD or Damage Control exercises, we would 'close the ship down', then, conversely, 'close the crew up'. Closing the ship down entailed shutting all (required) hatches and doors, to reach the required state. The higher the state, the more doors got closed off. You were then not allowed through these doors unless permission was given from DC HQ. All doors were fitted with up to a dozen clips, which would ensure that with the rubber edge, the door would seal perfectly, even if assistance was required by swinging off the clip, with a large bent piece of pipe. Not that we ever, ever smashed these even more firmly shut deliberately so that no-one would ever get it open again. Unless he was bigger than us! He would be significantly knackered, though, after undoing up to a dozen heavily closed door-clips. Just to really piss people off – as they undid one clip and moved to the next, we'd sit behind the door, putting back the one he'd just undone, making sure you just kept ahead of whoever was on the other side. That made for a really good wind up, though after some time, or as soon as you got bored, you'd have to get away quite fast, then 'act nonch(alently)' as he came through the door, looking for someone's blood, waving the pipe around.! "No", we'd say, "just got here ourselves – a greenie just legged it aft, giggling, dunno who it was – he had his anti flash on!".

The DC state corresponded with the threat, so the more likely we were to get attacked/sunk, the more doors we closed to try to ensure we continued to float and operate.

Conversely then, having closed down the ship, we then closed up the crews – Ops room crew, Gun crew, DC crews – all got closed up to match the threat, maybe Action Scractions, perhaps Defence watches. Confusing, wasn't it. But second nature after a couple of trial runs…

One of my 'action stations' was the radar office, where I got a surprise I wasn't prepared for. This office was deep in the bowels of the ship, through and down several hatches and ladders. This place was hot as hell from all the valves in the radar gear. However, the first time down there, on the headset to the ops-room, I was told to start the 965. I pretended I hadn't heard. When they finally sent someone down to show me – what took my breath away (in the new technological RN), was that I had to turn a wheel, which cranked the aerial. When it got fast enough, I could push a switch to engage the motor drive. Then I had to press a button to switch it on, to make it transmit. We had a similar set-up for the 293, only not quite so clumsy, and I think a further one in the ops room to start the old navigation radar.

We would also close up 'Specials', Special Sea Dutymen – experts who would navigate us in and out of harbour, and be ready to react to any potential emergency. It was important to be selected to do specials, as it meant you wouldn't have to get into blues and stand out in the cold and rain to enter/leave harbour. You'd instead be in the warm and dry, and in eights. Specials closed up for a variety of reasons – Ras'ing, entering harbour, anchoring to name a few, and would close up all over the ship, including the wheelhouse, DCHQ, gloomroom, switchboards, and tiller flat. That was the un-favourite place, hot, right aft, below the quarterdeck, above the extremely noisy steering gear, knowing that if we suffered a failure on that gear, that you'd then be working your knackers off, aligning the rudders, by hand pump. A terrifying prospect!. Whatever, entrance to the tiller flat was by a small hatch, again secured by clips to correspond to the DC state. And frequently, when the tiller flat pilot attempted to fall out, he'd find the door clips had been secured with enormous force, by persons unknown, meaning he had to bang on the solid steel door until someone heard him, and released him. Not a job for the unwary!

It would be shortly before this 'Specials' pipe, that the jimmy could make a broadcast, warning us of severe weather conditions ('blowing a fuckin' hoolie' was how it would normally be described), and telling us to secure the ship for rough weather. This could be merely lashing down everything that could move – ironing boards, tea-boat, blocks – to rigging the upper deck lifelines, and putting extra strops on everything else. We'd nevertheless rig the seaboat as a lifeboat, with the boatrope rigged, and all the gripes hauled taught(er). Conditions like this were fairly normal for Portland, at any time of year.

My first run ashore in Portland, was dressed in full twos', with complimentary white gaiters, and webbing belt, for I was one of the duty Shore Patrol. I had to sit in the Dockyard Naafi all evening, watching everyone else steam into pint after pint. The next night we were alongside, I actually got ashore – remember this was my first proper 'run' outside Rosyth or Pompey or Guzz – and I can still remember the main drag leading from the dockyard gate in Portland as it was, with alternating pubs and food shops. I still remember the atmosphere and smell too.

One lunchtime, I was piped to the gangway, and to my utter astonishment, my Mum stood there, with a friend of hers, both of whom were on holiday in Weymouth, and had decided on spec to come to the base to see if my ship was in. To their surprise, the first sailor they saw, wore a 'Zulu' cap tally, so after getting permission, they came through and aboard, where I entertained them in my mess, with my new mates. I don't know who got the biggest surprise that particular day, these two ladies who had never seen anything like us and how we lived, or us who suddenly were entertaining these two unannounced visitors!

On another evening we went ashore quite early (as soon as 'secure' was piped) to try to empty the place of scrumpy and Merrydown, and when we left the ship we were 'Channel Guard Ship', so there was only 'One Watch Leave' – meaning only half the crew were allowed ashore. We had done this before at Portland, often, as had all other ships doing their work-up. A different ship was 'guard-ship' every night/day. Further to this, 'Tribal' class frigates had two methods of propulsion – steam and gas-turbine. The Gas turbine (or G6 as it was called) could be flashed up within minutes, meaning we really could sail at the drop of a hat, in the time it took to fire up that turbine. That kind of information was nice to know, but meaningless to us. All we knew about G6 was the piped message before it was started 'Hands keep clear of the after funnel – G6 is about to be run up'. Followed by a muffled explosion, followed by an increasing roar as the turbine took effect. That would then be followed by a large shower of soot, covering anything down-wind of it. Not recommended, nor conducive to the health of the stoker(s) who wound it up just after we sailors had spent the last two hours scrubbing the wooden decks by hand. G6 was usually kicked up before sailing so as to provide a backup power plant in case of a steam plant breakdown. So as we stumbled back down the drag late one evening, we heard the muffled explosion, saw the flames leaping out of OUR aft funnel, thought "Fuck – that's us" and improved our speed, but not necessarily our direction back through the yard towards the gangway. As we did so, we were met by the Duty PO, who told us to get a wriggle on, as we were about to sail. Yeah, Yeah – we thought, another FOST Funny. Nevertheless, we hurriedly changed into eights, donned our foul-weather gear, and ran up to our parts-of-ship – and to our utter astonishment, we actually slipped and sailed with no more ado. Once we'd left with a partial crew (the rest had been left ashore still on the piss), we knew this was not an exercise or FOST Funny organised by the duty tosser. We were soon told by the skipper that we were en route to just south of the Isle of Wight, to a position just off St Katherine's Point ,where an oil tanker was stricken. We didn't get a lot of sleep that night, and as we had sailed without all the crew, we had to double up. The 'Pacific Glory' was ablaze from its rear end, and we could see the glow long before we located it on radar. We weren't the first ship on the scene, but our firefighters boarded it to assist bringing the blaze under control, and then assessed the considerable damage. Personally, I didn't see any of her dead Chinese crew, but we apparently picked a few up that night. As did the rest of the rescue operation. Even so, there were 27 very fortunate survivors from the tanker, and we Zulus were a lot less 'jolly' when we steamed back into Portland later to recover the rest of our crew. It is surprising how quickly a disaster like that sobered you up – in more than one sense. Mind you, it proved our training to be second to none – we showed we could respond instantly and professionally to any situation we were called upon. And that after only a few weeks training.

At some point, (lucky us) we had acquired our own helicopter – a Wasp (so called because of its' noise and nuisance factor, buzzing round you all the time I suppose), complete with pilot, and aircrew. As usual with Fleet Air Arm – they were a bunch of real posers. Always were – always will be. These were no different, all they ever did was get in our way. 'No Smoking on the upper deck – helicopter ranged'. 'No smoking abaft the after funnel – helicopter being refuelled'. 'No personnel on the upper deck – helicopter at flying stations'. Even going into and out of harbour – the blue queen bee used to pose on the flight deck, surrounded by its worker ants who would be smirking and smiling gormlessley. The only perk I used to get out of it was as helicopter lookout, on duty in the gloom room, when I would then go to the gun radar platform, to watch over the Wasp as it buzzed about. My job as lookout would be not only to track the thing with my mark one eyeball, but to scream loudly if it fell into the sea. Which it never did. However, I used to enjoy being up there in the fresh air, whilst we charged around the Portland practice areas at high speeds. On occasions, when we 'flew' at night, you were up there alone, in the pitch dark apart from the steaming lights, and while it wasn't noiseless, you'd really think you were the only person for miles. That far out at sea, for instance in the middle of the North Sea (or the Atlantic, or wherever we were operating, you'd have a ceiling of stars and no cloud, but best of all – no artificial lighting to ruin your view of the skies. The 'bins' then would be alternately trained on the lawnmower bizzy buzzing around, then on the skies. While it landed on to refuel or re-arm, you could lay back and stargaze. On that particular lookout post would be a gadget designed to direct the guns. This had a powerful set of bins in it, but was connected to the guns. We'd disengage the gun system (obviously – we didn't want to give the game away), and peer through the gunsights at whatever there was to see. Being electrically operated, you'd gently twist the handle on one side to go left or right, then the other to swing up and down – and be able to see for much further, even being able to stargaze without twisting your head up.

Back to the Waffoos – who used to work together, go ashore together, mess together, (probably sleep together) and generally be ignored by us real sailors – as they clearly weren't. Unless we thought there was something in it for us – like a flight in the budgie. There was a queue outside their office door the day they announced that, to enlist for a jolly in it.

We'd sometimes steam 'blacked out'. This meant covering all openings along the ships side, and even turning off all navigation/mast/steaming lights. Normally we'd do this to 'hide' from the Wasp, to ensure he would be guided back under direct control, rather than see the light and fly towards it. Doing helo lookout at this time was an eerie experience – you'd literally be in pitch darkness, charging through the oceans. Moonlit or starry nights were better, you could lay on the deck, gaze upwards, and spot satellites and shooting stars easy as pie. You could even see the helicopter outside radar range if you stood up again. But put clouds up, and make it rain a bit and the whole scenario would change. We were only meant to spend thirty minutes up as lookout – quite long enough in the pissing rain, but we'd draw it out if the conditions were right. Like flying stations midday in the tropics!!

A favourite retort to anyone who'd say to us 'You wouldn't do that at home, would you', would be "No, but there again, I don't get fuckin' helicopters landing on my fuckin' roof in the middle of the fuckin' night at home do I? "

Our shiny, navy blue helicopter lived in a little nest, called a 'hangar' towards the blunt end of the ship. On the Zulu – therefore on all 'type 81s' – this hangar had a hole in the roof where the deck used to be raised and lowered on a lift. Once lowered, i.e. out of sight (and mind), the idle waffoos used to do their hardest work ever – putting the covers on the hole above where the helo was now sitting. This repetitive task only used to take a few minutes, but being waffoos' they had to work out what to do afresh, every time they did it. So their evolution could take several hours, while we sandscratchers stood laughing. We did hear of a sister ship, where an even more stupid waffoo than normal, engaged the lift in 'raise' while the covers were still on, destroying the helo as it went up. Again – hearsay!!

At some point, we discovered why various items, mostly money, had been going missing from our lockers. Let me repeat, that sailors normally trust other sailors implicitly with personal effects, and rarely would anyone find it necessary to secure a locker, as no-one would borrow without asking. But we found stuff had gone missing. The mess we were in shared a ladder with the greenies mess on the opposite side of the ship. Our lockers were directly opposite the ladder. Things went walkies. We found some of the money one day, tucked behind a trap (toilet) in the forward heads. We had our suspicions, and had words with the Leading Hand of the greenies mess, telling him who we thought it was, and why. The chap was trapped with some marked notes, and eventually weighed off, curiously with bandaged hands, which occurred when a hatch he was going through accidentally got dropped – sorry, fell on his fingers. That was a navy tradition. It allegedly took several people to hold him there, and he apparently screamed very loudly whilst we were not present in the mess, having been earlier sent out.

We also did shore exercises, 'protecting' the island (of Portlandia) from insurgents and other nasties, who wanted to take over the place, marching around with SLRs' loaded with blanks, dressed in eights, boots, gaiters, helmets – the full bollocks, challenging anyone looking suspect. This was the excuse to stop every vehicle within range, demanding that the driver get out while we searched him and his charge. No matter that he was a docky on official business, or a pig on his way home – he still had to be stopped and searched by our (over) zealous shore platoon.

Chapter 11

Our First 'Foreign (Even if it was Only Hamburg)

Eventually the work up climaxed in an orgy of exercises and thunderflashes and smoke and disasters, which we apparently passed with flying colours. At least, the 'staffies' could find no more to whinge and whine about, so we sailed for Portsmouth, and from there straight to Hamburg for our first run ashore.

We arrived there at the top of the river at something like 0400, embarked the pilot up the jumping ladder, and closed up Specials, all the way down to Hamburg, where we finally moored against a large thing called the Uberseebrucke. This was miles away from the main town, but right across the street from a cuckoo-clock shop. I still have the clock – it still keeps virtually perfect time, and still cheerfully cuckoos, when allowed! As we went ashore for the first time, with our money conveniently changed previously into Marks, I forgot we drove on the left – although Germany didn't – and marched out in front of a large tram. How I avoided it – I do not know.

The next few days was a blur of Hamburg, Lowenbrau beer, German fast food, Lowenbrau, and more sightseeing. With more German beer for good measure.

It was only when we sailed, got to the top of the river, and turned into the North Sea that the snags developed. Too many sailors with a taste for English beer got a shock when, after drinking chemical beer for three days, we hit a force eight going back over to Rosyth. Me – I was sick as a dog for the first few hours of the voyage, but didn't know whether to put it down to my first real drop of 'roughers' (anything below a force eight was just windy, anything over was bumpy), or the beer... Whatever – I was not alone as we greenly pitched our way through high seas, with frequent trips to the aft heads (not so much motion as the for'rd ones'), back to the peace of the Forth, and then back into the safe arms of the jetties of Rosyth. Subsequently, I have always claimed it was the beer, as I was never, ever sick at sea again, not in any physical condition, not in any sea state.

This (being seasick) begged the insult "Not so fuckin' jolly now, are we, Jack?!", or "I dunno, last nights' ball of fire – this mornings ashes!"

One of our 'perks' as RPs' was our ability to go and stand on the bridge (in quiet watches), to gaze out over the sea on which we travelled, looking at the ships we had just located, seeing where they were headed. This of course was very much reliant on the current sea-state – in bumpy weather, with the bridge windscreen wipers at full pelt, watching the green sea smashing over the bow, thundering down the fo'c's'le, hitting the 'screen', bouncing up that, and then finally banging into those wipers was a truly amazing sight. Then, depending on the OOW, we would even be allowed to pass orders to the wheelhouse, or even acknowledge the reports from the rest of the watch in the ops room. As RP's we would still stand our steaming watch in the ops room, unlike the other seamen (Gunners, Sonars) who would stand 'watch on deck', providing bridge lookouts, stern lookouts (in case of man overboard), helmsmen, and seaboats crew. One night, a new young junior went onto the starboard bridge wing as lookout, and asked us how to report the light he had observed. Instead of telling him to say "Bridge – Port lookout, Green three zero, white light – far", we told him the reporting routine was "Bridge – port lookout, Yo Ho Ho little white light, green three oh". Then we legged it. He made the report, everyone on the bridge disintegrated into small giggling heaps – except the OOW who gave him a good bollocking, and taught him the correct procedure. The kiddy concerned gave us some stick afterwards, but we could handle it!!

Hamburg, then, our reward for getting through Portland, had been pretty much unremarkable, and we looked forward to Christmas 1970.

When it came, we set off for our main leave from Rosyth with our duty-free and rabbits from our Hamburg run – in my case my cuckoo clock, several bottles of vino collapso, several hundred ciggys and a large bottle of vodka. We freely imbibed from the carry-out shops, and were in fact three sheets to the wind before we got on the train at Inverkeithing. By the time we got to Waverly and changed trains, we had all had enough, and opened our dfs'. This we mixed with the coke/lemonade from the buffet, and I can remember drinking the last of my vodka whilst going through Berwick-On-Tweed. The next thing I remember was waking up at Newcastle, absolutely sober, but thirsty. I drank lemonade all the way to Birmingham, changed trains for the short run to Northampton, and arrived home quite safely.

Chapter 12

At Long Last – Off to the Fez

Going home for long leave, i.e. Christmas was a strange experience, for although nothing had changed – except me, completely and forever, nothing – in my eyes – was ever going to be the same again. And while I was ready for Mum and her question "When do you have to go back", I found that I had nothing much in common with my mates, preferring to demonstrate my drinking prowess – I was well into pints with whisky or rum chasers – rather than go dancing around handbags. We nevertheless continued to explore the pubs, bars, and clubs of Northampton, rebuilding old relationships within our gang. This gang still exists even after all these years – we still gather at least annually.

Leave soon came to an end, with a long trip back to Rosyth, followed by frantic last minute preparations, then suddenly we sailed to Portsmouth amidst understandable buckets of tears from Rosyth wives. It was not in anyone's interest to do any 'winding-up' of RA's on that trip, so it passed fairly uneventfully if dolefully. 'Countdown calendars' (showing how many days were left until we got back to Rosyth) had been created by RA's before we even reached Portsmouth. We re-stored, and sailed right away into the Solent, and the Channel, and started to consume the first of several hundred anti-malaria pills, which we ate, along with salt tablets, every day until we got back to the UK eleven long months later.

It had come about that we were to stop at Gib(raltar) first, and while in Pompey we had taken onboard several 'crabfats' (RAF Pussies) who were quite old and experienced relatively but were also very mouthy and mocking about their self-assumed superiority anyway. They were going to join us in WOD duties, and general upper deck pastimes, such as painting and cleaning, and were messed in with us RPs. Except that as we turned left at the end of The Channel we drove straight in to a force eleven gale. Bumpy – or what. We spent the next three days on the Bay of Biscay, tacking across seas, going about, sitting with the sea ahead, astern, abeam – with the skipper trying to find the most comfortable position and ride for us. Obviously we all had our sea legs, but the crabs stayed in bed for those three days, lifting their heads only to puke. Or to puke. Or to dash to the heads to puke and dump at the same time (called a 'grand slam', made even worse when you forget to remove your trolleys first) or for other reasons. Like puking. As I said – we were used to it by then, to the extent of deliberately and noisily sucking down and scoffing on greasy pork chops or bacon sarnies in front of them to provoke another attack of nausea. I can still picture Jock Norrie, giggling, holding one side of his extremely large nasal organ, pretending to sneeze, and letting go one end of a piece of bacon rind, so it looked like a large lump of snot had dropped. The target crabfat looked, then threw like a geyser, while we all collapsed laughing. All we had to do was mention 'bacon sarnies', or 'pork' after that for the crabs to turn greener still!! God how we laughed. They never did do any Watch on Deck duties, nor any other duties come to that, apart from clearing up their barfings. Well, we had no intention of clearing up after them – it was much more fun to make them do it themselves, retching as they did it. Useless wankers!

I might add we were all banned from the upper deck for those three days as it was considered too dangerous to be up there. There were provisions made for rough seas like these – we would put in place upper deck lifelines, to which to had to secure yourself if you went on the upper deck. And if you tied yourself to these, you had to tell someone you were going 'up', to where, and for how long. And you had to have someone watching. So we stayed below, battened down, as much as possible. Like for the duration. We were though allowed onto the bridge, where we could watch the waves – one minute high above and all round us, the next below us – smashing and crashing not only over the fo'c's'le, spurnwater, 'A' gun and bridge, but in, round and down everything in-between. While balanced on the top of the wave, we'd also hear the screw spinning crazily whilst well out of water, before we assumed yet another astonishing angle, meanwhile dropping like a roller coaster back between more rollers. This was, in my view, between the constant flick of the bridge window windscreen wipers, one of the most impressive sights I ever saw, but it was only when we neared the shelter of Gib that we found we had not only lost several liferafts in the storm, but also had decks and metalwork bent. Plus damage to the spurnwater (the shield in front of the forward or 'A' gun on the forecastle designed to 'spurn' water thundering over the forecastle), which was bent over backwards, causing the 'A' gun to be thrown off-line. By this I mean instead of pointing directly over the bow, the barrel now pointed some ten degrees to the right and several degrees up, whilst the aiming gear correctly pointed dead ahead... And the amount of work that had gone on in Rosyth to set the system up. Oh yes – and we lost the seaboat too – the one we had spent hours on, tuning the ancient engine, painting the old much used planking a pretty, contrasting blue and white mix. Floating around even now I shouldn't wonder somewhere in the Bay of Biscay.

Because it was something else I never discussed with anyone else, it is difficult to put into words the 'buzz' I always, but always got when entering any foreign harbour. Hamburg didn't count, as I was closed up and didn't see anything until I emerged once we were secure alongside. Gib was the first time I had been on the upper scupper to go alongside. The buzz I would get was an exhilarating mixture of anticipation and expectation and pure excitement – if that makes sense. In the UK, after you had a few 'runs' behind you, you got to know what to expect, so runs in Pompey, say, adopted a standard format of drink followed by food, followed by back onboard. Away from home the pattern was basically the same, but mixed in might be a sightseeing trip, new faces, new cultures, new food, different modes of transport. So my feelings were more along the lines of what might happen, rather than what would happen. We KNEW we'd end up several sheets to the wind eventually, it was therefore what would take place before then. I never lost that buzz no matter where I went. Of course, some visits to some ports were horrendous, retrospectively, but the anticipation on the way in would always be the same.

The most exciting part really, was that of standing on the upper deck, at procedure Alpha, or Bravo, watching everything that went on – the tugs, the maneuvering, the expectant faces on the jetty watching your every move, the frenzied rush of work to get the wires and ropes across, to get the ship secured alongside, to get the gangway across and rigged, then – as always – down below to change into working rig, to come back on deck to tidy up the wires, to lash ropes, to get awnings up, to repaint scars, to clean skirmish the jetty, then, finally, to secure for lunch before scampering off for that all important first run.

We moored across the harbour from the massive old sheerlegs (or crane), long since demolished unfortunately, and our first job was to paint the ships side. This is a tradition – everywhere the RN goes in a warship, as soon as the ship is stationary, out comes the grey paint, the stages and the bo's'ns chair, and up and down go the rollers, brushes and elbows as yet more paint is applied. This time, we had lost nearly all the paint from the stem, the anchors, and big lumps down the side, all of which were quickly covered as the Jimmy prowled the jetty looking at the repairs. One trick I learned during this ships-side painting, was that if it was calm enough, it was possible to stand on the 'cats' (large rafts between the jetty and the ship, ostensibly to hold the ship off the wall), and physically push the ship off the cats. This was handy when we had to paint the black strip on the waterline.

Ships Side Party, as it was known, was instigated by the Jimmy at 'Both Watches' in the morning, whenever we were alongside, and therefore – still. As soon as you got to BWH, and saw him leering over the side, you would know what was coming next, and immediately attempt to merge with the background. Fortunately, the way it worked was the better 'hand' you were at your normal daily work, the less likelihood there was of you being picked for SSP. Conversely, the bigger idiot/idler you were, the higher your chances got. So, SSP was generally staffed by the cabbages, who would have to go and find the stages and chairs, rig them, sort out their gear, don thick overalls (and in some cases lifejackets too) and descend over the side of the ship to wash then paint the side. The worst job was painting the stem, as this needed a bo's'u'ns' chair, and delicate balance in order to keep in touch with the job. And an urgent desire to stay out of the water. The second least favourite was to have to do the side below the bridge wings – they were immensely high (or seemed it when viewed from the bottom), but the worst was having to do round any of the sewage outlets, not knowing when someone would finish at their dumping stations, and flush their bowel contents out the side of the ship. You only did it once, after that you stayed above the drain and reached down.

By their nature, and due to gravity, the stages could only go one way – down. Meaning that once you were near the waterline, you then had to climb the ropes back over the freshly scrubbed or painted bits. It was catch 22 – whatever you did, you got soaked or filthy. If anyone with a score to settle knew you were over on a stage, the 'buzz' would go out, and it was not surprising to find buckets of icy water being accidentally poured over the side, or even the ropes becoming suddenly unsecured, allowing one end of the two man stage to tip its human cargo into the sea. It was general to walk past the rope securing it, and kick it or shake it, just to watch to stage-monkeys jump and grab the rope – as if that would be of any help to them if it all collapsed.

We had a small inflatable boat, big enough for, perhaps two people, called a 'copper punt' No prizes for guessing what we called it. This was brought into service whenever we moored, to either pick up side party, to get them to the pontoons, or to get someone right forr'd, to put paint on the 'foot' (where the stem of the bow disappears underwater). Paint would always be removed here – we'd always have to replace it. The copper *unt, then, was the easiest way to achieve it. It was very unstable – if you stood up, you WOULD be swimming.

Whatever SSP had to put up with while working, at the end of the day they had to re-stow the stages and ropes, return all their cleaning gear and paint, then go and get cleaned up using copious amounts of white spirit to remove the 'ships side grey' which now adorned their bodies and overalls, while we just washed our hands.

We had Rock-ape (Gibraltarian) dockyard mateys doing emergency repairs on the spurnwater, and I believe we flew out specialists to realign "A" gun. We obtained another seaboat, which was rapidly brought back into some kind of order. Finally, the crabfats slunk off, unnoticed, with a lot less mouth than they had when they first boarded us in England.

We were therefore forced (!!) to spend more days in Gib than we had planned to. Gib is a wonderful place – it made the perfect 'first foreign run' for us young sailors (having put the very friendly Hamburg behind us).

I will never forget my first proper run ashore, there – the main drag, surprisingly called Main Street, is reached by climbing up out of the dockyard, which puts you immediately in touch with all the pubs. I mean pubs, not bars. Gib is British in every aspect except one – the inhabitants. There are Gibraltarians, and there are the Barbary Apes. The pubs at that time lined both sides of the drag, for as far as you could see. We went on that very first run with Jock Arthur, who steered us from bar to bar to bra t rba to b are... until we couldn't stand up any more. It was in the courtyard of one of these bars, surrounded by colonial tables and tropical palm trees – I think – that Jock first introduced us to JC's (John Collins') – gin, fruit juices, and soda water, with a sugar rimmed glass. You could apparently drink these with no effect all day and night, which was most fortunate as that coincided with the opening hours – if you looked hard enough. We would start at the end of the drag with some Watneys Red Barrel (I did say Gib was a strange place), then as we moved further down the strip, we would venture into JC's', and pork pies (also sold!), and crisps, and end up at a place called 'The Hole In The Wall', where we would drink until we really couldn't stand – then get a taxi back to the ship in time for 0100, which not only ensured 'big eats' at a chippy on the way, but which was Ordinary Seaman's leave expiry time.

One day, just to be different, we boarded the cable car to the top of the rock. Well recommended – the view from there is unparalleled, from Spain to Africa, two continents and a bit more besides. A word of warning – do NOT leave anything unattended, and if you are holding anything -HOLD IT TIGHT – the apes (of the real, hairy type) will nick it as soon as they can, from handbags, cameras, anything. They look so innocuous and friendly on the postcards, but they WILL nick anything given the chance, if not anchored, firmly to your person. It was a scary ride on that cable car, it rises seemingly vertically for the first several hundred feet, over nothing at all, then from the next pylon it is over the rock, and the next stations, with the capability of getting out and walking up, or back down.

We walked through the rock one day, through old passages said to hold munitions in the war, clear through to the other side of the island, where the beaches (such as they are) are. Very dark and damp. The passages, not the beaches. There are also St Michael's Caves, full of brightly lit stalactites and stalagmites, very touristy but a wonderful sight. And the restaurants, of which there are many, for whatever type of food you want. We tried a steakhouse one night, accompanied by litre glasses of Lowenbrau lager, and appropriated the glasses too (which I also still have to this day) . Our friend Jock also showed us something extremely odd – a Wimpy bar in the middle of Gib – one that I recall sold alcohol. That used to be full of tourists of all nationalities.

The shopping is great too – the shops seem to have no set origin, you can literally buy anything there if you look in the right shops. And it is a duty free place too!

So far I have not mentioned a thing called a 'grippo'. A grippo is someone who is so enthralled by the fact that they have met a real sailor, that they willingly talk to you, buying you drinks and food all night. Obviously, the more they drink the drunker they get, but what they don't realise is that while they are getting faced, you probably are not, due to the fact your alchofrolic tolerance is way above theirs. Grippos can be met everywhere in the world, and it was in Gib we met our first. His family paid for our amusement all night until they had to get the taxi back due to their own inability to walk!! That made a refreshing change.

One day, me and a mate were detailed to put our best suits and white webbing on, to report to a building on the other side of the dockyard. We ended up as sentries at a court-martial. I have no idea to this day who it was, or what he had done, but I trust he was suitably dealt with.

Another thing Gib was famous for, was being able to tell when the Spanish Navy was getting ready to go to sea. A huge pall of black smoke used to rise above La Linea on the other side of the bay, as their warship (known as Smokey Joe) flashed up its' ancient coal powered engines, to finally sail creakily and slowly past our high tech gun loaded, missile bearing, freshly gleaming grey frigate called Zulu. You could smell Smokey Joe miles downstream.

Chapter 13

Africa!!!

It was with sadness that we left Gib, we sailed on a bright day, out into the calm Atlantic, and turned left towards... ...and the smell of Africa, and regardless of what anyone tells you – you CAN smell it downwind. It is a smell like nothing else, of desert and animals and...

...at some point we changed out of our 'eight' and into 'tens' or 'ten A', which was now shirts, shorts and sandals. What a lot of prongs we looked, being made to wear shorts at our age, showing off repulsive white hairy legs. We straight away moved into the swing of things, spending every spare minute above decks, usually stripped to our nix, trying to get more than just our knees brown. We also gave our issue sandals the float test, preferring instead to wear the lighter, more comfortable versions sold by 'Snobs' the Chinese shoemaker on board. He lived in the bowels of the ship, handmaking shoes for us. He would have crates and crates of these sandals ready to flog to us, at a very reasonable price, to be honest. Everyone turned a blind eye to our wearing of these non-regulation sandals – no-one in his right mind wore the hard issue version. I would imagine that the floor of the Bay of Biscay, should anyone care to dive to see, is covered in rotting pussers issue sandals. Best place for them too.

Throughout our travels, we changed time zones, and so we changed the onboard time as we traversed the zone. Now it became more important to observe good old Zulu time. Still, all meetings and exercises at sea between units were scheduled in Zulu, and we had to make sure we knew the right time to roll up for it. It also happened, that if you were going to lose an hour, i.e. put the clocks forward, we'd do it during the night watches thereby doing a short 'first', and short 'middle', whereas if we put them back, to gain an hour – this would be done during the dogs, so we'd do an extra half hour in each. Clock changes clearly happened more quickly the further east or west you went.

Many exercises and drills later, we neared Freetown in West Africa – Sierra Leone to be precise, and sailed up the distinctly brown, muddy river until we saw a ramshackle jetty in the middle of nowhere, which we promptly moored against, starboard side to (the jetty). Literally as soon as we secured the ship – two things happened. Firstly, we received alongside a fuel barge, I have no idea where that materialised from. The second was a lot of shouting from the remainder of our open port side. This emanated from dozens of hollowed out logs, packed with brown bodies, and fruit, and 'souvenirs'. The shouting was to attract our attention to their wares, in which we feigned total indifference. We casually pointed, asked 'how much' laughed at that offer and walked further up the ship, followed by that canoe, and more shouting 'how much you pay, how much you pay'. Having settled on a price, you would then lower a heaving line with a bucket attached over the side. The body would put in the bucket your wants, you'd haul it up, put the money in, and lower it back down again. In principle – brilliant idea, no-one got 'seen-off' (robbed), we got our 'bargain', the seller got a few more days money to spend before the next cruise liner (with more money to burn than us) pulled in. The natives would be seen swimming in the mud, round the ships' side, and climbing the jetty, but knew better than to come across the gangway, where several fierce looking sailors would be gathered. All except one native, shouting, soaked, obviously not at all happy. It transpired that one member of our crew got fed up with him, and accidentally released a huge, very old shackle which he was coincidentally holding over the side. As gravity took charge, the shackle dropped into the canoe. It didn't stop though, it continued through the canoe, out the bottom, and the canoe did its' final 'float test', along with all the goodies it carried. Which is why the native was so incensed. Our man had to give him something in the order of twenty pounds to shut him up. Well, the seller did have a machete which he brandished. He looked remarkably richer on his money, so we must have got near the price. The shackle-dropper then got immediate stoppage of leave – sad, really, as we were headed back to sea for the next several weeks…

We were allowed one-watch leave there, into Freetown for several hours. That came as a shock – it was the first time I had ever been that far from home, and we walked straight in to a third world country, replete with beggars, pickpockets and general assorted dwellers, all trying to make you part with what you had. So, we found a bar, drank minimally, and legged it back to the ship. Two visits down.

Again, we sailed, turned left at the end of the river – and got ensconced in more exercises and drills for several more days.

It was one sunset, that I heard the sun hiss as it set. I'd been told about this, but this particular evening, as we sailed south, and the sun set off our starboard side, and as we leaned over the guardrails, goofing at nothing in particular, but watching through clear skies, the sun sank lower and lower, getting redder and redder as it went. There are not many sights more spectacular than watching the sun set over the ocean, but as it touches the water for the first time, it hisses… Then sets further and further -as you watch it – until it finally disappears, leaving just a memory and a red glow.

On the 5th of February, at the point, where the water stops going round a plughole in one direction, and reverses, we 'crossed the line' at Longitude 08 degrees and 30 minutes West, and I am now allowed to cross the line at any future date, unmolested by any creature of the deep. I have the certificate to prove it. 'Crossing the line' is a full blown ceremony, involving all members of the crew (not on watch, but temporarily relieved anyway), where a member of the crew dresses up as King Neptune, who then oversees the ceremonies, along with the rest of his outlandishly attired 'court'. These ceremonies include being shaved with a giant razor, having first been foamed up with a deck mop, or being dunked in flour, or whatever, whilst the rest of the members of His court laughed hysterically. You would be perched on a 'plank' above a water-filled 'pit' on the quarter-deck (to be featured heavily later), whilst you were dealt with. At some point, you would then be tipped into the pit, emerging wet, but happier. The whole procedure took several hours, in baking sun one afternoon. Rank or rate did not feature in these proceedings, and there were clearly revenge attacks on certain officers and senior ratings, who were treated by the court with the contempt they fully deserved.

Before we sailed, those indolent swine at the Post Office had decided to go on strike, so after being away from home for nearly three weeks so far, not one letter had reached us. We would (and I still do) curse the Royal Mail roundly, for what we saw as a bunch of idle gits depriving us personally of any contact with our families. Normally, we would have had 'mail drops' from the long range patrol Shackletons, but all they would do was fly ponderously past us – eight propellers all told – four props spinning – four feathered, waving as they buzzed us. They were nice to see though. Or we would come across a fishing boat – literally thousands of miles offshore, and we would stop and check they were ok, frequently dispensing bottles of brown liquid in exchange for fresh fish, or, if we came across a merchant ship, we'd attempt to swap movies. However, as we sailed off Capetown, our Wasp did something useful (for the only time in it's life). Our pilot's father, an ex Rear Admiral, had retired to Capetown, and we had mail there sent 'via naval means' without any assistance from those lazy shites at the post office, and whilst picking up his father, he also picked up our mail. Or was it the other way round. Whatever – we actually had mail for the first time since we sailed. The RN had, in fact, set up its own mail system, collecting letters from recruiting offices and Navy bases all round the country , collated them at the services sorting office, then bagged it all for individual ships, and sent it commercially to the next port the ship was to visit. Large raspberries to the unfeeling PO workers.

We also at some point held divisions in our milkman suits. That was preceded by many days of preparing, of scrubbing cream shoes to whiten them, and of washing our white suits. The final result was, to say the least, dazzling in the tropical sun. But at least we had a breeze over us as the ship continued to cruise.

We were often pursued by porpoises, which would race alongside us right by the stem, so the only way we could see them was by laying flat out on the bows, head over the side. It always amazed us that they could swim from side to side, under our bow without colliding either with each other or, more importantly – with us. We took to laying there, gazing at them for ages. And the flying fish – shoals of them. We watched frequently to see if any would headbutt the ship, but they never did. We found one on the fo'c's'le one morning though.

The feeling I got right in the middle of that particular ocean, was one of our insignificance in our surroundings, plus our remoteness from shore. You felt that if anything happened, it would be forever before anyone reached you. We were literally hundreds of miles from anywhere – we could see nothing on the radar, there were no lights at night, nothing. Just blackness all round by night, and sea and sky all round by day. Little wonder people in shipwrecks go mad before they get rescued. Pending what was to happen to us on our way home, these feelings were probably justified.

After several weeks of drills, and the fact that on our approach, we actually cancelled our Sunday, in order to turn to, to get the ship sparkling for our arrival, we finally sailed into Durban – South Africa. The ship actually surfed on the huge rollers into the harbour. We refuelled on the way in, with a two hour stop at one side of the harbour, filled in by last minute preparations like Father forcing us to do un-necessary polishing of all the brass plates on the decks, then moved to the main quayside. We had been warned about Durban, but our reception was unlike any I have ever received anywhere else in the world. I will say now, that I have never been to such an openly friendly place as Durban – one day I will go back there. To start with we were 'sung' in by 'the Lady in white' Perla Siedle-Gibson. She had 'sung' Naval ships in and out of Durban since the Second World War, and, unfortunately, we were the last ship to hear her sing. It was a very sad occasion when, a week after we left Durban, she died.

The cutting from the Durban newspaper at the time read as follows

"When H.M.S. Zulu arrived at Durban on February 13, the lack of mail through the postal strike meant that the ships company were not at their happiest. Then they heard from the jetty the welcoming songs of the famous Lady in White, and the ship was hardly alongside before the hospitality began to pour in, providing the best week that most on board can ever remember.

Very regretfully, the ship moved on, the Lady in White being there again to sing the ship out of harbour. A week later she died. The Zulu had been the last of countless ships to hear her greeting and farewell, and the news was received on board with great sadness.

It was appropriate that the ship concerned should have borne such a local name, and the welfare committee paid for a huge wreath to be sent to the funeral. Their flowers were the centerpiece of the tributes, and could be regarded as the whole of the navy's token of affection for this gallant woman.

The story of the Lady in White – Perla Siedle-Gibson – began in the First World War, when she sang at Durban City Hall to some passing troops. In the Second World War, she was helping to feed about 500 troops, dressed at the time in a white dress and white apron. When the ship was pulling out, the boys called out to her to sing something and she cupped her hands to her mouth and gave them a song.

Afterwards she used a small megaphone, and her soprano voice was heard by millions of service men, in songs like 'Land of hope and Glory', 'Tipperary', and the like.

After the war the Lady in White continued her greetings, and thousands of men of the Royal Navy will remember and mourn her passing.

She was at the Zulu's cocktail party, and then went on to the ships companies dance.

As the Zulu steamed out, the Lady in White sang one of her last numbers for the navy – a request from the ship. 'Wish me luck as you wave me goodbye' is always deeply sentimental, but this time the words had a special poignancy of which none was aware. They gave her three cheers, as so many had done before, and thus ended an era founded on the personality of a remarkable woman."

Very sad looking back on it even now.

The papers were right though, we had been warned before arriving that this was serious 'grippo' territory, but we were totally unprepared for what was to happen next. Apart from the Lady in White on the quayside, there were dozens of sightseers, all come to welcome us. We were all in our (now) brilliant white 'ice-cream suits', having entered harbour at 'procedure alpha', i.e., everyone who could be spared upstairs, fell in... We also dressed up a rating as a Zulu warrior (bearing in mind South Africa is Zulu country, and we were 'the Zulu'), who was war-dancing on the bridge roof.

Even as we put the gangway across, we were getting approached by locals, asking if we could go with them for drinks/meals/tours. We just could not believe this was happening, we were still turned to, but that was only the start.

We had to wait until 'secure' which, as we were working tropical routine, meant being able to go ashore at around 1300. We could hardly wait to get into our suits, and get ashore. We were told to wear 'rig' here, and we did!!

I went ashore with my 'oppo', 'Sugar' Kane, and we'd got maybe three yards away from the gangway before a man with his wife asked if they could take us out for the afternoon. We graciously accepted, entered their car, and were whisked away to a large hotel on the seafront, where our grippos plied us with drinks all afternoon, then fed us 'sundowners' all evening. We attempted to stay sober, luckily, because we were then taken to dinner (at a Bar called the Smugglers) where we were served my first, and the largest T-bone steak I had ever seen, let alone eaten since, accompanied by fries, onion rings, salad and mushrooms – with the steak on its own wooden platter. I had never seen such luxury, nor eaten so much.

We met the same people the next day, they were on holiday from Jo'burg, and had two daughters, who we never met, but the mum and dad were adamant they'd like my mate and me to go back to Jo'burg with them, to marry their daughters, and that they would take care of work permits, jobs – everything. We thought about that one long and hard I can tell you, but declined the offer. Nevertheless, we had another brilliant day touring Durban – visiting the Aquarium, full of ragged tooth sharks, Garupas, and all kinds of other 'never seen before' sea creatures. We also went on the go-karts, rode a rickshaw along the seafront, pulled by 'a real Zulu', and went inland to a 'real' Zulu reservation, where we witnessed dancing, and drank 'Zulu' beer from a goat skin. In all we had a wonderful time. It was therefore with great regret that the next day we sneaked off the ship earlier than planned, ...only to be picked up by another grippo, who took us down the coast for the day, where we were again feted, and saw a monitor lizard cross the road, and it was only when I accidentally and painfully slammed the car door on my hand, that we drove back to the ship.

The next day, as sad as it seems, we were exhausted by the attention, so we donned 'civvies', ran across the gangway, and vanished into Durban, where we walked unmolested around the city centre, into Woolworth's and other department stores, bought our own drinks, then found a club where we drank 'cape brandy' all night. This is much like ordinary brandy, only it has alcohol and poke. We don't remember much about that night, except that wherever navy ships go, the ships company, as if by magic and a totally unarranged way, will always all appear at the same night-spot. That night was no exception. We did get "grippo'ed", all of us, by most of the crew of a passing cruise liner. We drank all night with that crew, and introduced them to the wonders of 'The Zulu Warrior', as now commonly practiced by most rugby players, thinking it is something new. We had the monopoly on it. We WERE Zulu warriors. After several lessons that night, the stewards from this liner tried it – to rapturous applause. Emboldened, one of the stewardess's thought she'd try it. In fact she claimed to be a stewardette, saying 'esses' made the beds, 'ettes' laid in them. Whatever – she started it off, not realizing it was what we'd been setting her up for all night. We had so far refrained from the endpiece of 'the warrior' – the beer throwing bit. We sang it, she stripped it, until one pillock in the bar made a grab at her – she panicked – end of 'warrior'. So we waited until the next volunteer to do the dance, and made up for it with him – I have never seen so much beer thrown over one person. We also gave the aforementioned pillock, actually a greenie, a good hiding for his stupidity.

On this night, we also demonstrated another traditional naval dance 'The Dance of the Flaming Arseholes'. In this, immediately following a rendition of the 'Zulu Warrior', we would have to hand a roll of toilet paper, one end of which would be tucked between the now unadorned cheeks of the naked warriors bum. He would then stand on a convenient table. The other end, several yards away now, would be set aflame. The 'dance' was the contortions caused by the warrior attempting to extinguish the burning paper before it reached his bum, without using his hands, nor anything else except gyrations of the lower parts. This dance is extremely comical to watch, and very safe to do (usually), as when the danger point is reached (some inches to go), beer is (again) traditionally thrown over the dancer, the paper, his bum – everywhere, to extinguish the flame. Unless the person doing it was unpopular, but THOUGHT he WAS popular. In which case much greater panic would set in...

Talking of popularity – it wasn't apparently, unknown for people to disappear off a ship during the dark night watches, so it really did pay you to be 'in', and not 'out'. I cannot pretend this ever happened on any ship I was on, though I heard several people who had "Don't be on the upper deck in the dark, will you" growled at them. This could have one of the reasons for the lifebuoy ghost, officially standing on the stern looking out for people swimming past, more likely standing inside 'Y' handling room, reading a book. As this was pre-GPS, we also studiously plotted our position by sun sights during the day, starsights at night, radar if near land and too dark for either, or DR (dead reckoning) if we couldn't do any of those. This, remember, was way before satellite navigation systems were installed. Back tracking like this, although difficult, meant that officially, we could go right over our previous positions, if the worst were to happen, and we actually lost someone, either by accident or design, and stand a fairly good chance of finding them. In theory.

Unpopular people actually stood out like sore thumbs. They'd try to cling on when when we wanted to go ashore, they'd skulk around the gangway, waiting for someone to take them. There were a variety of reasons for their not fitting in, they'd be crabby, or they'd be mouthy, or they'd be both, or just a plain nause. Whatever, they brought it on themselves: once branded, that was their lot. Except that if you needed a sub, or a loan, you'd ask them as because they weren't going ashore, they were clearly in a position to provide both!! You'd also ponce fag-coupons and beer-tokens off them. It didn't make them any less unpopular in our eyes, just more tolerable. At least we asked them to 'Do us a favour, Harry…'. There were those we totally ignored no matter what they did. As I said though, bullying didn't come into it, no matter who or what. At least, not that I saw.

One day we visited a 'white's only' beach, and exposed our own fairly white bodies to the hot African sun, complete with shark nets, and I remember we covered our bodies with 'Coppertone' sun tan oil. That was in the days when apartheid ruled Africa, and when Coppertone was not only brilliant, but affordable.

I must mention the naval tradition of 'cake and arse' parties, seen on Daily Orders as CTP, or 'cocktail parties' to the genteel. I should also point out the affection and esteem we held for our officers, politely known as 'the wardroom' but more generally called 'pigs'. Of whatever rank or discipline. No matter how well we pretended to get on with them, or they thought they got on with us. They were still 'pigs'. They had their own cabins while we slummed it in with loads of others. They were waited on, hand and foot by flunkies (stewards) – we had to get our own food, and wash our own smalls, then iron our own 'ones'. There always was, and – I am sure – always will be a great divide in between the lads and the officers. It used to really gall us, some of the complete tossers we would have to show our respect to by saluting them. It was made no better to be reminded we were saluting the uniform, not the contents. But when you got some pompous little sprog 'snotty' (midshitman) – who couldn't even spell H.M.S., much less tell you about it – on the P.O.S. as, for example Fo'c's'le officer, where he had as much experience as the newest SA (stores rating) or chef, but who was still expecting us to do what (dangerous) things he told us... Not that even some of the experienced officers had a much better idea. Mind you, those we DID respect were made aware of that respect. Seaman officers were generally safe, the rest – they could all go and shit in their caps for all we cared. Except those who had turned their back on the lower deck, and had been accepted as SD officers. They really didn't fit anywhere – originally used to messing and behaving like us, now elevated to being served, and having to behave politely!! HAH!!!!

Anyway, back to the cake and arse – these would be held usually on the first night a ship arrived, and would be held by the Skipper and all his officers who would actually host the affair, plus volunteers to 'staff' it (ferry drinks about). To remind you – Jack would NEVER do anything voluntarily unless it was for his own benefit, but once you had missed volunteering for one party, you most definitely ensured your name was down for the next one. I will explain. The parties would be attended always by the local naval officer in charge and some of his staff, then the town mayor or local governor, plus several hundred of the local dignitaries, rich or 'names' or 'hangers-on', who would be there like a shot for a free 'do'. What I didn't realise (although I was more involved in getting ashore that first day), was that it was an ideal place to secure a first class grippo, who would normally otherwise have been targeted by 'the wardroom'. You would therefore target a group of partygoers, or perhaps just one, appearing at their elbow after they'd taken a mouthful of either 'horses neck' (brandy & ginger) or G&T, ensuring both were light on the mixer. You would also drop some polite talk in about how nice it was here, wasn't it, do you live here? aren't you lucky being able to ... – anything to get their attention. Eventually, or maybe immediately, the alcohol you stuffed them with would take its effect and you could be asked out on a grippo run later. Job done, get illegally pissed with the rest of them, thieve and scoff some of the canapés, then get changed, get ashore. Easy life. Another small bonus – the 'hat check' person would sit with a bowl, with some large denomination notes/coins in it, so when the hat/coat owner returned, he would assume his fellow partiers had put it there, and add to it. More beer tokens, this time without working for them. As the party thinned out, so the guests would be easier to 'trap', but as they really got scarce, they would be bagged by 'the wardroom', and taken back in there for further drinks/food, before being taken ashore. Some goers knew this – the unwary didn't, as we could throw drinks around more than they could. Yet another perk after this was that if you were duty-watch, AND a CTP waiter, when the pigs had taken their guests back to the wardroom, their own chefs and stewards would prepare, serve and feed them on a 'special meal'. When enough people had eaten enough of this special meal, the remains would be distributed amongst 'the lads', specifically whoever got there first, that is to say the duty watch! Not only out of your tree, but a free takeaway too. And still without going ashore. On the Zulu, the wardroom chefs and stewards were Goanese, meaning absolutely gorgeous, juicy curries. Especially when these curries were washed down with the horses-necks we secreted into the nearly empty bottles as they became available, then hid for later collection once the fuss had died down. If asked, we would swear we saw a party-goer hoofing it with a bottle, that was why the wardroom flunky, sorry steward, couldn't tally the empties. Stewards were almost the lowest form of life on a ship – we would scream at them to 'peel me another fuckin grape, you', in order to rile them.

The down side of the CTP, was having to first 'rig' the entire fo'c's'le (or quarterdeck) with it's canvas awnings, then sidescreens, then the bunting (flag material draped everywhere), which would generally take the best part of a forenoon, assuming every sailor on board was turned to. Before that could happen, though, the whole area had to be repainted, scrubbed, or polished – depending on the surface involved. Only after this had taken place could the CTP take place. The worst part about it though, was knowing your' grippo' was out there, and that you had to unrig it all before being allowed anywhere, which is, of course, why you had a 'duty watch', who would normally do it. The bigger down side on the end of this, was although the duty watch would normally strip down all the awnings and sidescreens after the CTP, on occasions the awnings would all stay up until BWH the next day, at which time they would be removed. This took place normally only if the awnings got wet – a sudden downpour for example, and as it was a well known fact (!?) that wet canvas would spontaneously combust if stowed incorrectly, we would take no chances, and leave them up overnight or until dry. The even further down side of this, was that if you were 'duty', and the awnings were up, and it rained, then you – duty watch – would then be dragged out of your warm scratcher, and be forced to dress. The reason for this was two-fold. Firstly, most squally rain is accompanied by wind. Wind blows canvas. We therefore had to interfere with all the rigging holding the canvas to their stanchions. We either slacked them off, or tightened them. We would then throw our heaving lines over the canvas, to 'frap' the awnings. Again – this was a twofold reason – firstly it kept the awning from flapping loosely around (one thing that all 'jimmys' hated, was loose bits of ANYTHING flapping around), and secondly it prevented puddles gathering in canvas 'wells'. This then prevented us from releasing this water onto passers by, accompanied by great gusts of laughter and delight – especially if it was anyone senior to us, like from the wardroom who happened to by in the wrong place at the wrong time, as we prodded the 'well' from below with a broom handle. Eventually, much later, much wetter – we would be able to get back to bed, knowing that if anything else wanted doing to it, either the QM or the BM, at the most – the duty hands would be the only ones to be disturbed again. You see – there were always SOME up-sides to all the 'downs'.

CTP's were usually, but not always, preceded by 'Upper Deck Rounds', where the skipper examined in minute detail every square inch of the upper scupper. This meant we had to paint every square inch before he got there. Sometimes that meant stripping off old paint off decks, screens and lockers, and repriming and replacing it with new. More usually it meant painting over all the crud which had accumulated in all those 'difficult' areas, whilst making it look natural. It further meant painting every square inch of the decks with green, non-skid paint. This would normally be done over several days, but looked nice when finished. We'd then have to paint deck-clenches, fairleads, capstans, and everything else with either white, or red, or different green. Then, as the navy is fanatically against having paint splashes on anything made of wood, we'd have to very carefully – to avoid gouging the wood – scrape paint of things like the wooden covers used to protect bollards, and brass, then scrub the bollard covers and finally polish all the brass. Then, just to impress, we'd get out the cleanest headropes or sternropes (made of white nylon), and our best heaving lines, and carefully coil them all down on the freshly painted decks. All the main preparation would be carefully planned and carried out over a period of several preceding weeks, but would mean 'a busy time', and who says 'bullshit baffles brains'. Let me ask you – if you found 120 fathoms of very heavy, carefully coiled down nylon mooring rope – would you be bothered to move it to inspect what was underneath? Neither does the skipper.

CTPs' therefore, were regarded with great suspicion and very mixed emotions by the ratings, but it was at one of these "do's" that I first tried caviar…

All too soon it was, as the article says, regretfully time to sail, accompanied for the last time by the singing of the Lady in White, and we sailed into the Indian Ocean and turned left.

It was probably at about this time, that we finally ditched our church keys. Church Keys have been used for decades to open cans. Of beer, or coke, or other refreshments. Church Keys came free with crates of beer, but were grabbed by sailors eager to never be without a means to get to his beer. Keys (or can spanners) were carried about on the key rings, generally holding several keys to various kit and boot lockers, but could be taken to extremes with added extensions, to make them too unwieldy to carry about. Nevertheless, the spanners were now SNLR, as all our cans suddenly came fitted with ring-pulls. We now had new toys. Ring pulls, if broken off, and fired correctly, could be used as mini projectiles, and could actually hit with quite a painful ping. They could also be used as decorations, by stringing hundreds of them together, then hanging them in strips across the entrance to the mess, thereby doubling as intruder alarms. Sad really, what we used to do to pass the interminable hours at sea away.

Our next destination was off the coast of Rhodesia, to take over the duty ship on Beira Patrol – off Lorenco Marques, to support the embargo, and to stop the Rhodesians from getting any oil or supplies into that country. 'Beira' and its connotations for navy people can be summed up in few words. 'Misery' and 'Boredom' are two of them that spring to mind. We did four weeks, plus passage there, doing nothing but sailing up and down and up and down and up… For four weeks. With nothing else to do. Except steam up and down. We were in sea watches, one in four, but after a week or so, you became desensitised to anything but waking up, looking at your watch, determining if you had just been 'shaken' for your watch or if you were dreaming, going on watch, coming off watch, eating, working, sunbathing, sleeping. For four weeks. We would listen on the Ships Radio (or to our portables) to Radio Lorenco Marques, playing George Harrison's 'My Sweet Lord', over and over.

We sometimes crept off our patrol line, just to be different. I think we spotted less than a handful of ships in that four weeks, which we would make heave-to, before boarding and searching. Usually, whoever was trying to creep in, would either become aware of or be made aware of our presence, about turn, and scarper.

I distinctly remember being on watch on the gloom room one day, watching the radar, and generally getting bored stupid, when we decided to draw a picture on the old Surface Picture table. This surface plot was a representation of what the radar was seeing, and had a travelling light, which moved true to your course and speed. This meant any radar contacts on it also tracked at their respective courses and speeds. Except that where we were drawing was where the light was tracking, and pretty soon it all disappeared under our picture. At about that time, the OOW just happened to scan the bridge radar monitor, and demanded to know why we hadn't yet reported the contact – the one he could clearly see with his mark-one eyeball. We responded instantly that in fact we had 'just picked up the microphone to report it, and its' course was 'x', with a speed of 'y', and that we were re-appraising it at the moment. This quietened the OOW momentarily, until he worked out its TRUE movement, at which time we again lied that it must have altered course then, because we made it the same as him, now…

That was truly the first surface contact we had seen for weeks, and thanks to our drawings – it nearly sailed past us and got into Beira!! Ooops.

We had visits from the omnipresent 'shacklebombers', who would occasionally do a mail-drop on us. This entailed them flying to their patrol station over us, then near us, at which point they would drop bright yellow waterproof canisters into the ocean, at speed, but quite low in the sky. These would bounce and settle, for us to either recover with the seaboat, or by launching the paraffin parrot to go and get it for us. Then the joy of finding you had mail, and reading it over and over. Or the deep, deep depression of STILL no mail.

We would 'RAS' every couple of days, with the 'on-station' RFA tanker, they would either anchor for us to go alongside with fenders between us, at which point we would take on fuel the easy way, or we would meet with her, underway, and take fuel on that way. We'd both be flying the ships flag, no – not the ensign or the jack, but our own flag, but I can't remember for the life of me what the Zulu's was.

Ras'ing used to be fun, if you got the right job. Obviously working on the 'dump' where all the stores landed was a plum job, as was unloading each pallet in record quick time before the next pallet arrived. Generally, you'd have up to sixty seconds to do this, regardless of the cargo swinging over. If the cargo was large, easy. If however the load was 48 crates of ale – you would need to work harder and faster. To get the stuff away, human chains would again be organised above and below decks, with every available off-watch sailor being in these chains.

Unfortunately, things would go astray – like the odd box of nutty, or case of food, or even crates of ale. We figured that at the speed we worked, there was no way on Gods Earth that anyone was going to be stupid enough to count each and every one as it arrived at its destination. Especially as occasionally crates or boxes would accidentally 'burst' on being accidentally 'dropped', spilling the contents all over the deck beneath our feet, and so dangerously in our way. Of course, we'd be to busy catching the next armful to bother about picking up damaged goods, wouldn't we? …And the breakages were all immediately kicked over the side, weren't they? But the extra crates and food came in handy, and we'd often finish the RAS stinking of beer or chocolate, with more stowed in the mess or in POS lockers to look forward to. Perks of the job, we called it. Everyone knew it happened, but no-one could – or would – do much about it.

The harder work, was to be found on the lines hauling the load over be it light jackstay between two units, or heavy jackstay between RFA and us. The light one was just three lines – a main jackstay (rope) which was secured on one ship, but handled on the other, it being hauled in, or paid out to maintain the tension, depending on how near the two ships closed in, plus the two lighter lines used to actually pull the travelling block across and back. The block being fastened on to the jackstay. Still there? The traveller then had a sprung hook, to which could be fitted a well-tested helicopter lifting strop (used to get people out of the water) holding a person, or another strop to support equipment. The trick was to "Haul taught jackstay, two-six HEAVYYYYYY" until the person was in the air, his weight being supported by the four inch manilla, then signal the other ship to "Haul Away", which they did on the light line, until the person/consignment made it across. Throughout this, the jackstay party would be fighting the pressure, adjusting it to keep the load out of the water, normally rushing past beneath, at fourteen knots. No wonder we always had the seaboat manned and swung out, engine running during jackstay transfers.

We could normally carry out these light jackstays' with ten minutes notice, to swap movies, personnel (like Daddy-D or Admirals) or THELMA (The LMA/Doc) or the Surgeon. People were normally shit-scared and terrified of having to go across it, especially if they were ever so slightly unpopular, as it was well within the capability of the jackstay party to be a bit late in responding to the command to 'haul taught', thus allowing the transferee to get a dunking. Not that I EVER saw this happen…

The heavy jackstay was similar, only this used a wire on a winch instead of a manhandled rope, automatically tensioned by the RFA. We still used our line to haul the load across, but the RFA used a second wire on a winch to haul it back. Bear in mind also, that the RFA jackstay derrick was many feet above us, so used gravity to get the load to us, fortunate, as some of the pallets being thrown around could be up to a ton in weight. We had to rig shot-mats all round the dump, on the bulkheads, turret, 'sticking out bits' so anything heavy smashing into it would virtually do no damage. Except to us, if we were foolish enough to get in the way. We couldn't rig mats on the deck, or we wouldn't have been able to shift the pallets as they came over, with the jacks (thoughtfully provided on the first load) in time for the next one. When we collected enough pallets, we'd re-attach them and send them back.

Whilst on the dump, the guardrails would have been struck, meaning the only thing between you and the drop over the side, was a heaving line, thoughtfully rigged to protect you. It was for that reason, that everyone in the RAS party wore lifejackets. ...And we always kept well away from the ships' side. Actually, we did, and everyone always kept a good weather eye open for each other. You needed to – it might be you next time, precariously perched between a one-ton pallet and the gun turret...

All this called for some very slick co-ordination and timing. Plus an awful lot of hard work, except for the jimmy (who supervised, giving thoughtful advice...), the buffer (who actually ran the RAS), and the signalman, who, under control of the jimmy, waved his silly little flags around to request the next load(s).

We'd sometimes make use of the paraffin parrot to simultaneously do a 'Vertrep' (vertical replenishment), which would then scuttle between the RFA flight deck and our second dump, carrying loads. This meant the Waffoos had to be up and about too, much to their disgust.

Actually, thinking about it – when we did a big RAS, I would guess that nearly everyone on board was used, storing, steering, driving, whatever – the only goofers were normally the wives of some of the crew of the RFA. It didn't matter that it was your make-and-break, or that you had just come off-watch – you still had to turn to, in order to do the RAS. Even the greenies!!!

The easiest job of all, requiring no effort or brainpower, was manning the 'distance line'. This was secured at one end, manned at the other, and was simply a thin line with distance flags marked every ten (or was it twenty) feet, which showed how close the two ships' rode. The flags were always coloured in a particular way – we had a mnemonic to help us remember, which was :Rub Your Balls With Grease (red, yellow, blue, white, green) – so they could be told apart. It was very difficult making sure the correct tension was maintained, so the MUPPET (Most Useless Person Pusser Ever Trained) was kept to do this job. The skipper would then be able to take note of the distance, and order the helm accordingly. 'Specials' were always closed up for RASs', and we were always at a higher state of readiness (at 'Yankee') on the watertight doors, just in case.

Actually, to be detailed for 'specials' was considered to be quite an honour. If you were on the wheel, it was because you were the best helmsman aboard. Except that some ships used the Joss for this, which contradicted the previous sentence. It was, though, nice to know that if the skipper wanted you to steer a course of '142', that not only could you steer it, but that you could 'feel' the ship trying to drift, and that you could compensate for it before it actually drifted. I could do that. It took a lot of practice, but I could do it. No mean feat – the sea state wasn't always kind to us in during a RAS, except that if it got too bad, we'd cancel, or do what we could.

In the movies, you hear "Steer this" and "Steer that", and the helmsman instantly does it. That does NOT happen. There is a strict series of instructions and sequence of responses used, all of which are repeated, carried out, then reported back, just so there are no mistakes. For instance, to get five degrees of port rudder, the OOW says "Port Five". The QM repeats back "Port Five", and when he has five degrees of port rudder on, he says back to the OOW "Five degrees of port wheel on". The OOW then says "Very Good". Nothing can countermand that order then, until the OOW gives his next order (either "Midships", or "Increase to ten"). In my day, the steering compartment was amidships, below decks, well out of harms way, therefore the QM could not even see the sea, never mind take initiative and steer it himself.

When all was complete, we'd slip everything, cast off, let everything go, wave cheerfully, strike our skull and crossbones or whatever our 'flag' was, and go on our happy little ways, and – depending on whether we were 'dump', 'jackstay', 'line' or 'stores', we'd either be knackered, very knackered, extremely knackered, or just plain out-of-it.

On one occasion, while refuelling, we detected a ship on radar, and in order to intercept it we had to do an emergency breakaway, meaning we just smashed the retaining gear and slipped the hoses. It was a pity that the supplying ship couldn't stop pumping quite so quickly, and it happened that everyone in the dump party got a fuel dhobey. As did the fo'c's'le, the bridge – everything. It was weeks before we finally got rid of all the sticky black fuel, months before the smell eventually went from 'A' Handling Room.

We would still swap movies. Movies were very important to us in maintaining our sanity at sea, every night, except the nights when we would hold 'Tombollocks' (Tombola – bingo), we would have a movie in the junior rates dining room. We saw all kinds of movies, U, PG, X – anything, providing it looked appealing. We would jeer and scream like three year olds', especially if we had seen it before and knew what was coming. Anyone who died would be jeered at. Rudely. The more bloodthirsty or action packed it was, the better we liked it, unless it showed bits of naked female, in which case we'd demand that the projectionist showed that bit again, until – happy – we'd let him show the rest.

On reaching our assigned patrol station, we would rendezvous with the unit we were to relieve, with them sailing past us at high speed, throwing flour bombs, vegetables, blowing smoke, hosing each other down, generally relieving their tension. Also being flour-bombed and buzzed by their parrot. We would, of course, traditionally pipe each other first, and sometimes 'cheer ship', for fun, before carrying all this out. And we knew we'd pass the honour on to whoever then relieved us.

We'd then settle in, and would 'fight' either the ship we relieved, or the 'on-station' RFA for the honour of holding the 'Beira Bucket'. This was the mankiest bucket – bashed, battered and holed (currently in the museum in Portsmouth dockyard where I saw Zulu's' name on it many years later), for which we would compete in all manner of games and contests. We'd have a boat race. This involved a teams of sailors in a line, each with a can of beer. On the 'go', each would down the beer, before the next in line could see his off, and so on down the line. Rescrubs were popular on this game. Or the 'Duck-Run Derby'. This involves wedging coins between ones 'cheeks', running (like a duck, hence the name) to a pre-arranged place, before depositing the coin in a bucket, in order for the next to go. ...And of course, we would never heat the coins up first – would we... We did, obviously have 'sensible' contests – tug of war, with blocks rigged around the ship so you could pull parallel to the opposing team. You feared losing – your hands would be dangerously close to going through the block if you weren't careful. This whole contest would be held throughout an afternoon, finishing with a barbecue, and ice cold beer. We always had a large supply of steaks and sausages for the barbie, always had more beer than we needed, and always had plenty of ice except when the ice-machine broke down. It was always hot enough to cook eggs on the bare decks – we nevertheless always had ice. We would also be dressed in just shorts, and sandals, and would never wear anything else until evening, when we might decide to wear a t-shirt over our shorts. We quickly turned shades darker with all this 'bronzy'ing'.

The winning ship then took ownership of the 'bucket', and would then keep it in a safe place until challenged, or until passed on. It would be jealously guarded.

Another game we played, was 'blind man's boxing'. This is where two men are blindfolded, and put into a 'boxing ring'. It is obvious they cannot see each other to hit, so they are given a box of matches to rattle, to indicate where they are to their opponent. At some point, the penny drops that the louder they rattle, the more they get smashed, so they stop rattling, and just swing out wildly at where they feel their opponent may be. It is around now, some of us would rattle our own matches, to see one or both leg it across the ring towards the noise, blindly swinging punches in all directions. The winner is the one who is left standing the longest, where his opponent has got bored, removed the blindfold and gone below for a drink, while the one left in the ring still blindly swings after one of us walking round perimeter, occasionally rattling the box to liven things up! Great fun...

We held 'set' growing contests, from when we left Durban to just before we reached our next stop, we were allowed to 'grow', having asked permission first. The winner was judged on the fullest set, also the longest, also the absolute worst beard anyone had ever seen! Not a great privilege to hold that particular honour.

A navy tradition while at sea is 'quiz night', messdeck competing against messdeck, including senior rates and wardroom. The questions are set by the last winners, so the quiz was always extremely well contested. If you won, you would dream up even more devious questions for the next one. Surprisingly, the scores were always high, and the RPs' mess would always feature highly. Once you had answered all the questions (Fred Quimby was normally the answer to a question where absolutely nobody knew the correct answer, something I still do today…), the answer sheets were taken, say, to the SRE compartment, and marked. The results would be given, and a hooly would be held in the winning mess. Trivial Pursuit had not been invented then, but it could have been based on those questions we set!! And here, for all you afficionados of naval history, is a one of those questions. Name two things that run from aft to for'r'd on the starboard side, and from for'r'd to aft on the port side, of EVERY Pussers' ship?

We held kite making/flying contests, streaming miles of string astern as we chugged along at ten knots or so, with un-aerodynamic contraptions held up in the far sky by sheer willpower – well at least they flew.

We had Donkey Derby's', we cooked more eggs on the bare metal of the decks just to prove it could still be done, and we held knockout tournaments or leagues. Sometimes even inter-mess contests. These would all be based on card or board games, notably 'crib', at which I was particularly good, or 'uckers' at which I developed an unerring skill. 'Uckers' is derived from ludo, but has none of the associated genteelness. It is played on a square table, painted in the form of a ludo board, then covered in clear plastic. Uckers is played either in fours (in which case you help your partner), or head to head in which case you go all out to win at any length. Uckers is an extremely tactical and to some extent psychological game (as in before you would agree to play, you would need to go through the 'You are not good enough to play me' scenes, followed by 'By the time you are good enough, you'll be too fuckin old', or the worst, on getting challenged to play, you would reply "I won't actually play, but I will give you lessons". This would pre-empt the ignominious loss, whereby you would announce "It was a lesson, not a proper game – just letting him see what winning is like. Anyway, I have 'winning fatigue' "), which must be thought out many moves ahead – or you would lose. No question. Before playing, you would decide on the appropriate rules, either 'far east', or another. You also agreed the battle cry, generally "UCKERS YER FUCKERS", followed by screams of "HACK!!, HACK!!"

(meaning 'remove your opponent's pieces'). Having decided the rules and cries, you then needed a six to get out, but instead of travelling round the board a la ludo, you may put one (or more) pieces on top of each other to make 'blobs'. 'Blobs' block your opponents passage – they have to throw many sixes to remove them. If you have a 'mixy blob' (caused by all your different coloured pieces being stacked behind a blob), you lose your go until the opponents blob moves, and all his pieces can go over yours. This blob is usually held at the end of the run-in, but once that blob splits (and depending on the rules in force) your opponent may 'suck back' your 'bit' from the final run. It could also be possible to take off ALL your opponents mixyblob, giving you three bits to move in, while he has no bits 'out'. This was the whitewash, THE most satisfying form of inflicting defeat, and the one most likely to get you headbutted. I have seen vicious fist-fights develop following these defeats. I have seen people thrown across messdecks for alleged cheating. I have seen 'the uckers table' smashed up and all the bits thrown over the side, and I have witnessed blood being spilt due to 'misunderstandings' of the rules in force. The maxim – If you can't take a joke – DON'T PLAY.

One evening, we detected a cruise liner going about it's business – we hailed it by radio, and asked if they could drop mail off for us at their next port of call. Obviously it is not easy for a Shackleton cruising at over a hundred miles per hour to stop and pick mail up for us. The liner agreed, we had 'Mail will close in thirty minutes' piped, we all excitedly dashed off or posted our mail, and we stomped off after the liner. The skipper hauled us in at speed from astern of the liner, and we passed a line across with our adapted rifle as we dropped the revs right off, bringing us to match exactly the liners' speed. By this time the deck of the liner was awash with goofers, all watching us. We passed the mail, we passed the obligatory whisky, we exchanged movies, we then went up to full power, did a 'hard-a-port', tilted alarmingly, but most impressively, and sped ahead, off into the deep red sunset, soon leaving the liner and it's passengers far astern. Judging by the 'flashes', we were photographed countless times on that little jolly.

One day we had a whale surface close by – THAT passed SEVERAL minutes...

We also had the biggest laugh I ever had, before – or since. I have mentioned the pit on the rear of the ship, which is where we stowed all ropes, wires, fenders and other junk whilst we steamed about. This would be covered with boards and tarpaulin for protection. But when we were off Beira, we emptied it of this junk, and filled it with sea water from the fire-main. We were then able to step in and out of it between browning sessions to cool off.

One afternoon when we were stationary, we nicked a joint of beef from the galley, a large hook, and several fathoms of strong string. Also a barrel of fire-fighting foam, used to extinguish oil fires. This foam, allegedly derived from ox-blood, was reputed to be a brilliant shark attractor, not that they needed that – we usually steamed with a 'gash-chute' rigged over the stern, down which went anything deemed to be gash. We opened and poured out the contents of the foam, holed it, and threw it over, for the traditional 'float test'. Unsurprisingly, it failed. But the foam was now in the water. We baited the hook, threw it in, and waited, but not for long – we had a take. The shark we recovered was extremely surprised, exceedingly violent, and took a lot of smacking around the head before it was pronounced dead. Even at his size – nearly 2 metre's, he looked awesome. We stroked the skin, marvelling how it was smooth one way – like sandpaper the other. We argued over who was to have the teeth – or the fin. We decided we would give the fin to 'snobs'. 'Snobs' was wary of us sailors after someone had ordered a pair of shoes, collected them, promised to pay on payday – and left his name as 'M Mouse'. We never did find out who – but we had a good idea. Along with his tailor mate who made suits, shirts and trousers by hand. And the Chokey laundry crew. They were referred to as 'Number One', and 'Number Two', unless you weren't feeling too friendly, then you referred to them as 'Number Six' (after the very popular cigarette of the age). We decided they all would share in the shark. It was then we noticed the baby clanks lounging in the pit, and before we could stop ourselves – we threw the dead shark into to the pit alongside the stokers. Except that the shark had been playing possum, and as soon as his head went underwater – his tail wagged, and he started to cruise, with apparently the mother of all headaches, and a severe dose of arseache. The stokers came out of the pit vertically, screaming, and disappeared below decks... We wet ourselves laughing. When we calmed down enough to be able to stand without any pain, we sorted out who should go to get sharky out again, and a rather large gunner went in, grabbed it, and emerged holding it by the tail end. He then proceeded to smash the eating and biting end against the after gun turret until this time we knew it was dead. We processed it in the galley, and ate shark steaks that night for supper. You needed to be there to believe it, but it happened. I have genuinely never laughed so much in my life. I don't remember the stokers concerned, but if you read this – I apologise!!! Honest!!

Flash Cards made their presence felt, just to enliven our lives. Flash cards HAD to be carried at ALL times. In the shower, ashore – any and everywhere. If you were challenged by a so-called mate showing you his card, you had several seconds to produce yours, or you forfeited a can of beer. It quickly taught you to carry it!

We always had a barber onboard, whether it was a rating 'trained' to cut hair, or whether it was one of the Chokes – but most evenings, there would be a small queue formed in the regulating-office flat, for hair relieving. For we still had to conform to 'the naval standard', even though we were miles from civilisation. But we had sent off for one of those 'razor in a comb' things, much advertised in the press. When it arrived, we all tried it out, hacking off large hanks of hair, leaving ridiculous looking tufts, at which point the 'joss' would go spare, ordering us all to get it cut properly. It took ages for our hair to grow back properly, and we never used the thing again. At least, while at sea for long periods, a) there was no point in confiscating station cards, and b) your hair would grow almost sensibly back.

We were eventually relieved, and zapped up the coast to Mombasa for some recreational leave, by watch, for several days each, and we were allowed to go to a service R + R place called Silversands – if we wanted to. We moored in the middle of the river in Mombasa, amongst much ceremony and maneuvering. We completed our 1 in 4 duty, and boarded a coach for the ride up-country to wherever or whatever Silversands might be. The journey probably took the best part of an hour, through the dense green undergrowth, along dusty 'roads' and over a marvel of engineering – a bridge built by British squaddies after the Second Worlds War. It was only when I got back to the UK and described Mombasa and this bridge, that my Dad told me he'd been one of the people who had helped build it. That was a strange coincidence. We arrived at the compound wondering what we'd let ourselves in for. We soon found out. We were 'barracked' into huts, sited amongst coconut trees, but more importantly directly on the starkest, whitest, softest beach I have ever been on in my life. The beach bordered the bluest sea I had ever seen too. To say it was idyllic would be an understatement. We quickly unpacked (i.e., threw our gear out), and went exploring, only to find the Naafi open. This was a bar (called the Casuarina) which was fortunately open. Before we could stop ourselves, we found ourselves rapidly downing large quantities of JC's, before going for more exploring. We found the Naafi shop (most odd, to find a Naafi in the middle of such a remote place in Kenya), and lo and behold on the beach was the 'beach bar', where we drank some more as we strutted round in our new swimming costumes and totally, totally lairy shirts. We had bought these local floral, highly patterned shirts during our one night ashore, and then worn them on every subsequent occasion. We discovered the beach bar closed late afternoon, but that a third bar then opened. We thought we were in heaven!

When that one shut, the Casuarina re-opened, and we sat there all night getting more and more inebriated.

When we retired early the next morning, we apparently took the remnants of last nights drinking with us, for we woke up to warm and flat, but still palatable JC's for breakfast. That was after we had negotiated our way out of the voluminous mosquito nets. Mosquitoes' in theory didn't bother us – we had gobbled the anti-malaria pills several times a day since leaving England all those weeks earlier. However – those African mozzies bites itch – badly!! The JC's were followed by the short walk to the dining room, still overlooking the beach. I have never eaten breakfast in such a place. The waiter seemed only to speak two words of English, although he understood everything you said. He was the tallest person for miles around, with more white teeth than I would know what to do with. They were filed, according to custom I suppose. You would ask for toast, he would grin, lazily, and drawl 'Yiz Barsss', and trot away for it. He would return, you would eat the toast. That was if you weren't persuaded to give it away to the masses of longing brown eyes making you feel guilty at every mouthful. These eyes belonged to the resident troupe of monkeys, all of whom had a bright green-to-blue bum. Very distracting, however we would feed them toast, they would scamper off to the nearest vantage point, eat, and return to start over. It was the most entertaining breakfast I ever had. Asking for more tea, more bacon, more anything was also met with "Yiz Barsss". I can picture him now, and I am sure I would recognize him again…

We then started the rounds of the bars again, interspersed with lying on the beach. By the time we had left Beira, we looked like natives anyway – this was merely topping up, and making the most of our rest and recreation.

All too soon it was over, we returned to the ship for our next duty, whilst the opposite watch took their leave at that wonderful place.

We got a couple of runs ashore in the main town, chiefly remembered for the huge tusks crossing the main road. And the Sunshine Bar, which coincidentally sold a local beer – called Tusker!. Also the market in the centre of the town, where you could buy anything you wanted. As long as it was made of carved wood. Plus the gaudy shirts worn by everyone in the area. Mine was bright green with migraine inducing orange and yellow jazzy 'stripes'. I wore it to death – this was a thousand-and-a-half-miler. I then got chased out of the market for offering too little money for what I wanted – just table rings carved into animal shapes, but I overdid the bartering and obviously insulted the stallholder badly with the price I offered. I got it in the end by sending a mate back to buy it at the asking price. I had no intention of facing him again!!

As I said – we moored, properly in Mombasa. This took the best part of an hour, and was probably THE most technical seamanship evolution ever carried out by any ship, though we had practiced previously. Mooring here meant securing between two immense buoys floating in the harbour, but with the sailors working hard, the rest of the ships company would be stood at 'Procedure Alpha', all hands in number twos paraded by department on the upper deck. Except for the waffoos, who would have previously launched the budgie, which would then fly round the ship and harbour with all his lights on, and be trailing about a large ensign on a wire, with a heavy weight on the end of the wire to stop it getting embarrassingly entangled in the rotors, causing a sudden end to the display. You see – things like this always impressed everyone watching – lots of noise, lots of visuals. We (sailors) also had to drop the seaboat and cutter, then send off buoy-jumpers – a job over-volunteered for – to secure the anchor cable to the buoy, the cutter crew then went to the stern, and secured to the aft buoy, then we would use the capstans to winch ourselves in-between the buoys. Once we were initially secured, and on hearing the 'still' piped, both accommodation ladders (laboriously made up over several hours previously) would be carefully lowered, both booms would be swung out, the jack, and ensign would be run up, and the ship would normally be 'dressed overall'. That is, all the flags displayed from stem to the mainmast (the foredown), with a further run between the mainmast to the stern (maindown). The flag waggers would be responsible for this, with loads of them hauling on the halyards to raise the dressings. All this swinging out, lowering, and hauling would happen in perfect unison, and was – I have to admit – impressive to watch. Except the day we failed to secure the accommodation ladder, which slipped gracefully beneath the waves, necessitating our divers to don drysuits to go and get it back.

Once the sailors secured, the greenie department would then all be kicked out of their beds where they would have gone for a rest having been made to stand upright for longer than ten minutes (procedure alpha, remember?), and they would have to rig floodlighting on booms along either or sometimes both sides of the ship. They used to hate that, as it meant not only having to work for a living to rig the large number of booms poking out in the right places, AND get them all exactly level and even, but worse – that one of them would have to remain on duty all day and all night just in case someone called them out to replace a dead bulb. Not that we'd ever get them out of bed to show them a bulb which was, oddly, working again. Well it was duff the last time I looked at it – it must have been a loose connection. If they got them level in daytime (checked by the chief greenie by boat), the chances were that once they were switched on that night, the chief greeny would be back in the boat, ensuring they looked nice in the dark too.

Sometimes at 'alpha', we'd have to do a gun salute for the local dignitary, which meant (only the correctly trained) gunners would haul up the saluting cannons, and secure them to the quarterdeck. They'd then put on their stern and serious faces, and with perfect timing (chanting BANG"If I wasn't a gunner, I wouldn't be here"BANG"If I wasn't a gunner, I wouldn't be here"BANG – try it yourself!!) between salvoes. They would fire the designated number of rounds, be covered in thick smoke, then have to put it all away again, again lots of noise, lots of attention drawn.

Being moored in the middle of Mombasa harbour meant it was difficult to get ashore, so we had to get liberty boats from ship to shore and back. However, we weren't to concerned if we missed our own seaboat, as Mombasa harbour used to crawl with small, brightly coloured 'K-Boats' – water taxis for hire – very cheaply. It became a point of honour to get as drunk as possible, hail a K boat, and demand to be allowed to drive it back to the ship. Or in my case, directly at the ship, ignoring the owner, who had to forcibly remove me just before I made the sudden, final, violent contact against 3000 tonnes of grey painted steel. I won that particular battle of nerves. I was fortunate to get that far, that night. Having had far too much to drink, I'd fallen asleep in the toilet of the local chateau, and my mates had thoughtfully all gone back on board without me. I woke up at sometime in the early hours – I rephrase that – I was woken up by chattering, and on opening my eyes discovered many small brown faces looking over the top of the 'trap' at me. I ran out of there at a great rate, and hightailed it down the main drag, under the famous elephant tusks, back to the quayside.

Jack has a fondness for leaving fingerprints – we 'imprinted' – everywhere we went, we would add our names to our illustrious predecessors signatures, in pubs, on jetties, on dock walls – everywhere we could. I'll bet if you got to Mombasa today, you'll find "H.M.S. ZULU, 1971" painted in at least one place!!

Again, all too soon we left 'Mombers', and once more turned left out into the blue, blue Indian Ocean, amongst the flying fish and porpoises once more. We steamed, turning always left, until we finally reached Bahrein in the Persian Gulf.

On the way, we discovered more new terminology – 'sneezing', or 'caught a cold', or 'blobbing up', or 'catching the boat up', or 'squeezing up', were euphemisms for having ones leave stopped for several days – but only until the penicillin took effect, and cleared it up... This was in the days when the worst you got was Syphilis – not completely life threatening, if treated, or

'Gons', which went quickly with the injections. We were though warned about 'Tokyo Rose', which was tame even by today's standards. The painful part though, was having leave stopped until THELMA (The LMA) considered the patient fit to go ashore again. Having never been affected, I never found out – although I knew plenty who did! They should have taken the free noddy hats from the gangway…

Another unpleasant side effect of living in close proximity to other people, was that if one person caught wildlife, zoo-creatures, crabs – whatever you want to call them, we would all, eventually – succumb to them. This was partly because our towels and washgear used to be in close proximity, but mainly because the bastards would put a couple in your pit while you weren't around. So, if you discovered one of your so-called messmates could walk unaided, you'd steer clear, and inspect your pit closely before shaking it energetically, then climbing into it. It is paradoxical that we should get crabs anyway – we must have been nearly the cleanest people in the world, what with our daily shower and all.

We discovered three cures. One was to go to the sick bay, talk to THELMA, and ask him for some crab powder. Both the illness and the cure used to itch, so if you saw anyone with his mitts on his bits, you should guess he was attempting to dislodge his pets. Second, was to sit in a swimming pool/water for several hours until they drowned. But by far, the most effective, was to invest in a small bottle of scotch, and some sand. First you'd rub the scotch into the affected area, the crabs would all drink it, getting pissed in the process. Then you'd rub the sand in, the crabs would think it was rocks, and throw them at each other in their drunken party, until they were all dead.

Being called a 'crabby bastard' was an insult. Being called anything else from the Anglo Saxon phrase book was quite permissible.

Crabs, and doses were actually the only reason anyone would normally report sick, stand fast accidents. It was so extremely rare we got colds, 'flu, measles – anything. We were therefore quite a healthy bunch all round.

We still also had messdeck rounds, where everyone was expected to polish, paint, scrub, or wash in order to get all the messdecks, bathrooms, heads, and 'flats' ready. On this major cleanup we discovered a crate of Tiger beer hidden above some cabling. It must have been there since the last commission, when the Zulu last went to the Fes, however, it didn't last any longer – we soon got rid of it the correct way., but how in hell the dockies had missed it during their alleged refit, I don't know.

Messdeck rounds were still, notoriously unpopular, it was like being invaded as it meant we had to make a thorough clearout of our lockers, beds, behind the bunks, and in the (every mess had one) 'glory hole' – an unpopular place to have to clean. Mind you, there was always the traditional cake to look forward to, IF you won.

Also unpopular was that even as upper deck workers, we'd still have to clean the heads etc., for messdeck rounds. We always wondered what greenies and clanks ever did apart from slouch round with their hands in their overall pockets – whatever the rounds were, it always seemed to be us sandscratchers who ended up cleaning up. The heads were bad, but at least you could throw a hose round in there, then dry it all off, having repainted the graffiti on the walls and doors of each 'trap'. The bathrooms were the worst, they stank of thousands of washed (and sometimes unwashed) bodies, and the only way to get them clean, was to literally scrub and clean every, every bit, of every, every surface in there. Then chuck several gallons of cleaning fluid and disinfectant around.

We started up a small group called MAFRO, or Messdecks And Flats Resistance Organization around this time – it lasted several weeks, wound up a lot of people, then died a natural death. It was, however, quickly replaced by SPONGE (Society for the Prevention Of Niggers Grabbing Everything). We all walked round with bits of sponge on a safety pin, to indicate our support, until we were ordered not to. We then wore bits of the wrappers from 'fudge' bars, with just the letters FUD showing. Like I keep saying – anything for a decent wind-up, and as long as someone reacted – we were happy.

Telephone No.: 37518

Careers Office,
Royal Navy and Royal Marines,
Newilton House, Derngate, Northamtpon

Date **24th March 1969**

Dear **Michael,**

With reference to your application to join the Royal Navy/Rxxxxxxxxxx, I am pleased to inform you that, provided you are in all respects still fit, you will be offered a vacancy for entry to:-

H.M.S. Raleigh at Torpoint near Plymouth on

xx Monday 8th September 1969

Further details will be sent to you nearer the date of entry. In the meantime, if you get a job or change your employment, please forward the name and address of your employer, the date you started and the nature of your employment.

Yours sincerely,

for Lieutenant (Careers Service),
RN/RM.

How it all began – March 1969. My letter of acceptance into the Royal Navy

Been there, done that – February 1971. The certificate I received when I crossed the equator for the first time

Your friendly BP Station. Zulu *fuelling abeam from a Royal Fleet Auxilary Tanker, November 1971.*

This was what Beira patrol was all about – intercepting one of the sanctions-bustings tankers that refused to stop, November 1971.

You don't get this many spectators if you catch a fish on the canal bank at home. This was the shark we captured in November 1971.

Away seaboat's crews, November 1971

Prepare to tow for'ard. This was not just a drill, but for real, when Zulu's *main gearbox seized in the middle of the Atlantic, and not an AA man in sight, December 1971.*

HMS Zulu *in Grand Harbour, Malta, spring 1972.*

Flag K at the dip – HMS Tartar *preparing to take her helicopter on board.*

The author – 'every hair a rope yarn, every finger a marling-spike'. This was the photograph that caught my future wife's eye.

Ceremonial divisions Tartar's *ship's company parades on the jetty, alongside the ship in Vera Cruz.*

Steam past for the Queen, Tartar's *ship's company cheering ship for Her Majesty and Prince Philip, off Vera Cruz, 1975.*

A real bringer of tears to the eyes of old matelots – the 'Gully Gully' man, Port Said, December 1977.

Between the wars there was a famous recruiting poster for the Navy which featured two jolly jacks in uniform, riding camels, over the slogan 'Join the navy and See the World'. I did and I have, AND ridden a camel as well.

Chapter 14

Bahrein, Sand and Desert Wellies

One fine day, as we neared Bahrein for the first time, and a mini-refit, we held a RAS with a Gulf State warship – who promptly got too close, and created a large tearing hole in our ships side (the one we had laboriously and often painted). This was repaired with a large plate as soon as we got alongside.

The jetty we secured alongside was probably half a mile long – we would moor at the very end of it. On the other side was where civilian ships would moor. On a weekly basis (we were based there for four months), we would see the same cattle ship load and unload. On the middle of the jetty was a small shop, selling fresh milk, some food, and extra long king size cigarettes, which we would smoke to extend the length of our monthly allotment of 600 'duty frees', as these shoreside packs were cheaper than we paid. When you consider that we were then paying something like 10p for a pack of twenty, these extra length ones were better value!! We did catch our toe at the shop- first night ashore, back to the ship, wake with hangover (we worked 'tropical' routine those days, start at 0700, finish at 1300, leave up until 0645), over to the shop, pint of milk, funny taste that, what's that brown sludge at the bottom of the carton, 'shit – it's goats milk'. Mind you, it grew on you, and certainly was good for clearing last nights' hangover...

One job I always volunteered for was 'mast painting'. This entailed drawing all the 'safe to transmit/safe to rotate' keys for all the radio and radar aerials for the ship (just in case on overzealous but stupid flagwagger or greenie decided to transmit megawatts of power from an aerial near you, or decided to rotate the radar with you standing on it), getting several pots of paint and brushes, drawing safety harnesses (which were as useful as chocolate teapots, given that you tied them below you as they got in the way otherwise), then climbing the main mast complete with heaving lines (to haul up paint and brushes) ready for a several day skive. Once up there (where no-one else could come and check on you without being spotted fairly quickly), we'd do a spot of painting out on the yardarms – hence the harnesses, standing or swinging to get to the awkward bits. Luckily, the yards were over the ship, otherwise we'd have got wet if we fell off them!!!!! From the top of the mast to deck level was around a fifty-foot drop, but it was eighty from top to waterline. We'd get odd looks when we descended – we'd be covered in paint, but brown too! The view, though, was worth the effort.

We also 'volunteered' to wash and repaint the funnels. This was a filthy job, but worth doing. We had to climb up the inside of the funnel, and come out of a very small hatch on the top. Then we'd carefully creep to the edge, drop the heaving lines, and haul up the paint stages. Having ensured they were totally secure to our satisfaction, we'd gingerly edge off the funnel and onto the stage. Having got there, we'd have a fag, in the knowledge that anyone who wanted to bollock us for doing so could have a bucket of stinking, sooty water upended on them – completely accidentally of course – before we got on with the job to hand. We'd take days and days doing the funnels.

The first night ashore, we went to the Naafi at H.M.S. Jufair which was at the end of the jetty and then some. It was probably a mile walk to get there, but being a duty free area – all the booze was DF too. Which meant a Bacardi (a double, obviously) would be far less expensive than the coke to throw in it. Actually, you could buy a bottle of spirit for less than a couple of coke mixers. We would sit and drink all night up to the point where we would cheerfully drink in excess of a forty ounce bottle of Bacardi, and walk back to the ship quite happily, and steadily. There was not much else to do at Jufair... One night of the week, we would be permitted to use their chipshop. It only actually opened one night of the week. We were also not allowed in one of their swimming pools, but would sneak in anyway late at night for a dip on the way back from the town. Until the night I nearly drowned in there, at which point we didn't use it any more. The only reason I got out, was because even through my Bacardi sodden drunken haze, it occurred to me that if I sank to the bottom, I could kick, hard, and get back to the surface and shout for help. Which I did, and my mates got me out. Like I said – we didn't go back in there. Another 'near death'.

The night we first met the USN crews (Elmers as they are scornfully named) – they moored where they belonged: astern of us with further to walk. The rumour says that before the yanks meet 'jack', they (the USN) are riot-act'ed – told not to try to outdrink, outsmart, outfight or outfuck us under any provocation, as they would fail on all counts singly or collectively. They knew best. Except some wouldn't listen, and as they came into the DF bar at Jufair – we saw it as our birthday and Christmas rolled in together. The USN run 'dry', whereas the RN don't. We had been used, by then, to heavy, prolonged drinking bouts. They had been used to their onboard luxury of 'coke' and ice-cream. They would start to drink with us, and lose track of reality not even half way through our normal session, at which time we would leave them to sleep until we wanted to go back onboard. We would carry them back, relieve them of their 'Popeye' hats, dump them at the bottom of their gangway, and go back ashore, into the town in a taxi to continue our sessions. I still have a 'Popeye hat – somewhere.

We were astounded (though pre-warned by old hands) about their silly habits, and funny old 'pipes'. Where we would 'pipe' an understandable "Clean up messdecks and flats for rounds", theirs would be "Now hear this, Now hear this – Sweepers man your brooms, sweep from for'r'd to aft", or something equally odd (to us). We would laugh every time we heard it, and extract the urine every time we saw them, except that their gangway crew would be apparently armed. We would only have (or need) the 'duty hands' as backup, armed with large fists, and heavy boots.

We were further forearmed with 'the ready answer'. It was a foregone conclusion, that while in his cups, a yank would feel the need to ask us "How does it feel to be in the Second largest Navy?", to which we'd reply "Great, how does it feel to be in the second best?" That would always piss them off, they'd skulk off thinking of something else smart to say...

The 'de rigeur' dress code then was 'Levis' (well worn and faded, but only Levis), shirts (button down collar, short sleeve, any startling colour, made by the Chinese tailor), and desert wellies. It was the desert after all – we felt entitled. Oh, and socks. We only ever wore pussers issue socks, therefore either black or navy blue. This, we reasoned, dispensed with the necessity to buy any other colour, 'cos whatever we wore, it either went with the blue socks, or the black socks. Except if we wore brown, which we rarely did. Nobody did, except the wardrobe. We wore black, blue, or anything else provided it matched our socks. We would wear this, constantly, returning to the ship, throwing it all in to the laundry every fourth day (when on duty) for refurbishment, or 'dockyard job' repairs if necessary.

We would 'secure' at 1300, have lunch on board (the RP's still did, everyone else still had 'dinner'), then go ashore either to illegally laze around the pool or drink at Jufair, or go into town to the markets to pick up some absolutely wonderful 'rabbits' (souvenirs), ranging from gold to linen to real Persian carpets, to anything else we fancied. The smell and the atmosphere in those back street markets was something never to be forgotten. We would never drink in the town, we were too wised up for that, but would occasionally venture into the Gulf Hotel, or the Moon Plaza Hotel, both of which had a nightclub. Full of sailors. From the Zulu. As I said – you couldn't get away from them. We did, however, find a back street cafe which served superb food, and we would make it always a stopoff point between the hotels and the ship to eat the local food. I can still taste their gorgeous prawn masala with japatis freshly cooked in front of you in the stone oven.

We held 'banyans' (beach barbecues) sometimes – we would pile into the whaler or cutter, and drive them to a lump of sand which became exposed for some hours a day. We would (of course) pack the boats with beer, the barbie, and food, and clear off until we got bored, or it got dark, or the sand started to get seriously underwater, or until we ran out of beer. Guess which one usually drove us back. We would play cricket, or 'bronzie' (sunbathe), or snorkel around the crystal clear water, marvelling at the sealife which was plentiful.

We didn't just sit alongside making the Zulu look pretty, we toured the gulf from one end to the other, ostensibly looking for smugglers carting diamonds or drugs or currency, and we would spot them on radar, heave them to, then search them I remember the search team finding something one day, but I don't know what it was. However, whilst on patrol, we would stop at a remote island to banyan. It became a standing joke that wherever we stopped, you could guarantee that within hours, a dhow would also stop, the inhabitants would decamp to 'our' party, to beg for food, which we would normally give them. At one of these stopovers, the dhow stopped, off came the gopher, and we gave him the bread. He reboarded the dhow, and sailed off into the sea. We cracked laughing at what would happen to him – we used to carry a chemical with us to check our fuel for water contamination (or was it to check the water for fuel contamination), which was harmless, but if ingested would cause severe gastric disorder for some time. Which may or may not have been laced into the loaf of bread donated to the crew of that Dhow. I wonder if he ever caught on – or scrounged off another warship?

We frequently took 'hands to bathe' which, as the temperature was usually around 110F would be very welcome. We would stop the ship, lower the whaler complete with an SLR-armed sentry, put further armed sentries at strategic points on the ships' superstructure, lower the scrambling nets (in case of a shark appearing and causing a reverse Titanic effect – i.e. boarding the ship at great speed), and dive (yes dive) off the highpoints of the ship into fathomless water. Then we'd climb the nets, climb the superstructure – and dive off again. The 'midships' decks would be ten to twelve feet above water, the Seacat launcher decks twenty, the bridge wings nearer thirty. We would happily dive off all of them. The wimps would jump, the total wimps (i.e., the greenies and stewards) would climb DOWN the scramble nets. Whatever, we would enjoy ourselves thoroughly, and look forward to the next 'hands to bathe'.

We did 'sea days', where we would take local dignitaries, Commander Naval Forces Gulf, or Commander British Forces Gulf, to sea for the day, where we would be 'attacked' by aircraft, play with the minesweepers, fire the

4.5s', disturb the fish by dropping mortars, maybe loose off a Seacat, do a RAS, tank along at high speed, then return to base, hopefully having made a sale…

There was a permanently deployed fleet of our minesweepers at the landward end of the jetty – it was a point of honour to be 'called round' there, which one day I was. I don't remember getting back on board that night, but I'm assured I did.

Minesweepers, unsurprisingly, sweep up mines laid by other people. To do this, they stream large paravanes off the blunt end, which are connected by long lengths of wire. It's the wire that sweeps or catches the mine. Minesweepers (and other ships) carry 'dancans' (dan-buoys), which are carried rigged, ready to throw over the side to 'mark' items on the seabed, or for another excuse, as required for seamanship evolutions. In order to drop the dancan, you had to chuck a large weight over the side, which was attached to the can by wire. It follows then, that the weight could be dropped long before the can was slipped, and thus needed a lot of wire, especially if the water was deep. Normally, wire on ships ready to work, was laid down on the deck in correctly overlapping lengths, called 'bights', so when the weight (or whatever) was on the end, you kept well out of the way in case you got caught in it, and watched guardedly as the wire unravelled itself, and disappeared through special fairleads on the deck, right on the edge of the ship. Just to make that clear, the weight is chucked over, the wire then pays out by itself until it's all gone, at which point the dancan is slipped. It was related to us that one of the sweepers had to rig a paravane for a sweeping exercise, and did so, readying it until all they had to do was drop the weight. Coincidentally, it seems, they had on board an illegal monkey, which they had been told to get rid of. I'm relating this, remember, I don't know if it really happened. Allegedly then, they tied the monkey halfway along the wire, threw the paravane over the side, and the monkey apparently sat watching, interestedly, as the wire vanished before his very eyes, until with a rush, the monkey was taken through the fairleads, into the sea, never to be seen again. We had wet trousers when we heard that one.

I celebrated my eighteenth birthday whilst at sea, and again when we got back to Bahrein. I also bought my first 'duty-free' – a Seiko watch which lasted many years.

Not that it was all drunkenness – we visited other ports in and around the gulf. We went to Bandar Shapur, and took some station leave to Isfahan. A place, I remember for several reasons. The first, and most memorable, was stopping the coach halfway there (in a village where Moscow was signposted), and buying Fanta Orange from a tub of iced water. The last place I would have expected to buy Fanta was... Secondly – the hotel we stayed at fed us – on request – soft-boiled eggs for breakfast. After months of either fried, or fried – you would never believe the unexpected luxury of soft boiled eggs...Third the beauty of Isfahan – old buildings and bridges, and the most eye-catching mosque ever – exactly what you would expect to see in Persia. Fourth – learned to dive properly there – by running along the board, hitting the end, going off head first, somersaulting, and eventually hitting the water feet first – I could always 'perform' that one!! On the way to Isfahan, we crossed miles of desert, but actually saw snow at the top of the mountains. There we were still in 110 degrees plus – and there was snow visible. We also bought more Fanta and Coke out of icily watered buckets, from shops in villages in places you wouldn't even have put a shop. Miles away from 'civilisation'.

We went to many more Gulf ports, none stranger than the one where there used to be an RAF base called Sharjah. Nothing there except the RAF. We did boat races, had darts matches, played footy, did all kinds of civilised things. Then went to the bar...

We visited Dubai – where we played volleyball against the sons of Sheikh Rashid Bin Said Al Maktum (the Ruler of Dubai), to Bandar Abbas, Qatar, Abu Dhabi, Muscat, Damman – and nearly every island in the Gulf ... *and all the time we wore our desert wellies!!!*

One sunny day, my mate Arthur had a berserker, and refused to obey orders. That meant being thrown in the 'brig' if you like – actually a secure compartment at the stern of the ship. The wobbly started when he was dumped on after being offered a 'blue card' job (Navigators Yeoman, making sure the clocks and watches were right, making changes to and updating charts), later rescinded. He took exception. He was quarantined in the diving store, and the story we got after he was carted off to DQs' was that when he was ordered off the bridge wings where he was waiting, into 'Captains Table', his response was 'make the bastard come out here to me – I don't want to play any more – stick the Navy up your arse.' Unsurprisingly, he came out of DQs' some months later, and was subsequently discharged – SNLR. A great shame – he was a nice bloke who I missed greatly, as it was he I had met on the train from Paddington so long ago...

Captains Table is held weekly, normally, at sea or in harbour, but can be held for sudden serious 'crimes', as for Arthur. The Table is held to answer request forms, or to punish defaulters. Everyone wears 'blue suits'. Requestmen are marched on, have to salute, and have their request read out by the Joss, have a few kind words read out by their Divisional Officer, have a few more patronising words spouted by the Captain, then (generally) have their request granted. You 'request' to grow a beard, to shave off a beard, to be promoted, to have a long service/good conduct badge, to get married, anything 'pleasant'. Defaulters, however go 'on' after all the good boys, are marched on, then are 'off caps' (hence the expression 'get your cap' when you need to 'troop' someone, or "get two hats, an' take a lifejacket – 'cos you're in DEEP") as they then stand before the Captain. Normally, if they've got this far, it's because nobody has believed their fibs told to wriggle off or they have admitted what they allegedly did, so, their 'offence' warrants captains punishment, or worse (i.e., court martial). It also means you've been through Officer-of-the-days' table, and been passed on, and possibly through 'Jimmys' table' too. The defaulter's charge is read out by the Joss, his DO tries to say some mitigating things, then the captain awards his punishment. If you are in front of him – you are guilty – no two ways, unless you can spin the shit to such an extent that he believes you. At OOD or Jimmys, you are given the opportunity to plead Guilty, or Not Guilty, or No Plea. The latter means it wasn't your fault, and that you intend to blame someone or something else in the hope that you won't be so severely punished. If the captain finds you guilty, you get stoppage of leave, or reduction in rate, or stoppage of pay, or a fine, or any combination of the above. He can also send you for a 90 day 'holiday' (in DQ's). Anything more than that, he'll offer you a court martial. That means going ashore and being 'weighed off' by total strangers. You then stand a fifty-fifty chance of having your 'pun' increased, drastically, or of getting off altogether. This second option is most, most unlikely. You really have to come up with something good at this stage!

Perversely, a favourite pastime is trying to second-guess the punishment, with an appropriate sweepstake on the outcome. We would take great pleasure in winding up 'the accused', telling him sea stories – "...when I was on the XYZ, we had a bloke did that – he got 90 days...". We would normally be fairly accurate, with practice, though various other factors would need to be taken into consideration, like whether you had the skipper up in the night, or if he 'got a bit', or if the last person in front of you gave him a hard time. Remember, the skipper was judge, jury, audience, everything. If he said 'jump', it wasn't 'How high?', it was 'When can I come down?'.

It helped if your recent appraisals were good, too. Periodically, you were lined up in front of your DO, where he would read your report, on what a good boy you'd been or how you'd performed in your work and attitude, and also your behaviour. If, therefore, you were a snivelling arse-licker who had never been trooped, and never got into any trouble ashore or aboard, your summary would be VG/Sup(erior). For the rest of us, we'd get VG/VG or G/G or a mixture of them. You always knew what you'd get before you got there, it nevertheless was a great help if you stood in front of the skipper, to hear your DO plead your exemplary record, and your VG/Sup record. So a good appraisal always reduced your sentence. Slightly. Otherwise you'd end up losing 'badges', money or leave, or a combination of all three. Stoppage of leave while at sea was a waste, but acceptable, but any stoppage did mean that while 'under pun', you had to rise early, muster, turn-to, muster, work more, muster etc etc!!

Talking of lifejackets, you had one issued as part of your joining routine. They were worn at Action Stations, Emergency Stations, RAS's, and Boat handling. They were pretty good, except that you had to blow them up first. A fully inflated lifejacket is a dangerous item, especially in confined spaces. You also had a smally whistle, and a smally light with a battery, which had to be plugged in if it was dark. You thenceforce totally screwed up your night vision every time you caught a glance of it. You weren't allowed to take it off though – OOOOH no. You could sometimes manage to 'find' an automatic lifejacket, which was furled in its bag, and only inflated once you fell overboard. Much more sensible, and far safer.

Then we lost a crew member, who died in a freak accident involving a lorry. This was a terrible shock to us, and something we never expected would happen to a mate. It seems we stopped acting the OD for many weeks after his death, but memories fade, don't they, and we eventually got back to 'normal'.

Navy tradition after a death requires an auction, where everyone bids for various items of the dead man's kit. Even if you don't want it. Once purchased, you then return it to the auction, where it is bid for again, and again. The money raised, along with his kit and possessions, is then sent on to the family. As I said – that frightened and shook us badly, making us realise how easy it was, and that we weren't as tough as we thought.

We came back one night, and, as usual, the hurricane fan at the top of the mess was whirring away, and turning slowly from side to side. This was our only form of air conditioning, so we would run it continuously. Jock Arthur, in his bed nearest the fan, threw himself out of bed one night, drunkenly, screaming about the rats in his pit with him. We all turned out, put all the lights on, and nervously scoured every nook and cranny in the mess looking for our new pets. After some time, someone noticed that Jocks' sheet was flapping every time the fan pointed at it. "There's your rat, you prat". And we all returned to our beds, Jock very sheepishly – or should that be rattishly…

Peculiarly, every week, an old battered freighter/steamer would stagger towards the jetty, tilted drunkenly. Eventually it would grind to a halt, generally by hitting the jetty, then disgorge (seemingly) hundreds of sheep and people. After a few hours, it would stagger back to sea, and disappear for a further week. God alone knows where it used to go.

Occasionally British freighters would tie up, and we would make our acquaintance with them. They, you see, could have as much booze as they wanted on board – very handy after closing time.

We finally sailed from Bahrein in late summer (our time), and headed for Singapore. We did, though stop at Cochin in India, which put me off going to India ever again. We moored, as usual, but within minutes were besieged by onlookers, raggedly dressed women, men, and kids, all holding their arms outstretched begging. Many of the beggars had missing or hideously deformed limbs – it was a pitiful sight and I will never forget it. Apparently (though we never took them up on it) the women were offering themselves in exchange for a bar of soap. We threw them the soap anyway, plus anything else we could raise. We went ashore in the afternoon, to one hotel, near a market. We spent all our allocated money on some terrific rabbits, got back in the rickshaw, and went back to the ship in time for supper. We were only allowed to 'change back from rupees' what we had 'changed into rupees', so we didn't spend a great deal of it. We were offered many, many times the going rate by the taxi driver for our sterling though. When we got back, there was a man on the jetty with a mongoose and several snakes, one of which was a cobra, which he thought we ought to watch fight. For a sum. A very large sum, in fact, we thought. We watched the mongoose 'fight' another snake. The mongoose was winning when the man hauled it off. We never did see the cobra – we refused to pay him his fee, we got bored and wandered off. The smell from Cochin was appalling – it took a long time before it cleared from our nostrils. A very sad visit to a very sad port.

Chapter 15

The FES, at Long Last

We reached Singapore after navigating the straits, and eventually moored at Sembewang dockyard. I was 'specials' that day, so I missed all the sights, except that I saw them all on radar. We were still working 'tropical' routine, fortunately, as every day, without fail really, it hissed down with torrential rain, then cleared, and was nice for the remainder of the day. We secured alongside H.M.S. Triumph – an old carrier converted into a factory ship, and commenced a month long mini-refit. This entailed moving the whole ships' company into H.M.S. Terror for some weeks, while work was carried out on the ship. We were back into the routine of trekking down to the ship for 0700, turning to until 1245, securing, back to Terror, then see what developed. There was a terrific swimming pool at Terror – mostly for families, but we could get in if we promised to behave. Or we would go to one of Terror's bars, drink pints of draught Tiger beer (only available otherwise in bottles), watch the 'chitchats' (small lizards) climbing walls, ceilings – everywhere, and generally laze around. Chitchats have an aversion to glasses being thrown at them, which is why you could never hit them. Or was it the fact that after several delicious glasses of ice cold Tiger, your co-ordination went. Totally.

On the Triumph were several 'shops', one of who's owner I remember raided our messes as soon as we secured, looking for clothing to launder or repair. His name was Peanuts and he was a naval legend at that time, however, he would haul your gear out of the communal locker, throw it disdainfully on the floor, screaming "Fuckin' do'yard job". i.e., badly needs repairing/cleaning. You'd negotiate a price, he'd repair/clean it, and return it in far, far better condition than it left. Or the tailor, who would tout his wares and examples. You would order some shirts, in a particular colour, of a certain style, for a fixed price. Without fail, he would return next day with the shirts, all exactly as you expected, all a perfect fit. Emboldened, we also purchased immaculately tailored trousers and suits. And the snobs who sold many, many pairs of shoes. Also, there was a 'drinks' man, selling different flavoured milks. However, you ended up asking for "cho'la miw", or "grin miw", or "ping miw" which is what he called them. These were lifesavers for clearing the effects of the night before, having missed breakfast, but desperate to clear the remains of the 'Tiger'.

We had to spend duty watches on board, in better conditions than Rosyth, however, with the dockyard canteen just across the jetty, we would send the junior watch person with a 'fanny' to fill it with Tiger – which we would dispose of quickly. We would mess from Triumph – queueing in batches to eat our evening meal on board.

H.M.S. Intrepid was there at the same time, and my mate Glen (from Raleigh) was aboard. We exchanged pleasantries, ale, stories, and separated once again when she sailed.

There was a duty free shop on the base, which is where I bought my first sensible camera – a Pentax, with which I took thousands of photos. I finally decoded the manual, learned how to use it properly, how to exchange speed for aperture – and it rarely left my side throughout the rest of my naval career.

The trend (in those days...) was for multi stereo systems, portable ones looking like briefcases, with cassette/radio/record player, detachable speakers, battery or mains – which I think everyone bought except me. And in the markets in Singapore, you could select some records, return later, and the stall owner would have recorded them for you, in perfect stereo. We spent a fortune there too.

Sembewang village was just that. Several bars, shops, 'restaurants', and assorted other stores. It looked like a cross between a wild-west town, and a suburban high street. However, the choice of entertainment was limited, though cheap. I should say Cheep, as the song blasting out of every bar was Chirpy Chirpy Cheep Cheep (Or 'Sembewang is cheap, cheap' as we paraphrased it.). We would therefore fill up with Tiger in Terror, adjourn to Sembewang until closing time, then move on to the city for the nightlife. This would normally be a place called Bugis Street, which was THE place to go. Populated by Kai Tais' (transvestites) who would parade up and down all night, trying to scrounge drinks. Off us? More chance of being hit by a meteorite. It was, however, one of the best black cat's of all time, to be able to say you had started a session at lunchtime, played it out all afternoon, gone ashore that night, ended up in the city – SEEN THE SUNRISE OVER BUGIS STREET WITH A BOTTLE OF TIGER, then gone back on board courtesy of a very fast fast-black, and actually made it without being adrift.

There is a strange place called 'The Tiger Balm Gardens' in Singapore. Tiger Balm is (was?) an (apparently) illegal substance, something like Vick mixed with Heroin. It allegedly cures many ills, and was freely available in Singers. These gardens are full of contorted statues, montages of wild cruelty and hideous 'apparitions', all representing legends and folklore. The gardens were unlike anything else in the world – but absolutely enthralling.

We attempted to get in to Raffles one day, to sample Singapore Slings – but were adjudged to be too incoherent, and rejected.

We would normally return from a run, via an open air 'restaurant' in 'the vill' (-age of Sembewang), where we would sit alongside an open sewer, watching the chef prepare what we wanted. Normally Heinz Tomato soup with Bread and Butter, followed by Nasi Goreng, washed down with more Tiger. Eventually, replete, we would go back to our rooms at Terror, and catch a couple of hours sleep before starting over again. One night, one of our number rolled off his café chair into the ditch – and had to be rushed on board for emergency medical treatment (mostly injections!).

At some point, between the torrential rainy season daily downpour, and the duty watches, and the runs ashore, and the camera learning – I passed my tests, and became an Able Seaman. I also upgraded from a basic RP to an RP3 (third class). What glory – I was 'one of the lads' for sure now, an AB, not an OD, and a star above my radar badge. New badges all round, get the tailor to sew them on for me. Jolly Jack – bin there – seen it etcetera etcetera. With the sea-stories to go with it.

Our rooms in Terror were first class – we all had an open balcony, four to a mess, it really looked like the colonial apartments you would expect in such a place. We took to spending our off-duty aboard time dressed in multi-coloured bedsheets which you could also wrap round your waist (like the natives), and which were considerably cooler than even shorts. We wore these for months until it became too cold on the way home. As I said – they were bedsheets too. Multi use for such cheap items.

It was at about this time, that due to our prolonged use of locally made jockey shorts (a novelty at that time), that we started to suffer with 'dhobey rash'. This was an affliction of the nethers, which you got no matter how much or how well you washed either you or your shorts. It would itch like crazy for weeks, then go, suddenly. It always looked odd – the sufferers could normally be found with their hands clutching their goolies, appearing to be doing rude things, but actually only scratching! We also used to get 'Chokey foot rot', known to millions as 'athletes foot'. How we managed to get that whilst only ever wearing sandals or flipflops, I'll never understand.

We eventually moved back on board, and sailed for Hong Kong – the highlight of our eleven-month tour, and something I particularly looked forward to. I had heard so much about the place – was it all true?

Unfortunately, something had bitten me in Singers, and I spent two weeks in sick-bay with severe pain in my knee, extremely swollen it was, and had to be massaged frequently to remove the pus build up inside it. Accompanied by large doses of antibiotics into my bum, several times daily. Admittedly I got out of the exercises we took part in, but I was desperately disappointed to miss the first few days in Hong Kong.

When I finally surfaced, limping, we went to the Fleet Club, where we met the Yanks again. We took the ferry to Kowloon, played in the bars and clubs (accompanied by Creedence Clearwater Revival -" Hoid it thru the grapevine" – or Santana – "Oye Como Va", everywhere, bar after bar). We toured the shopping malls, we took a bus trip up country to the China border, where we had mud thrown at us (right through the bus window). Fortunately – the bus driver had the good sense to drive off, otherwise there is no telling what would have happened to the person who threw it, or what the repercussions would have been for beating ten bells out of the locals.

We went up Victoria Peak in the tram railway. Almost vertically at first, and through the flats of the residents, but once above the skyscraperline, the view improved. By the time I got to the top, the view over the whole of the harbour was absolutely amazing. And you could see in all directions – for miles. One of the best views on the world.

One night, having saved up with the beerboat for this for months en route, we visited the Tai Pak floating restaurant, having previously made the reservations. That night we ate an eleven course meal, comprising Lobster salad, abalone with green kale, Fried stuffed crab claws, Sweet corn with crabmeat soup, Steamed fresh prawns, Deep fried chicken, Baked lobster with onion sauce, Steamed garoupa with chicken fat, Fried rice, Wan tun soup, and Fresh milk punch. We were in there for hours, and hours. I remember the menu exactly – I kept it.

We were full when we got back from that night out, then discussed it and relived it for weeks afterwards.

On the other side of the harbour, in Kowloon, there seemed to be a club or bar every second step you took. We would find a different one each night, and drink in there. Occasionally, we would find one uninhabited by Jack, but each one would be playing CCR or Santana…

We'd also sing our own song "Fly me to Nee Soon, and let me play amongst the bars", to the tune of "Fly me to the moon…", Nee Soon being a very popular area of the colony, along with 'The Wanch' or Wan Chai.

In those days, there was no tunnel across the bay, you either got the ferry, or got stuck when they stopped running. Or you could pay an exorbitant rate for a sampan, and be rowed across. That was the usual choice – that or be adrift, and fined more than the sampan price!

Attached to H.M.S. Tamar (the base in Hong Kong), was the jetty where we moored, and no sooner had we tied up, apparently, than we had an offer to paint the ships side. As I said earlier – doing the side was a total absolute drag – you needed to be volunteered to do it – you avoided it at all costs. 'Jenny's" Side Party happily turned to, primer'ed, undercoated and repainted the whole lot whilst there – it looked magnificent when they finished it.

At most places we visited, there would be a market set up on the jetty alongside us, in order to induce us to part with our dosh. Hong Kong was probably the only place where the markets were allowed on board, in both 'waists', spread around, much as car boots are nowadays. We got some good last minute rabbits from there.

Chapter 16

'Time to Go Home, Time to Go Home . . .'

We sadly left Hong Kong for the return trip (and home) counting the days now until we got back to Rosyth.,and now we were 'Homeward Bounders', but not the sewing version. We stopped at Gan, in the middle of the Indian Ocean – another RAF base then, inhabited solely by RAF people, where we had the inevitable banyan and game of football against the sad gits otherwise known as 'the inhabitants' – then sailed, rapidly. I don't know if crabfats would volunteer for Gan, or whether they were volunteered, but there was nothing, and I do mean – nothing to do there.

We spent a week at Victoria, on the island of Mahe in the idyllic Seychelles, where we spent all our free time disappearing in taxis' to the far side of the island, where the sand was as fine as flour on the beaches, which were unparalleled. We tried to locate the famous turtles, but never saw any.

While we were in Singers and HK, we had started to lose our suntans, and were now glad of the opportunity to top them up. So we left Mahe, and sailed back to Mombasa.

This time, no station leave. This time it was the safari. A real safari, upcountry to Tsavo Game Park, with new, real camera and several films, in a minibus, scouring the park for different animals. We saw and photographed, elephants, lions, crocodiles, antelopes, zebra, cheetahs, giraffes, more elephants, monkeys, gazelles, hippos', hyena, impala, more giraffes, more antelopes – and ended up at Lugard Falls. Another truly awesome spectacle, however, when my 'slides' came back, most of the animals were so tiny, you had to really search for whatever it was. I still have all my slides, and sometimes go through them to see what I can remember. This safarai meant we had to get up extremely early in the morning to do this one, and we didn't get back to the ship late in the evening. But it was one of the best remembered days I spent.

We sailed from Mombasa, straight back to Beira – another month at sea, scanning the radar, topping up the tan, fighting again for the 'bucket',

Then back to Durban for another few days. We left there, and sailed to Simonstown to refuel, then to Capetown harbour – just to see Table Mountain, then set sail PROPERLY for home.

It is a fact that while you serve in any ship, you become so used to the background rattles and noises, that you actually become attuned to the ship, that you instinctively know when something amiss happens before you are told about it. Or even before something happens. So it was one night, as we sailed northwards up the West coast of Africa, while passing the mouth of the river Gambia, we were laying in bed awaiting the 'shake' for the 'middle'. I think we all woke up without exception, and looked at each other in the lights from our bunks, then there was a loud muffled bang. The Zulu shuddered, the propeller stopped turning – and we cruised to a halt. Hundreds of miles from shore. We had had a major fire in the gearbox – quickly extinguished. Those practice drills, daily for eleven months served their purpose that night – it was 'out' before it knew what had hit it. However, due to the resultant damage, we then sat motionless for several days, while (extremely fortunately for us) the same 'sweepers that were in Hong Kong with us caught us up. They were returning from their deployment too. They arrived one morning, hitched up tow lines, and dragged us to the nearest 'port', which was Dakar, in French West Africa. As soon as we arrived there, we were well entertained by the French Navy, who could not have been more helpful unless they had actually held the wine bottles to our mouths. It was a pity they didn't tell us (or was it that we failed to understand what they were saying, even when they demonstrated it) the wine was supposed to be mixed half and half with water though. We had an extremely drunken barbecue on a beach that day, with so much food and drink we had to turn it away. I still can't drink red wine even now without thinking about that beach…

It was very close to Christmas by now, and we had specialists flown out from Rosyth to come and make the gearbox better. They couldn't, immediately, and it became high priority to get several of our crew home to UK, understandable as they had weddings arranged. They were flown back – we sweated over whether we'd make it. After several days (and several large hammers) the 'mateys' freed up the gearbox enough for us to connect G6, and we came home all the way on that. Unfortunately – G6 was a thirsty beast only used sparingly, so we had to RAS, it seemed hourly but was probably daily, all the way back to England. We were also curtailed to the maximum G6 speed – well below normal cruising. We arrived in Rosyth just days before Christmas, actually only slightly later than expected, and headed for home for well earned leave.

We were all loaded with rabbits, all looked deeply sun-tanned, all had new suits from the tailors (mine had a rich red lining), and all ran like hell to get the taxis to Inverkeithing for the train to Edinburgh, for the fast trains south, via Birmingham in my case, to get home to Northampton.

Once more, nothing had changed – my parents, my mates, Northampton – all exactly as I left it eleven months earlier. Once more, only I had changed. To my eyes, nothing would ever be the same again, as nothing can prepare you for a year away from home, closeted with the same faces watch after watch, day after day, month after month. Like or hate – you HAD to coexist and rely on them all the time. I had seen things, done things, smelt and touched and eaten things that no-one I knew would ever do in their lifetime. It was difficult to come to those terms – coming home then was like coming into an alien world. My mates had girlfriends, my mates drank pints, slowly. My mates had the run of the local. Again I had to slowly get re-acquainted with all this, plus do the rounds of the relatives, plus get ready for Christmas. And there was the inevitable and constant 'where did you go', 'what was it like', ' is it really like it looks in the pictures', over and over. Mind you, with my new handmade suit with its deep red lining, and the handmade shirts and shoes, and the deep, deep suntan which we all sported even though it was December – I felt I could put up with it!!

Chapter 17

After the Lord Mayors' Show . . . Comes the Med

Christmas was over far too quickly, and back I went to Rosyth where the clanks, along with the dockies finally disentangled the gearbox bits from the engine bits through a large hole specially created in the ships side, rebuilt the lot – and we were then patched and away again, after the inevitable 'basin trials', power trials and many other engine tests.

We sailed to Portsmouth, and while on duty one night, we were told by returning libertymen, that Southsea Pier was on fire, and looking that way we could see the glow. That was a waste of pier, allegedly during the making of a film. We refuelled, and left once more for Gib, and the prospect of three months in the 'Med'.

We were designated Gib Guard Ship for a whole month, and in that time we were twice called out to 'escort' fleets of Russian warships through the 'Straits. On one of the 'escort' duties – as apparently the two fleets were changing over, hence our escort – we saw a brand new Russian aircraft carrier – the Moskva, though when we next saw it – it was apparently the Kiev. Or was it really two ships. Whatever – they were operating helicopters which flew oh so close to us for a gander, whilst their version of our Harrier jump-jet took off and landed behind them, as – for once – WE were the observers. Our EW chaps had a field day then, taping various signatures, as I'm sure they did the same.

We were also interested in the escort vessels – brand new Kara class warships, all bristling with weapons and radars. All of which, incidentally, we were told was rusty/unworkable/made of wood/undermanned... But there was always Smokey Joe to look out for.

One day, whilst at sea, I was 'piped' to the Air FMR, and told it was my turn today, to be a passenger in the parrot, while it did a one-hour sortie looking for surface contacts. I was briefed (do NOT jump out), strapped on to it (the rear seats were removed – we sat on the floor with lap belts), and we launched with a jerk. For 'flying stations' the ship hurtles into the wind at high speed, to get extra lift for the parrot. As you lift, therefore, so the ship clears from underneath, the parrot breaks to port, and up you go. Like an express lift, so your stomach is still on the flight deck. The pilot then demonstrated the art of high speed maneuvering, so if I looked to the right,

I could see the sea, though I should have seen the horizon, really. I forgot – they also removed the doors. There was nothing but a lap belt then, between me and the sea. It was totally exhilarating!!!

All too soon we landed back on. To land, the Wasp would slowly catch up with the ship, hang over the port quarter, wait until signalled, then scat across and down. With one hell of a bump. I volunteered to go again, but was never so lucky.

During one exercise, we were in contact with an American Orion, which was flying and flitting about reporting surface ships back to us. Later in the afternoon, we were called by an American, warship, asking if we had heard from the Orion recently We had to confess we hadn't, not for several hours, but said that as we weren't controlling him, and as he had only spoken to us sporadically, we weren't surprised that he might have gone 'off task' without telling us. It was then, with great shock, that we heard later, of reports that an aircraft had been seen to fly into a hill. We legged it there, but too late obviously. The Orion had for some unexplainable reason, flown straight into a mountain, killing everyone onboard. We never did find out how they'd managed that, all we saw was the smoke from a distance.

We also engaged the local MFV to take a large party of us across to Tangier for the day, another unmissable experience wandering round the souks, looking at the sights, buying souvenirs, smelling the spices and tasting the food. A terrific day, especially the camel rides!

We went to Naples, where the local kids, as expert pickpockets, would tap your pockets as they walked alongside you, and then took a ferry across to Capri, going of our own accord to see Gracie Fields. In 'rig' of course. We hadn't consciously planned this, although we were aware she lived there somewhere. Therefore we found out where. We went to the front gate of her villa, knocked, explained who we were, and why we had come there, and were let in to her home without hesitation, spending a wonderful afternoon talking to a lovely lady. We had tea there, and returned to the ship. We took a weekend to Rome, driving up in a coach to a hotel on the outskirts. We ate all the native, real, proper, genuine Italian food, we toured the city in the coach and saw every tourist trap going. We walked the Coliseum, the Trevi Fountain – you name it – we saw it, and took the photo to prove it. We visited a cameo factory at Pompeii, where a man was making jewellery out of silver, with cameo settings. I bought a beautiful ring, with the head of a centurion in it, but sadly it broke one day, and I could never find anyone who was willing to repair it for me.

The night we were there, we had the obligatory party in our hotel room (I can't for the life of me remember how many of us shared the room), but we found a bar nearby, after we'd got back from a short 'run', and purchased several bottles of the local devils brew. It was warm, so we put it in the wine cooler in the bathroom ready for the proposed evening party. The first person who saw our Roman wine cooler collapsed laughing – we had used the bidet. We ate much more real Italian food during that time, and I really enjoyed that weekend too. The wine, incidentally, WAS nice & cool, and tasted fine…!!!

We 'stern-moored' in Naples, meaning we approached a very narrow jetty backwards. When we got close, we dropped one anchor, veered to one side and planted the other one, then reversed so that only the stern was on the jetty. We'd then secure the stern, set the tension on the anchor cables, and stay there. Leaving was just as hairy – let go aft, winch in on one anchor whilst releasing the other, raise the first one, winch over to the other, raise that, Simple, but time consuming. At least the mud was warmer than Portland's.

When we visited Pompeii, we saw all the sights including the man apparently zapped by the lava – he was displayed for all time in the museum, prone, as he was when the lava hit him. We spent hours there, and it was amazing to remember that people actually lived there – there was the graffiti, and there were the wheel ruts in the road, and there was the mosaic saying (in Latin) Beware of the dog… a memorable day out.

We finally left Naples, back to the exercises. We had by that time teamed up with a Mediterranean fleet of warships from Med nations. The idea was that we exercised constantly with them, but weekly we would sail into a host port for some leave. Hence the start in Italy. We then visited Patras, Thessalonika, Messina, Taormina, saw Mount Etna in the distance, Malta, Cyprus, and Izmir. Whilst in Izmir, I was the duty boat driver – we had moored some miles out of port along with the other ships. I drove the boat ashore one night to pick up libertymen, and wondered why the rest of the fleet boats were all alongside even though they were full of their own respective 'tars'. I put our boat out of the harbour – and sailed slap bang into a typhoon. Well, it felt like it – it was a severe squall, and by the time I had got the whaler back to the Zulu, it was slightly full of water, the libertymen were all drenched (including the officers who traditionally sat at the front – waves break over the front!!), and exhausted from baling the whaler as I steered through the driving rain back to the ship. We emptied the boat of men (up the accommodation ladder), hoisted the boat a little way on the falls, took the bung out, then sat back and watched the water drain. And by the time we had it fully hoisted, the squall went as quickly as it came. So we put the bung back in, lowered it, and returned for all the crew who were by that time wondering how they would get back.

On board all navy warships, are 'booms', which can be swung out from the ship's side. At procedure alpha, or when anchoring, all the booms, accommodation ladder and boats would be swung or dropped at the same time. It looks impressive, but that's where the fun starts. The ladders require very many sailors to position them, even after the many hours required to build them. However, the booms are lumps of wood, with ladders and ropes and wires everywhere. If the ladders are where sailors climb on and off the ship to the boat to/from ashore, the boom is where the boat is itself moored whilst doing nothing. So after dropping off the libertymen, the boat would approach the boom boatrope, and secure to it. The crew would then disembark the boat via the ladder hanging from the boom, then get back inboard by traversing the boom. Piece of cake. Usually. However, it was more usual to have to do this in a swell, sometimes in a heavy swell. That would make mooring the boat difficult, as you would need to judge the approach to the boatrope exactly. Then hope the bowman could actually grab the rope AND secure it before the boat dropped away on the bottom of the wave, dragging him overboard if he wasn't careful. Once secured, it then got dangerous. You'd have to go to the pitching bows of the boat, pull the boat up on the boatrope until you could reach the jumping ladder. You'd then ascend the ladder to the boom. Except that the boat would want to drop back with the tide, which meant the ladder developed its' own malevolent personality. Even dry – those ladders were evil, wet – they were virtually impossible. We'd also be wearing plimsolls to attempt this. If you managed to leap at the right time, you'd be half way up the ladder, then have to get from beneath the boom on the hanging ladder, to above the boom so you could seize the guy wire, and carefully walk sideways until you got back aboard the ship. By which time it would be time to take the boat back again for more libertymen.

Getting back to the boat was slightly more dangerous – cross the boom, feel for the ladder, swing underneath to it, keep your weight on the ladder until the boat appeared beneath you – and let go. All things being equal you'd fall into the boat, start the engine, propel it forward, and let the rest of the crew in. As I said – couldn't be simpler. Now throw in driving rain, a heavy swell, and do it again at 0200, in pitch dark, having been roused from sleep five minutes earlier. Soak your plimsolls in the oil and grease from the bottom of the seaboat, and try it again. And I used to volunteer for that?!

It was in Izmir where I ran out of money, and swapped an expensive looking (but actually extremely cheap) watch, for a genuine Afghan coat. Unfortunately, on getting it back to the ship, it turned out to contain its own zoo, and so was consigned to a carrier bag full of 'crab' powder until we got back to the UK before being declared 'safe'.

All these visits were reinforced by the odd banyan, none odder than the one in Crete, where, by the time the boat came back for us, the tide had dropped, exposing rocks which the whaler clearly could not now navigate! We walked several miles up a cliff, (I fell down the cliff – we had expected to be picked up, not have to walk miles – the tinned beer had taken its toll on everyone), walked down the other side, met the whaler, and eventually returned to the Zulu.

...And then we had to change back into 'eights' from 'tens', and what a bunch of prats we looked with long trousers again, and how uncomfortable they felt after the freedom of shorts. And as for having to wear boots again, instead of the sandals we were used to...

We had a final few days in Gib to buy souvenirs, where I finally cracked and bought a stereo, which I promptly blew up – I didn't read the 'voltage' label. I returned it, swore blind it was duff when I got it, and had it replaced. I also purchased an Omega watch – the like of which I have never since seen, and which still keeps perfect time. That watch didn't leave my wrist or pocket for the next eight of my naval years, in case someone fancied it more than I.

We sailed back to Rosyth – some glad to be home, but most of us were sad to be at the end of the commission. We had enjoyed thirty months of each other's company, seen some wonderful sights, bought great rabbits, got older, and much, much wiser. I was sad to leave the Zulu – she contained some good memories. I never saw her again. I wonder if anyone ever found out about the pumpkins and other odd fruit we used to ferment into wine? ...Or found any of the crates of whatever we stowed away during RAS's, and forgot about? And whatever happened to her anyway? I spent thirty very formative months on there, and enjoyed almost every minute of it.

Chapter 18

A Shore Draft

I left the Zulu, had several weeks well earned de-commissioning leave, and re-joined H.M.S. Dryad (only this time I knew where it was) for a 'twos' course, intended to make me into a 'second class RP', instead of the 'third class' I was then.

Before leaving a ship after an overseas tour, all crew would request a draft to a unit they fancied. I fancied (and was recommended for) the 'twos' course, but was still pleasantly surprised when I got on it.

After my long leave, I travelled to Portsmouth, joined Dryad on the Sunday evening, rose on the Monday, changed cap-tallies once more, and met my fellow attendees on the Monday morning, ready for several more weeks of concentrated lectures on radar, the principles of how it worked, how to spot this, how to report that, and at the end of the course, graduated well.

I must first say, that after two and a half years of not being able to look out of a bedroom window and see daylight, it made a very pleasant change to draw curtains and look over fields. The 'hands' mess at Dryad was at the edge of the base, and overlooked pastures, and it was cows that now kept me awake (if sober enough) rather than stabilisers and steering gear. Looking back, being in a steel box was more like sensory deprivation.

The nightlife at Dryad was now at my fingertips – I was nineteen, had seen the world, had the T-shirt(s), worn them frequently, and read all the books. Surprisingly, my fellow course-goers had not between them been to as many places as I had by then. I counted myself as fortunate to have been on the Zulu for that commission. They had, though, their own wealth of experience to recount, and we still learned an awful lot from each other.

We would frequent 'The Beast' in Southwick, where Sid and his missus would run a loose ship. The Beast was a five minute walk there, but anything up to an hour back. The Beast didn't sell shorts, only Gales Ales, and wine. All different flavours. A different one for every day of the year, I think. We would either buy by the glass, or by the bottle, or we would hold a bash, and get Sid's missus to fill a large bucket with assorted bottles, lemonade, beer, and fruit slices. We would (as the evening wore on) augment the contents as the level sank naturally, with wine, more wine, crisps, nuts, scratchings, and more wine. The further through the night, the tastier the bucket got, conversely the weaker the taste apparently got, until the mixtures of lemonade were omitted, meaning what was left was pure wine, albeit many different flavours. We had some great nights in there, as there was no defined bar – just a couple of rooms, one of which had comfortable armchairs, and an open fire. We would sit there for hours. 2230, closing time, (the one thing Sid rigidly adhered to) was followed by the crawl up the back road to Dryad, followed by a visit to 'Dots' for the inevitable SRE sarnie. With a side order left for tomorrow morning. Occasionally, we would race back to the Naafi ready for last orders, or send an advance party there to get them in, prior to our arrival, so we could sit there until the 2300 Naafi closing time.

Just for a change, we would go to the other pub in the village, which was a 'normal' pub. Very infrequently we would go into Pompey for the night, but there had to be a good reason for that. Like going to see live bands at the Guildhall. I saw some top 70s' bands there. – The Strawbs, Uriah Heep, Wishbone Ash, Black Sabbath, Rory Gallagher…

And we had divisions every weekday morning, followed by a dash to 'Dots' in the five minutes we had available to get to our first lecture.

We had the inevitable duty watches there, charging from one end of Dryad to the other pulling the 'fire cart', stamping round the grounds on Estate Patrol, or through the buildings on Security. Funnily, we were permitted to patrol in the wardrooms quarters, but still never allowed in Tampax Tower. We used to have a good look anyway, just in case. We would often find matelots and splits in compromising places though.

The weeks there passed in a blur, punctuated by weekends at home, or weekends in Pompey if there was a good band on. The course members were fiercely team-spirited, and we would rarely go round with other courses. We would however team up with WRENS, and it seemed an unofficial contest to get the largest bunch of tables together in the Naafi in the evenings, in order to create the biggest 'gang', whilst seeing how many 'hangers-on' we could attract. My course would normally win that, with all our tables haphazardly arranged, but deliberately placed right up the middle of the club. We would drink in rounds, with everyone religiously getting theirs in. Sometimes, thee would be 'club night' (live band/disco), or 'folk night' which was merely an excuse to sing, volubly along with the man holding the microphone. The war-cry in those days was "Cheese Toastie". ALL through the evening, the Naafi served sarnies, and would put them in the toaster, hence THAT cry, which used to really get on our nerves. We would also monopolise the juke box there, playing what we wanted, 'nudging' it if someone tried to play something different, or something we didn't want to hear, but normally repeating Status Quo "Sweet Caroline" (one of our course members was 'trapping' a Wren with that name), or Dylan's "Knock Knock Knockin…", or Chuck Beret, sorry Berry's "Dingaling" all night and the football table which we would play until we dropped. We also played darts quite a bit.

Eating at Dryad, in the approved dining hall, was always fun. As usual, we would queue for food, sometimes starting an orderly rabble outside the dining hall well before the right time, merely to allow ogling. This would take place between WRENS and sailors, and go on until the doors were opened. It was also traditional to get there even earlier on 'new intake day' as new WRENS arrived from their initial training at H.M.S. Dauntless, to be the first to scan them for anything interesting. We, then, would normally be the first sailors they'd ever seen, live, and we would clearly often take advantage of that.

According to legend, there lived a cat in or near the galley, its name was 'Cooking Fat'… …as in 'Where's that fooking cat?"

The Folk nights were popular, and an excuse to sing, bawdily, rudely, and loudly. The louder, the bawdier – the better. We therefore knew all the correct words to 'Wild Rover' and other traditional Irish/drinking songs, plus plenty of not-so-traditional ones. We also knew the ruder versions of everything. Apart from all those, we'd make new ones up. For instance, Old Macdonald's Farm. Apart from all the animals, he also had a lighthouse, which used to 'flash'. Very entertaining. Plus all the actions for all the animals. When that got too boring, we'd then go off at a tangent, singing 'The Music Man (who comes from down your way…)', and if at the end of the 'what can you plaaayyyy', you were being indicated, you had to get up and pretend to play a musical instrument. Or pretend to play anything else. The most popular was the trombone (ask someone else – I'm not going to explain it). Oh All right – tromboning was navy slang for…, and the actions therefore were very explicit. Or the easy cop out was 'I can play the big O.D.', followed by 'performing' all round the room. If you attempted to do one someone else had already done, you were loudly booed down, before getting a very traditional beer shampoo.

Zulu Warrior was always favourite, depending on who you could coerce into performing it. As was that (now hijacked) old faithful 'Swing Low Sweet Chariot', which we knew ALL the words and ALL the verses to. We would, for variation, hum it, then mime it. If you have never seen anyone, let alone several dozen (or more) people in a line, miming silently but in perfect time to Swing Low…, then one day, you are in for a surprise. It is though very easy, and you can make anyone understand the chorus, amidst much, much laughing when the mimes become apparent.

Interspersed with the serious drinking songs would be gentle melodies about a crow in a tree (my favourite – rarely did I ever find anyone else who knew the words to that one), or about 'Chiefy put me dayman (you can have my tot)', or about a gentleman called Sambo and the bee. We even knew the 'Eton Boating Song', clearly with our own words, mainly involving hard boiled eggs…, and several others about 'My Brother, Sylvest' and many, many more. It was clear, then, that the more songs you had in your repertoire, the better it was for you. All were guaranteed to get a laugh, especially if performed in front of a previously untainted audience. Like we used to seek out, time after time after time!! It never got boring though!

Weekends at Dryad, if you stayed there, would be (if not on duty) laying in bed all morning, going to the Naafi, sleeping the afternoon, then back to the club (or the beast) in the evening.

Going home, entailed catching a coach to another naval base nearby, changing coaches, catching one more up to Northampton, getting dropped off there with a cab home, followed by 'when are you going back', followed by straight round the local, then sleeping all Saturday morning. Getting back was more problematic. I had to be in the centre of Northampton for 0200 on Monday morning, to get a very smelly (all sailors fart frequently, it must have taken them days to ventilate the coaches they used), very packed coach back south, and sometimes I got a seat. Normally you just sat in the aisle. We arrived at Fareham at 0600 (ish), changed coaches, and got back to Dryad around 0700, just in time for breakfast (the only time we would normally make it), then roll up for our first lecture, totally exhausted.

After many weeks, we took final exams, did our final 'models', got our next drafts, said goodbye to all the course mates and Wrens we had come to know over the preceding weeks, and disappeared into the railway stations.

I thoroughly enjoyed that course.

Chapter 19
Another Shore Job

I left Dryad, and was drafted to H.M.S. Victory (as the naval base was called before it changed much later to Nelson), then volunteered for, and was put on an educational course to top up my GCEs'. This meant being in class all day, just cramming for English and Geography. For this period, I had a blue card, which meant 'no duties'. Great, ashore every night, home every weekend I could afford it.

Along with Glen (who was coincidentally on the course) we sailed through all the exams.

My first day job after that was being attached to the registry, where I carried round all the internal mail throughout the base. That opened my eyes, especially when I had to make the daily delivery to DQ's , which was reputed to be not too dissimilar to Butlins. The euphemism was 'going on holiday, for ninety days'. It seemed a harsh regime there, not one I fancied volunteering for, so I'd skid in then out, quickly. The 'warders', all senior rates from the navy and marines, were seemingly hand picked as the most unpleasant shites the Navy ever paid. Even when I went in there to deliver their mail twice daily, you could not even start a conversation let alone get one to speak coherently or pleasantly. Made for the job.

One of the duty-watch jobs here, was 'cinema attendant'. You had to get to the on-base cinema some hour before the film was due to kick off, and check the 'float'. You'd then argue about who was to be 'cashier', 'usherette', or sweeper upper-afterwards. Having decided that, you'd then see the film for free.

Another job was main gate sentry – a lovely job, standing outside the barrack gate, saluting anything with rings, sneering at passing civvies, and cursing all the matelots going ashore. THE worst job there.

I was detailed after that to another (unfortunately) blue card job. I worked with one of the last Navy 'sailmakers', in the sail loft, where we would repair marquees, sails from the RNSA boats – anything, but not too hard, or too fast. The reason it was a blue card job, was that we used to hire out marquees to local functions, at a cost, and not only have to deliver them, but also erect them. The three of us – Chief Sailmaker, me & another AB – along with as many volunteers as the hirers could muster would take the best part of a day to do that, generally on a Friday. We would then have to go back either on the Sunday, or first thing Monday morning to drop it, and stow it. We would then have to air or dry it, before taking it out the next weekend. Not that it was all drawbacks, the hirers would normally 'treat' us, not only while in progress, but generally afterwards too.

As 'the loft' was off the beaten track, we would rarely get visitors there – we were exempt from rounds due to the nature of the job, and exempt from duties due to the weekend work, so life was pretty easy.

I was 'messed' right across the road from the Naafi, Dining hall – very central, and, as usual, a clique developed, with the whole gang trooping around together, going on jaunts here and there. One of them ended up in the Fire Brigade, with a village mate of mine – I don't know who was the most surprised of the two when they realised they both knew me.

It was an extreme shock to me when one day I discovered that – blue card or not – I had been volunteered to take part in an honour guard for a visit by the Prince of Wales. And an even greater shock when I started to drop the SLR every other movement. I had a rapid visit to the sickbay, who x-rayed my elbow, decided to schedule me for an operation on it, and promptly excused me from the guard. That was close.

A couple of my 'run ashore oppos' were at that time guides on the wooden H.M.S. Victory, in permanent dry-dock in Portsmouth Dockyard. In those days, that was the only place civilians could go in the yard, and they would spend hours queueing to traipse around the Victory, peering at where Lord Nelson fell, at where the crew existed. All having a jolly good time. We would infiltrate these tourists on occasions at weekend, and be attentive to everything our oppo would have to say, prompting questions here and there, pre-empting the usual dumb questions. We would then be first OFF the ship, but in full view of the assembled tourists, we would loudly announce our thank-yous', and in full view of all visitors, we would give them some money. Usually a fiver (borrowed from them some hours earlier). That would normally precipitate a shower of further dosh from the grateful grockles, which we in turn would thankfully divvy up later, ready to go ashore on the proceeds.

On a Sunday, we had major choices. We could either stay within the base, go to the Naafi, and watch the (ostensibly) live folk singer, which was guaranteed to get a laugh, especially the day one announced he was going to sing a song by Tam Pax..., sorry TOM Paxton. The splits didn't find that at all amusing. Or we could go ashore, then after the pubs shut at lunchtime, we would catch the Isle of Wight ferry, and make one or two crossings on that to while away the hours until the pubs opened again. The fact that the IOW ferry bar opened as soon as they left the jetty was neither here nor there – we just used to go for the sightseeing...

During the week, a 'club night' would take place, which could be anything from a live (but not very well known band, such as a Navy band called Shy Talk (you work it out!)) to wrestling (where the wrestlers' would talk to each other, choreographing the contest before going into the ring). Each night would be well supported by us, we'd go and see anything for a change. Plus disco night, known as 'grab a granny', or 'widows hop', or 'gronk night'. And we would bet each other to dance with the ugliest... Maybe they ran a sweepstake too!

Sweeping was a favourite game, at closing time. We'd 'sweep' or mop up all the glasses with anything left in them. This was in the days when you wouldn't think twice about drinking out of someone else's' glass. It would not matter what was in there – beer, lager, shorts, mixers – we'd drink it all. Of course, you wouldn't do it sober, but you regarded it as perks of staying until closing time. Or if you were supposed to be clearing up. Or duty shore patrol, supposedly looking out for, and hopefully stopping any trouble from developing. You'd only really do it inside the base.

It is a strange thing, but when your duty watch has you down for 'shore patrol', you never, ever got any trouble from anyone inside the club. But go ashore and see someone else's shore patrol, and they immediately become targets for venomous attacks. In the club – great, permission to have a quiet drink (or six) whilst on the lookout, sit and chat to your mates – no bother. Go outside the base – watch other ships companies go looking for 'cementheads'.

Actually, most matelots avoid 'reggies' (the polite term for naval police) like the plague. They are seen as traitors to their own branch. They are normally defectors from something sensible, or apply because of the instant power, providing they survive the personality transplant/charisma removal. They generally, though, 'go through' because they do not have the requisite skills to go any further at their original profession, lowly as that may have been in the first place. They normally have their own mess on large ships, but have to mess 'with the lads' on smaller ships. If it is in with you, you have to hide every fiddle you have, for example the 'beer boat', just in case 'it' drops you in it.

For two weeks in mid summer, I was temporarily drafted to H.M.S. Baccante (known as the Bagshanty) which was designated as Guard Ship for Cowes Week that year. I was enlisted as boats crew, meaning we had to run between Portsmouth and Cowes over the sandbanks to fetch/return crew/stores, then at night we would graciously ferry yacht crews from wardroom – sorry – ship to yacht, or back, taking great care to avoid causing a wake enough to rock the sleeping yachts and their crews. Not that we'd do that of course. Unless provoked by lets say – not getting a tip. Those weeks passed quickly, and it was soon back to barracks. Many years later, while touring H.M.S. Victory (the REAL one) with my wife and some friends, I met the man who I crewed with , a chap called Simon Battisby – we recognised each other immediately, which dredged up all kinds of memories.

A burning memory from that duty, was the cutter we ran, which could hold dozens of passengers rather than the several we used to carry with our whalers, was equipped with bucket gear. This is an old, cheap way of ensuring you don't have to fit a reverse gear on the engine. The bucket was controlled by a handle you used to wank round, rapidly, which closed a bucket behind the propeller, forcing the wash back the other way, meaning the boat theoretically started to go backwards, assuming you remembered to rev up the engine to full power first to counteract the forward momentum. Except that it all took longer than it takes to read about it, and when you suddenly find you have to go backwards, hurriedly, it is easier to just to hang on for dear life, and go through the motions, so when you finally smash in to whatever it was you were heading for, you can at least swear blind you were doing your best. The cutter was extremely well built – much harder than anything it bounced off.

Ships refitting in Pompey did what we used to do on the Zulu in Rosyth – live ashore and march to the ship, and it came to our notice that the officers of the ships would traverse Victory, short cutting to their ships. We especially came to like one officer, a very green, obviously straight from University lieutenant, very small and inoffensive, with an oversized cap, held up only by his protruding ears, it seemed. We noted how he would blush when saluted, so we took it upon ourselves to line up one behind the other, purely to get the blush. We would also hammer round the blocks to do it again. I don't know if he ever caught on, but he must have generated plenty of heat, and arrived with a tired right arm!! The blush, incidentally would be followed by a very sheepish grin. He was lucky – for a start, we'd normally go miles out of our way to avoid saluting 'pigs', but fortunately the 'rule' was to only salute the same officer once per day. And if he carried his cap under his arm, we'd totally ignore them, like a bad smell.

The only other time we'd have to 'chop one off', was whilst reporting for rounds, or being 'trooped'.

Towards the end of the summer, in amongst more 'concerts', weekends, and other mixed fortunes, I received another draft. Bearing in mind that the 'scare' ships this time were the Blake and the Tiger (known to be real 'spanner' drafts – not popular), I was extremely pleased when I was told that mine was to H.M.S. Tartar, another 'Tribal'. Based in Pompey, but more importantly – YIPPEE – cracked it, *it was going on tour of the Windies*.

I then served out the rest of my time at Victory still in the loft, with weekends mostly at home, but with several others teararsing around in Vic Jelleys' old MG, visiting the motor museum near Southampton, the New Forest, or wherever else we could scrape up enough petrol to go.

Chapter 20

The Tartar *(of the Title – See, I wasn't Lying) in Pompey*

I was extremely pleased to join the RatRat – I was actually welcomed on board by my peers, (especially by motorbike mad Ray Dentith who was QM on the gangway at the time) as, as an RP2, it meant I was in charge of the Ops room watch, along with the other seven RP2s', meaning that when we sailed, we were actually one-in-eight (watches) instead of the one-in-four the rest of the crew were on.

Also, as a '2', I had credibility, could play 'uckers', and talk sensibly about a wide range of naval topics, and expertly spin the shit when I had to...

Unfortunately, within weeks of joining her, I was taken off to have my elbow sorted, and went P7R (navy term for unfit) for six weeks. More unfortunately, I had to go back to Dryad to recuperate. More beast, more 'toasties'. Dammit...

While I was up there, the Tartar did basin trials, and in doing so, the hawsers holding her parted, and she took off towards the caisson separating the ocean from a dry dock. Containing a submarine. She was stopped following some extremely quick thinking by the OOW, who had the engines reversed in record time, so no serious damage was done. It gave an extremely serious fright though.

Of course, I was sat at Dryad on 'light duties' and didn't find out till I got back.

Tartar had just completed a long refit, and my first shock was to see the officer we had tormented through my 'Victory' days was the Electrical Engineer, and, although he didn't recognise me – he still grinned and blushed...

Portsmouth was at that time divided into two drinking areas – 'the strip' where I had previously been, with the pubs full of students and sailors, the floors of which would still be covered in sawdust (to save putting it down after the event...), and the main drag, where I had visited during my Victory days. Even I was amazed when my mates on the Tartar introduced me to pubs even I wasn't aware of. We quickly made mates on there, George (later to become my best man) and me were virtually inseparable for nearly three years. Of course, being an RP2 had made it easier to be accepted. That and the fact there was a 'juniors' mess on board, which kept them out of the way!!

Attitudes changed quickly as you ascended through the ranks! It did, though, mean I could now pass on my knowledge and experiences to these juniors. It was strange to think that only two years previously, I had been on the receiving end, also to think how much knowledge I had actually acquired in such a short time!!

Comradeship was rife on there, and we would go ashore, gangs of us. If one person was broke, he would have a 'free' night – we would buy his ale. The next night, you might be skint – you'd have your ale bought. Bearing in mind that even then, you COULD go ashore and get smashed on a couple of quid, including the snack on the walk back to the dockyard. We obviously had our favourite pubs, and would be queuing outside the preferred ones at 1755, waiting for opening time. My favourite was the Borough Arms – full of students from the local Poly, and matelots. That particular pub had three things going for it. First – the best jukebox I have ever seen in any pub, before, during or since. Secondly – most matelots kept away from it, as it had a dubious reputation even for Portsmouth. Third – they still sold scrumpy from the wood, and if you were fortunate enough to get the last pint, you'd find you got a free meal from all the bits of apple at the bottom of the barrel.

We used to occasionally 'smooth it', either by going to grab-a-granny night at the weekly disco at the dance hall in Pompey, where we'd wear a tie with our short-sleeved shirts, jeans, and jackets. That place would keep a stock of ties on the door, just for passing trade – like ourselves. Or we'd go to the Still And West in Old Portsmouth, where we'd drink Guinness (for a change) sitting outside overlooking the harbour entrance, shouting 'encouragement' at passing warships or ferries. They sold wine (like at Sid's) there, and scrumpy and beer, and Guinness. I had never dunk that before, but quickly appreciated its smooth taste, and bitterness. Oh yes, and its ability to get you pissed quick! The first night me and George had leg failures on Guinness, we also woke up to find a whole length of flashing lights, which used to guard a hole in the road in Old Portsmouth. I have absolutely no idea how they got there, how they (or we) got past the Mod Plod guarding the dockyard gate, or up the gangway, but they made a terrific splash as we gave them a float test only moments before 'colours' the following morning.

We also got into the bad habit, but naval tradition of stopping for 'big eats' in the form a Chinese meal virtually every night, or if we weren't at that end of town, we'd prop up the (still there) snack bar on The Hard. At one time, we also frequented the Kentucky place, but that went downhill faster than we did.

The Chinese was favourite, the one we used was close to the station, and run by one 'Charlie Chop Suey', who would see me and George walk in, and get the kitchen staff cooking our standard evening meal before we'd even ordered. Charlie was terrific, nothing was too much trouble for him – he would even let us put our meal on the slate if it was near payday – he knew fine that we'd be back and pay for it along with our next meal.

If we felt really flush, we'd go down to Southsea, spend the evening among the bars and discos, get a Chinese in the best 'house' in Southsea, then stagger round looking for a taxi back. We'd usually demand a stop at the snack bar to ensure a supply of milk for the following morning, although if you spoke nicely to the QM, normally a messmate, he'd ensure he skimmed some off the top of the milk churn delivered daily so we sailors could have fresh milk with our cornflakes, and in our tea. Fresh milk was obviously unobtainable at sea, but we ensured supplies by freezing vast quantities and thawing it out periodically. Apart from that, we'd have 'metal cow' (powdered milk), or the least favourite – tinned milk, something I still avoid eagerly.

Whatever – scarcely a weekend in Portsmouth went by without being called 'up-homers' by one of the locals, where he and his wife would give you a good Sunday dinner. Our special favourite was to go to 'Blackies' house. He was a gunner, with an incredible fondness for and ability to dispose of Bacardi. His wife, Barbara, made a splendid Sunday lunch, uncomplainingly when we got back from the pub late. We'd sit around in armchairs at Blackies, eating his food – all of us chatting away. Great times. Blackie left the ship sometime while we were in the Windies, never to be seen again. I heard subsequently that he had accidentally had his back broken. I really hope not, or if he did that he recovered sufficiently. However, standing in a Trinidad bar, drunkenly calling for 'Blackie' is not recommended!!

Budgie was another favourite – we lost count of the times we went to his single room flat in Portsmouth for meals with him and his wife. Budgie was so called 'cos his surname was Burge. However, if he had been named after a bird, it should have been a vulture – I don't know what it is about large proboscis' and the Navy, but Budgie certainly had room for several families to dwell in his!

Not that we needed an excuse to get away from the food on the Tartar – it was, quite simple, the best food I ever had in all the time I was in the RN. We would normally have a choice of at least two different joints of meat for lunch, with amazing suppers. (Not many 'veggies' in them there days) You could normally tell what was being served – the length of the queue back up the Burma Road would be in direct proportion to the 'goody rating' of what was on the menu. Mixed grill was favourite (especially if we got hold of mushrooms), but strangely that was only ever dished up on a Saturday. Second in the running was Chicken Supreme – something the (now Chinese) wardroom slaves would knock up easily, but something I have never since been able to recreate without resorting to 'packets'. Breakfast was always good too – we were usually allowed to fry our own eggs rather than eat the mass produced ones, or carve a lump from the scrambled tray...

Actually, my taste in food was (and still is) wide-ranging and varied, but I could never hack Spanish omelettes, which went on the menu regularly, when the caterer ran out of ideas. Disgusting looking things.

As a sideline, when we did the 'morning', one of the chefs used to be treated to a cup of tea when we woke him at 0430 (ish) to start cooking – he would then bring us fresh bacon sarnies later, right before we slid off for the first of two breakfasts. The chef we used to do this trade with was a bit of a wag (for a chef), and if he was 'duty chef' for 'nine-o'clockers' (supper every evening), you had to be a bit cagey what you ate. For example, if it was 'cackleberries' (hard boiled eggs), you had to make sure you cracked the eggs somewhere safe – or you might just get one of the several uncooked eggs he had thrown in for fun. We got wise to that after a while, and would either threaten him, in which case he'd keep yours separate, or you'd use the old trick of spinning the egg quickly on its base. If it fell over – uncooked. If it continued spinning – cooked perfectly!! Try it!!

Nine o'clockers (actually served at 2000) is a Navy Tradition, like rum was... ...and it could be anything. It could be cake, or sandwiches, or crackers (at which point you would have a side bet as to who could actually empty their mouth of three cream crackers inside one minute. Impossible to do...), with cheese, or ham, or eggs, or corned dog, or 'herrings-in', or meat paste – whatever lay at hand when the duty chef decided to get it ready. We would, generally, toast the bread first, and lash it up to plenty of butter, or we'd nick as much as we could of whatever there was available, to take back to the mess if it was our 'turn'. If you were tardy getting there, bad luck – it would ALL be gone in moments. Like a flock of vultures descending. If you were lucky, the duty chef would still be about, and you might be able to con some out of him. More often than not, they'd put it all out, and that was it. During the in-sail-movie, we would shut down the projector so as to allow hungry sailors to get their nine o'clockers, even though they'd been troughing nutty since suppertime anyway. Once the last hand had sat down again, we'd recommence the movie.

There is a standing joke in the Navy, there are cooks and chefs. Navy cooks like to think they are chefs. We, however, would point out cooks are still being trained, and that no matter how good you (cook) think you are, you'll never be a CHEF. Having said that, the food I had in the navy (apart from the garbage to be dished up on another ship I had the misfortune to later serve on) was some of the best I ever had., especially when you knew who to butter up (or who not to!).

Again, we had cafeteria messing in a central dining room on the Tartar, four rows of tables, with benches either side, on which we use to sit, having queued for our scran. We would then eat as quickly as possible, for two reasons – firstly to let someone else sit and eat, secondly to get back to the messdeck for a rest/clean up for rounds/continue the card school/have a fag/anything else not listed.

It has been a habit forced upon me, that due to the small amount of time we had to eat, ever, as there were always others waiting to eat, or a card game to continue, or a watch to sit, that I have ever since eaten fast. This appears to be caused by greed, but it is totally due to the restrictions imposed by the Navy – and is still a hard habit to break. I still savour my food, and enjoy it as much as anybody, it's just that I keep looking up for someone else, hovering with tray in one hand, rods in the other, waiting for my still warm seat!

In the dining room was a speaker for the SRE – Ships Radio equipment. The SRE usually played world service, or local radio, or tapes from home radio, or records (The Navy Lark was always a good bet) on the ancient 'deck' in the SRE Office. We used to be able to take our own LPs' in there and knock out a 'show' for a couple of hours whilst off watch. The dining room SRE, however, could be a bone of contention, especially for George. If there was something playing which he took exception to, or if he judged it to be playing too loudly, he would go to the SRE, and turn it off, saying "This is a dining hall, not a fucking disco. If you want to dance fuck off to your mess and do it there – I want to eat", and go back to his meal, defying anyone to turn it back on again. And woe-betide anyone who did! Of course, we (George and me) knew he was only winding everyone up, but no-one had the nerve to turn it back on until he left the area!

Similarly, if George approached a mass of bodies blocking his way – either ashore or aboard – and depending on what frame of mind he was in, he would either holler "Make way for a Naval Rating" fairly politely, or "Gangway 'afore I carve a bastard". Both ways produced a parting similar to that which Moses achieved...

Of course, all our meals were planned in advance, and promulgated on the notice board outside the galley. Therefore we always knew when the best food was going to be there, and got in the queue. Navy shorthand decreed that RB+Y/P was roast beef with Yorkshire pudding – you get the idea, so we would know whether to eat on board, or get ashore early for a pork pie, with a chinky later.

The meals were planned by the ships caterer, normally an overweight, sweaty Chief PO, never anything less than a PO. He would sit in his office planning the menu along with the CPO or PO Chef, then have to ensure the food was fresh and available for us to scoff at scrantime. One of the 'high points' of eating navy food at sea, after several weeks without fresh supplies, was that we would fall back on tinned junk. Like powdered potatoes known as 'pom'. Disgusting. Warned with that, you'd know the next few meals could be tinned veg, tinned meat, powdered egg, everything 'out of a tin'. Bread would be non-existent, so a chef would have to be on duty all night baking fresh for us. Of course the tantalising smell would permeate the whole ship, especially the gloom room, where we would be the first ones there to congratulate him – 'brilliant bread chef- any chance of a couple of rolls...with a bit of bacon in. We'll wet the coffee, see you in the ops room in wot, ten minutes?'. We'd also by than have run out of fresh milk, unless someone was careful enough to freeze some. We'd otherwise have to drink 'metal cow' – powdered milk, which tasted as bad as it sounds. OK in tea and coffee – crap on cornflakes!! Sometimes, we'd really suffer, and have to resort to drinking condensed milk. YEEUUUGGHHHH!!

We'd get stews (potmesses) and unidentifiable mismashes, just to ensure we used up the old food, to save having to ditch it when we got back. Other delights created for supper, to clear the older food supplies, were 'trainsmash' – a mixture of tinned tomatoes, cheese and eggs, 'babies heads' – individual steak and kidney puddings out of a tin, 'cheesyhammyeggy' – egg on cheese on ham on toast, – still something I'll eat at the drop of a hat, and 'shit on a raft' – kidneys on toast.

If we thought the food then was crap -we'd voice our feelings, and if we didn't get any sense from the caterer, we'd bitch like hell at the next 'welfare' meeting.

There are many offices aboard navy ships, from where Scribes sits (doing very little), to the regulating office (where the cementheads used to sit reading QR's & AI's (Queens regulations and Admiralty instructions) all day, and then contemplate who to pick on next), the radio office (where the flagwaggers sat playing with themselves all day, and the one compartment nobody was ever allowed in, unless you were a flagwagger, or a pig), with special other offices for various heads of department. You could always get five or ten minutes in an office, apparently disappearing off the face of the earth. Eventually, you'd get 'piped' to wherever you were supposed to be, in which case you'd already have an excuse for your boss. Your excuse would be "Well, I went down to stores, for a new pair of bats, but he wasn't there. I was JUST on my way back, when you piped me... 'Another fuckin' 'JUST' rating'...

We spent weeks attached to Middle Slip Jetty in Portsmouth, and being summer, we used to be turned-to on the upper deck, keeping a watchful eye out for the 'belles' sailing past, packed to the gunwales with grockles all on their tour of the dockyard. 'See the ships' the sign would proclaim, 'Sail on the Southsea Belle' and there they were. Our game then was to jump up and down, waving frantically at the grockles, screaming 'IF YOU GOT A BIT LAST NIGHT – WAVE', knowing they couldn't hear you above the din of their engines and the constant cackling of their tour guide. They would inevitably wave back, at which point we'd wet ourselves with laughter – it had worked again! The grockles went away happily, thinking what a happy bunch of people 'tars' were. If only they knew!!

We used to enjoy ourselves though, apart from going ashore every available night. We had a mixed mess, with all ABs' and LS's in. We got on well, we could predict who would say or do what next, and two of our games involved catching people off-guard. One way, was to wet the tip of our forefinger, creep up behind someone not paying too much attention, then ram it into his earhole. This would crack everyone else up, except for the poor sod who now had an ear full of someone else's spit. The other, was to wait until someone sat down, then drop on his lap, and fart loudly. This also used to guarantee full crack-up. Unless you were the one being sat on. Occasionally, we'd hold the target down, and THEN fart. Or we'd hold contests for the loudest, wettest, longest, brightest burning and longest burning...

Talking of annoying people, when we wore shorts, we'd sneak up behind someone, grab a handful of leg-hairs, yank hard, and run off with them. The pain from that is immediately worth smacking somebody for.

We'd also, on getting fed up with someone, take them bodily down to the tiller flat, and tie them up (or upside-down) leaving them there for some time, until we thought we'd go back and release them. I will point out right now – bullying did NOT happen, it wasn't allowed, not by QR & AI, but especially not by us. If we thought one of our 'wingers' was being picked on (and we'd all take on a couple of juniors to mentor and shepherd), there was no place on board to hide. There was then, nothing malicious in those actions, we'd do it to let off steam.

One day, we were tasked to go to H.M.S. Vernon, where they trained the 'torpedo/anti-submarine' ratings. We had to go into models there, to back up the TAS guys on their training. We cracked that within hours, and were faced with the prospect of stuff-all to do for the rest of the day. We therefore, with the full permission of the officers etc, all swapped jobs for a bit of fun. Me and my mate ended up being thrown in the deep end, with a 'torpedo' coming straight at us. Much to the surprise of the organisers, we threw the 'ship' round until it was pointing towards the 'torpedo', and casually continued to 'search' for target submarine, knowing it was now most definitely ahead of us. We located it, and 'destroyed' it, and when we got to the debrief afterwards, we were asked how we knew what to do. We replied that we'd obviously watched too many movies, but had the impression that we'd actually made the 'correct' response to the 'threat'. We swaggered out of there...

Being in Pompey also meant we were close to all the shore bases – Vernon amongst them, which was famed for its 'midweek hop', where, it was said, everyone went. Not the night we got there.

Lucky me (not) I was drafted into the 'Tartar Rifles', otherwise known as the Internal Security (IS) platoon. This was to back up the ships detachment of booties. For this, we had to go to Whale Island daily for a week, to re-learn how to strip, re-assemble and fire SLRs. Plus in the dark, by touch – whatever we were told. Also how to prevent natives from furthering their proposed riots. This was achieved us marching up and down in Whale Island, waving our rifles in a threatening manner. We re-learned how to fire them on the ranges on the edge of Portsmouth creek, then learned how to fire 'shotgun style' (open sights) at night, then finally got to Jack's delight – firing SMGs bootie style (at anything – anywhere, as long as everyone else was behind you), then finished off by manning and firing GPMGs'.

Remembering that this range overlooked the upper reaches of the estuary (The Creek), it is fair to say that if any civvy sailors up there saw a red flag flying on any range – they would stay well clear. Especially while we were about...

Then we went to another base (H.M.S. Sultan – where the navy attempted to construct engineering mechanics, to make our engines push us through the water) to practice riot control. This comprised several dozen ratings from this trainee stokers' base pretending to be yobbos – our IS platoon task was to control them. We did, but not before it got slightly out of hand, and our baby gunnery officer (Sub Lt Buckley, in charge of us) tried to stop a house brick with his chin. The brick was deliberately thrown at him, We knew that as all the other house bricks thrown were pretend ones, made from heavy sponge. Obviously 'Baby Guns' came off second best, bringing the proceedings to an abrupt pause. We did get our own back on the little moron who threw it. We were taught total self-control even though we would potentially be surrounded by hundreds, possibly thousands or irate rioters, and how to run snatch squads. We combined the two, waited for the re-run, bided our time until the right moment, and grabbed the brick-chucker. We then gave him a thorough slapping whilst official eyes were averted. We were also told to remember that we would be armed with weapons which would fire a round through a human body, and the effects it would cause. We were shown films of the effect of a round fired from an SLR through a tub of soap (said to be fairly comparable to the human body), and told to remember that while we knew our weapons would be loaded, it would come as a surprise to any rioter when he felt a 'sharp stabbing pain in the right eye, followed instantly by a fucking big hole in the back of his head'. We were told NOT to aim for legs, that was only in the movies. If you fired, you fired to kill, NOT to injure – an injured person could still do damage, a dead one could do nothing but lie there. We were also told that by law, we had to warn someone running three times to halt, before being 'allowed' to open fire. Hence 'STOPSTOPSTOPBANG!!!'

Volunteers were called for to go to Loch Ewe, a remote Loch in Western Scotland for a week, with the ships booties. We volunteered. Before we had got out of Hampshire, one of the married men was at it in the train toilet with a lady he had just met. We drank all the way to Waterloo, crossed to Kings Cross, got the overnight SLEEPER (luxury – lucky us) all the way to Inverness, where we then caught a further train across Scotland to get to Achnasheen. We detrained there, into a coach, which took us through Kinlochewe, up Loch Maree, and Gairloch before heading up Loch Ewe through Aultbea and up the coast to where we were to reside for the week – in an old naval base, unused recently, but it was an anti-submarine or torpedo something or other. To say this place was desolate was a severe understatement. Fortunately, we had taken some sensible precautions, like bringing much beer and whisky. This, however was not really necessary – there were crates of the stuff for us to quench our thirst on. Although we did have to open it ourselves…

We also noticed that where we were was a short bacteria flight away from Gruinard Island, where anthrax had been tried many years before, rendering all the sheep population slightly dead, and preventing life of any sort on the island for a lot of years after that. We'd sniff the air very cautiously after we found that out.

We quickly found the short cut back to Aultbea – a seven mile walk back down the road we'd just arrived on, so we passed on that one just now, preferring to stay in the base. We weren't prepared for the next morning – the booties physically dragged each of us out of our pits, throwing us into that nasty, cold Loch. And all this before breakfast. I should point out, that in those days, if the marine was told to jump off the ship as it sailed, he would – such was his belief in 'The Corps'. It did though let them in for stick – we'd tease them with remarks like "Royal Marines, running round the World – GO. What kept you laddie", or "Royal Marines, Jumping in the air GO. Who told you to come down". It never failed to get a bite from them. Mind you, they got their own back with this throwing into the Loch business.

We spent several relaxing (!) days there, swimming, crossing the Loch to the island in it, exploring there, here, everywhere. Even walking steadily to Aultbea, and unsteadily back, after hunting for cockles on the beach whilst waiting for the pub to open.

The booties then decided to go yomping up a hill – An Teallach – 3000 feet and more. And what was more – they expected us to go with them. We got back into the coach, drove to the base of the mountain, and camped out, with all the survival rations etc. Next morning we tried it, but with our sailor senses dulled by weeks of inactivity (and alcohol) we gave up and left it to the booties. We returned to the croft and attempted to tickle some trout instead.

We got back to the base, and found we were going back to Pompey next day, so we had one final hoolie there, which I remember our own three-badged-AB Dago Robson clearly calling the wife of the ships bootie officer a 'Dumb Cluck', because she couldn't understand what he was gibbering drunkenly about. Fortunately for him it came out as above, instead of what he really meant to call her. She was actually quite fortunate to receive speech – Dago normally could only manage a high pitched whine when pissed. We, though, could understand by the pitch what he wanted – it was either a waz, a drink, or his pit. Dago persistently drank Bacardi, asking everyone – for some reason – "How's yer neck, rabbithead?".

That was a good week.

Every morning on board, if we were duty watch the night before, we would have to do 'user checks', where we would close up all the gunnery, sonar and ops room crews, to test out all comms, radars (if we were allowed to transmit), sonar (same as above) – which all took up to an hour if we stretched it out amongst the coffee and late breakfasts nicked from the galley on the way past, and would help stabilise the obligatory hangover. We would hear, from the gunners "Test bells buzzers lamps and remote firing circuits", whilst we would run round checking every communication circuit between the gloom room, and anywhere we talked to. The plots would all be run up and tested against all the radars in use, the gun turrets and Seacat launchers would swing and track invisible targets, and this would all be done with our 'serious' faces on. However it would normally degenerate afterwards, with everyone on the various intercom sets taking the waz out of everyone else.

Our new PRI – Mac (MacDonald) was newly passed out from Dryad, from his 'I' course, and had a lot of time for us. He'd been a Leading Seaman on his last ship, and was still very much aware of 'the ropes'. He also drove a TR4 or 5, and was thus poplar when it came to getting lifts anywhere. He would organise who would test what (we had more-or-less identical radar to the Zulu, only newer). We weren't normally allowed to transmit the bedstead radar within so many miles of shore, as it tended to have an adverse reaction on television pictures, so we either pretended, or just checked the surface radars.

Our forays into Pompey – down the 'strip' or what was left of it – continued, we would eagerly look forward to the weekends, for the previously discussed 'homers', but if we didn't fancy that, or a weekend up the line, we'd do our Friday duty (or 'sub' someone), then turn-to on the Saturday morning. This is something of a misnomer – turning to on a Saturday, means everyone on board. (So as a diversion, we'd stop overnight at the Sailors Rest outside the dockyard gates. This cost something ridiculous like five bob a night). If we were aboard, we'd turn-to, skive off somewhere, then sit drinking coffee, smoking, telling sea-stories all morning. Until stand-easy, at which point we'd go and get a cup of tea. Saturday morning also meant the chefs weren't too quick to clear up the galley after breakfast, which we could get (if you knew what to say to them), most of the morning. Having eventually made it to secure, we'd gobble lunch, change, and be ashore PDQ. We'd start in the nearest pub to the ship, then crawl up the Hard, or up to the 'strip'. It was then left to see what developed. Sometimes it would be drink to closing time, hit the 'offie' for a carryout – preferably sherry, cider or lagers, then take them down the (Southsea) front to continue the session until the pubs re-opened. Remember – this was in the days when boozers didn't open all day!! Otherwise, we'd get ratted, and trawl the shops, annoying the shopkeepers, trying on clothes to pass the time, with no intention of buying anything. Or we'd go to Billy Mannings (funfair) on the beach, and spend mindless time shooting ducks, spinning the shit (telling stories) to anyone who'd listen, throwing darts, throwing up...

Bored, we'd go back to the ship, crash out for a couple of drunken hours, then attempt to get up again to go back ashore. This was never as easy as it seemed. In theory – terrific – get shake off mate at 1700, shower, supper, back off to shore. In practice, get shake, get another shake, get several more shakes. Get up eventually, extremely grumpily, sit in very cold shower for long time, attempting to get sober. No effect? Never mind – big supper, then ashore. There was a brilliant drink around then, called 'Thunderburg'. I have no idea what was in it, but it was, most definitely, kill or cure. You either felt better immediately, or you tossed your ring, THEN felt better. We found other cures – if you were afflicted with the tom-tits, you drank Barley Wine:

actually an extremely strong, potent beer, in a very small bottle. This acted like the cement you got from the 'doc on board. Barley Wine was otherwise consumed by topping up your half-empty pint with one. Eventually, your pint would be Barley Wine – and no 'bitter'. Got you very drunk, very rapidly.

The Tartar was re-commissioned in January 1974, and was the tenth to bear the name – the first was launched in 1702, and lasted until 1755. The motto was 'Without Fear'. They got that right. We never ran away from anything! Further, the Tartars, led by Genghis Khan, were renowned for their ruthless ferocity and fighting expertise. That would certainly come into play during the commission ahead. We also had our ships mascot – "Dago", the three badged AB, who would dress up as Genghis for each event, such as the CTP or Open Day, or for sailing at 'alpha', standing on the bridge roof brandishing sword, straggly beard (his own actually) and shield.

Chapter 21
Another Crack at Portland

During the weeks leading up to Portland, we did the same things as I had done on the Zulu – basin trials, compass swing, hurtling up and down the Channel and the Solent, staying out overnight, working up various ops-room crews and all, while the riffraff stayed below out of the way. We also, one weekend, were all sent to live ashore at Victory, whilst the whole ship was defumigated and blitzed, against the inevitable, well travelled cockies. We'd see them scuttle away whenever you switched on the dining hall, or galley lights, so we knew it was well overdue. Funny, I hadn't seen any on the Zulu – must have been that they couldn't survive the Northern atmosphere. Or Mac's guts.

Eventually we sailed for more time in Portland, for our work up.

As I said, we had newer radar than the Zulu – we had 993 which was very uprated 293, and 1006, which was very much better than the 978. It still didn't stop us reporting 'Nab Tower' in the middle of the Solent as a contact on a course of … at some knots. It took us all a while to get used to that one. Any RP who has ever forgotten to take account of the tide will appreciate this gaffe, followed by derisive laughter from the bridge, and severe tormenting from their colleagues when off watch. Of course I never did it…

We would also be able to get the lighthouse off Portland travelling. Mind you, we NEVER reported 'the Nab' to the OOW deliberately to hear him say 'Roger – report'.

Being i/c of the radar watch at steaming stations was great. I learned how to tell the course and speed of a contact (another ship) on radar, by eye (after much practice) without having to work it out on the old mechanical plotting tables (this was a long time before computers assisted the operators), which made me favourite for any exercises we did with other ships, where we had to work out what they were doing, and report to them, We would get points for 'near', and massive points for spot on. Which I could do within moments of them changing course.

I also got good at playing with the air radar. The day we exercised with a shore base, reporting all air contacts within a 12000 square mile area, my team did such a good job in the air-side, that the shore controllers were forced to admit they had never heard such accurate or good reporting. Our 'air' boss – Lt Johnson – was over the moon that day – as were we. I got him a beauty – I would do raid reporting over the radio, to other ships and units.

I had to wear a headset to do this, which I would talk into, but as the transmitter (pressel) switch was on the floor, I had to consciously press it with my foot, which meant leaning forward slightly. As part of my 'net controller' duties, I would be talking over the radio pretty much incessantly, reporting the air-contacts which we could see, to other units without the radar, who could therefore not 'see' them. I had to break the 'chat' every few seconds, to allow other units to butt in, if necessary. All the time, we would use callsigns to attract the attention of the other units. Occasionally, this 'butt-in' would be a deaf dimwit asking me to re-report something, which I would do. Once when Johno was engrossed in my reporting, I 'broke', waited a few seconds, leaned forward as if to transmit, 'called' his callsign, and said "Are you fucking deaf – I'll tell you this once more, then swim over and smack you one" The rest of my team cracked up, Johnos' headset flew off as he dashed over to me, screaming "Whacker, did you really say that, did you? Did you?". I then confessed I hadn't actually transmitted, at which point he saw the funny side, and laughed, with relief. He was a good officer who COULD take a joke. His opposite number was known as 'Golden Bollocks' (Gordon-Lennox), who could also be relied upon to be on the receiving end – if he was in a good mood.

I have to say that while we were on watch, with anything between four and twenty plus people closed up in the plastic palace, we would all talk incessantly, about anything or nothing. Most likely, the subject would be what we did on our last run, or how we'd spent the past few days winding someone up, or how we were going to 'fit' someone who was winding us up. The conversations would last for hours and cover all manner or topics, all running from one to another. The best topics were either 'when I get ashore in…', or 'my pasha back home…', or we would resort to the inevitable black-cat'ing. 'When I was on the…'

When we met another navy ship at sea especially one of our own (we'd normally do this on a prearranged time to rendezvous), we in the ops room would normally have to hold an exercise of some description. Before closing with them, we'd be talking to them on the vhf radio nets. But before we could do that, we'd have to prove to each other we were who we said we were. How we could possibly be anything else in that particular place, at that exact time – I know not. Nevertheless – we'd have to exchange details. We'd normally use our unique international callsigns, but if we felt anything like compromised, we'd use previously published other, coded callsigns. Whatever, when we finally got though on the net, we'd 'authenticate' each other using a numerical code. This entailed asking the other unit(s) to 'authenticate' a two number/letter code. If he responded with the correct

every night. We found the best mosquito bite preventative was lots and lo of rum. Taken internally. Mixed with other strong liquor, and flavourings Well it worked for us…

By now we were in the pattern of marching past the Admiral, at which point we would be instructed -one -two -three "Good Morning Ethel" at the absolute tops of our voices. Sometimes, Ethels head would appear from the window, accompanied by a wan smile, and a weary wave.

Towards the end of the week, it had been noted by Guns that I was taking loads of photos, and after some discussion, I was persuaded to take the official camera, use official film, and be the official photographer for the parade and march past. I agreed, but I really would have preferred to be on the parade rather than observing – honest!! Nevertheless, when it came to the parade proper, I put on my ice-cream suit along with the lads, and attended – snapping away like a maniac until both cameras ran out of films. It was a wonderful atmosphere for the whole of those proceedings. Something else that will live in my memories for a long while.

That final night in English Harbour, while waiting for the Tartar to come back for us – we put together all our remaining BWI (British West Indies) dollars, hired a local reggae/steel band, bought loads of food and booze, then invited all those people who had been so kind to us during our time there to attend. I have to admit the turnout was not what we had anticipated – we expected a few, but word got out, and we subsequently couldn't move in our digs for bodies, there were hundreds!! Everyone, apparently, had a good time, and it was with great sadness we shouted our final 'Good Morning' to Ethel as we made our final journey in the dilapidated coach back to St Johns to meet with and reboard the ship.

Next stop was Chaguaramus in Northern Trinidad, for a mini-refit. We carried this out alongside a civilian dockyard, moored against a large floating dock, in which ships were bottom-scraped, before being repainted. This was done at such a furious rate, it seemed a new ship went through every other day (or two), and the noise was literally deafening as they did the scraping bit with shot-blasters all day, and all night.

Across the bay from the jetty, was one of the very few proper beaches boasted by Trinidad, with the inevitable bar. We would either launch the canoe, and paddle that across, or we would dive off the ship, swim across the bay, dry off and drink, then walk back to the ship. Or we'd walk round to keep our dollars dry, even though the barkeeper happily accepted our wet ones.

The canoe was the ship's own, bought – I think – by the welfare committee. It was lashed under the seaboat, or somewhere for most of its career, and anyone could use it. It came to pass that me and George took a ing to using it as a taxi between us and this bar, and we discovered the fastest way to achieve our objective was to carefully drop the canoe straight over the side, chuck the paddles in the sea, then jump in after it all. This meant we got wet, but those BWI dollars were still acceptable wet or dry. Once in the oggin, we'd mount the canoe from the rear, slide up until one was in, then the other would follow. We'd recover the paddles, and hurtle across the bay to the bar. …But I can't remember how we ever got it back, due to the absorbtion of too much Carib, and Mount Gay.

One afternoon, I started swimming around off the beach, complete with obligatory mask, snorkel and speargun, looking down, as you do, when something moved underneath me. It looked like eyes, but on closer investigation, it had a long tail, and was – in fact – a very, very large ray of some description. There is a scene in JAWS where the bathers burst from the sea in panic. I walked across the waves to get out – followed by the population of Trinidad. I'm sure the ray was scared to death by all this, but it was a while before anyone plucked up courage and went back in to see if it had gone away.

We also had a weekend banyan, taking the whaler several miles around the coast to a bay, setting up camp, then realising we had loads of Mount Gay (rum), but no mixers. Seawater isn't really recommended but did at a push, but 'Carib' (the local gorgeous beer) boilermakers are. We spent a strange weekend there, as one of the first things I did was stub and break a toe. I hobbled everywhere for weeks afterwards. Potentially more rewarding though, was as the boats co'x'n, I was offered several thousand dollars by one of the locals' for our whaler, but could only wonder what my excuse would be for losing it, bearing in mind that wherever I would need to lose it, the ships' divers would eventually go and take a look for it, with an official view to getting it back. With this in mind, and after much thought, I declined his offer.

In this tiny bay, we were surrounded by the islands' rich, who would 'powerboat' to this bay each weekend for recreation. Even though it was heavily populated by barracuda, which we drunkenly chased with our spear-guns' as we swam in circles. There were also strange noises, later identified as being local monkeys, and flashing lights in the evening, which had us wondering at the Mount Gay, until we realised it was fireflies! With them and the humming birds, it was a real wildlife place.

One fine day, George and I went into town, and had our photos taken in the passport office, on a whim, but really because we had an ulterior motive. We had dozens of copies made, which we collected some days later, and took away. We then placed an ad in Melody Maker for young ladies to write to bored sailors. We had thousands, and thousands of replies, and ended up dishing them out by area to nearly all the unattached – and to some o. attached – ratings on board. That passed several hours, and led to c writing, who ended up by marrying me after we had corresponded for man many letters.

We found a 'Seaman's Mission' too, one that did real chips, and proper cheese (NOT Spanish) omelettes, which we would eat whilst watching Sesame Street!

The favoured local food in Trinidad, though, was 'Hot Roti, which was made from something we never did identify, but it didn't taste like anything we knew. It was meaty, very hot, and went down well after a night out. As did the local chicken, cooked on street corners, or in the small shops which seemed to be open at all times of day and night. Also the goat curry – freely available, if you felt brave enough… There was a drawback, the following days would prove that if the bottom hadn't fallen out of your world, the world would certainly fall out of your bottom. And again. And again, until all traces had gone, and once again you could entertain the Carib and Mount Gay.

We sailed from Trinidad the first time, and went to Tobago, and from there we sailed for Barbados for Christmas.

After first attempting to water ski off the back of our Dory in Tobago, I decided I didn't want to do that any more, so I aqualung'ed off the beach, and was attracted by the conch shells littering the sandy sea bottom. I decided one would be nice as a souvenir, but was not ready for what happened. I dived down and picked up the conch. As I did so, several thin black fingers emerged from the open end, grabbing MY fingers. I almost dumped in my trunks. I dropped the shell, instantly. However, I was not going to be put off that easily, and eventually the hermit crab in residence was forced to swim off to fight for another home. I still have that conch shell, and smile whenever I remember the surprise I got.

I had never spent a Christmas away from home before then, and never expected in my wildest dreams that I would ever go to Barbados – but to fulfill two at once was fantastic, given our circumstances and where we were.

We moored opposite the omnipresent cruise ship, put the Christmas tree on the top of the '965', then after we'd added the hurricane hawsers (just in case) we legged it away on two days station leave. We headed into town, and once past there, we started knocking on hotel doors to see if they had room. "We", was George and me. We felt like Joseph & Mary, but ended up in a self-catering apartment overlooking the swimming pool, the beach, and the sea. It was amazing there. We stocked up with some food, but didn't expect to eat it. We also laid on booze – then invited the rest of the mess round for a party. We ate soft boiled eggs and toast, washed down with Bacardi and

e. It was odd – sailors our age sitting in these extremely plush apartments the very (then) exclusive Barbados, complete with fridge and cooker, booze p to our eyeballs, totally relaxed, troughing boiled eggs.

The next day, we ventured as far as the hotel pool, and spent the day in there, climbing out only to relieve ourselves. The pool, you see, had a bar in it, which you swam round, whilst clutching your Banana Daiquiri. Far too much temptation!

All too soon we returned, on Christmas Eve, and rose bright and early Christmas Day. As I said, I'd never experienced this away from home before, but the day started slowly, with breakfast, then decorating the mess, then prezzy opening, then lunch (served by the wardroom), and all kinds of abnormal, traditional naval things. A really excellent day. Oh yes, and extra beer rations, plus the extra rum and Bacardi which somehow appeared, it having previously been carefully and inconspicuously smuggled aboard. Eventually, much later that evening, we crawled ashore.

At that time, there was a new item of informal wear, called a personalised T-shirt. Barbados sold them – you could have anything you wanted printed, provided a) it was available, b) it wasn't offensive. I wore mine, with a cartoon dog, emblazoned with "Whacker" (my official navy name – all "Paynes'" were called that), until it rotted away. Then I bought a new one! There was also a brilliant market inside and out of the 'Customs House' at the top of the harbour, where we brought some terrific rabbits.

One thing I always remember, is that whenever I was away from home, either for a birthday or at Christmas, I always received (from 'Elizabeth the Chef' bakers via my Mum) a huge fruit cake from home, in a tin, nice and fresh, which we would all tuck in to, washed down, as usual, with nice cold beer!

We sailed from there – and realized that was the first Windies stop we had made were it HADN'T rained.

A 'letter home' published in the ships magazine summed up one persons feelings about our trip so far.

My Dearest Flower

I thought you might like to hear how I was getting on, as it has been three months since I left. I hope you are not still waiting at Southsea to see us leave, as we slipped out at night,. The Skipper said it made it easier for some of the officers that way.

We've been to some rotten places – Bermuda, San Juan, Tortola, Antigua and Trinidad. I hardly ever go ashore, as they are all so different to Pompey. They are all full of half built houses, and everyone moves very slowly – except for the one who stole my wallet. And the taxi driver who almost ran me over. I tried to stop the thief, but one of my shoes had earlier gone through a window when I kicked a fag packet. Pity, they were your brothers' shoes, the ones I borrowed to get married in. Anyway, it was difficult to run in just one platform shoe, and I lost all my money.

In Tortola, the Governor asked me up for a cocktail party. He was very nice, and I think his wife liked the joke about the male parrot with no legs holding on to his perch. Perhaps I shouldn't have told her in front of the Commodore, as I got a job change next day – I am now 'captain of the heads'. All of them.

My messmates are ok, but they go ashore too much for my liking, and come back smelling of rum. I prefer to stay on board and save up to buy you a present, and also to pay the repair bill to Mr Mopedman in Bermuda. The jetty there was very narrow, and it was difficult to decide what to do when it started to skid like that.

Your letters are a great comfort, but please resend number 53 (which didn't arrive), as my messmates want to know what happened to the daughter of the old witch at number 8.

I may not have time to write again before we get back on the 3rd of April, as we have to work very hard, however do not worry too much, as the master at arms says he is taking a personal interest in my welfare.

Please imagine your Christmas Present this year – it is a diamond ring.

Yours, Everloving,

Bill Barnacle.

...although I 'm not sure he was being totally truthful.

After a fantastic Christmas, we went back to work, exercising frequently off Puerto Rico, doing tracking and gunnery shoots, and one day arrived in Roosevelt Roads one fine morning, and moored opposite our sister ship – the Eskimo, full of old buddies. Roosy Roads, we were told, was where the Royal

Family would have been evacuated to if things had gone badly during WW2. Or was it the US government?

Back to the Eskimo – they had been there a couple of days, apparently, and we either called round, or were called round for beers in respective messdecks, to swap stories. We queried the unusual amount of facial and other injuries they sported, and were told how they'd been to the PX (US Forces NAAFI), the previous evening, but had been physically attacked by the resident, predominantly non-white USN population. We were told even the rest of the USN (white) guys backed off – even the Shore Patrol.

We went ashore that night – two ships companies worth of libertymen, in several coaches, to investigate. We travelled in coaches because it was a very long way to walk. When we arrived at the PX, we started to chat to both the (white) US servicemen and Eskimo's already there, and exchanged beers and pleasantries. For no reason at all, (apart from he was dancing with his bird), a large different coloured guy started to verbally abuse one of ours, which was just what we had been waiting for. The result was like the Clint Eastwood 'Dirty Harry' film, where everyone in the bar exploded into a fight, with the inevitable glasses being thrown, chairs being smashed on people, and tables collapsing. In all, really good fun and just what we needed to let off some of the steam which had developed whilst at sea. After several (!!) minutes, the Yank Shore Patrol, accompanied by our own duty SP (complete with helves although the Yanks were gun-totin'), moved in, but stayed on the edge, not really wishing to get involved. While we were on top, and to prevent further injuries to the 'troublemakers' the SP moved in, arrested and carted off all the trouble-makers (none of our crews though), escorted all of us back to our bus, grinned and shook their fingers – and sent us back to the ships. The fight was never mentioned again, and there was no more trouble any time we ever went there again. A good, successful night ashore then.

As an aside, there was an RN 'pecking order', as perceived by us as RPs'. At the bottom of the pile were waffoos of any description. Above them came middies, then tiffies, then other pigs, then S&S (pen-pushers, stewards etc). Then greenies, then stokers, then flagwaggers, then us seamen. And amongst seamen, gunners, then 'TAS', and finally us RPs'. So we looked down on every other branch. There was always considerable further rivalry between the various branches, and we would always slag each other off to a considerable extent. If that extent meant going to action stations (fighting) to prove the point, then we would. This rivalry was only exceeded by inter ship rivalry, where we would defend the honour of our ship and, therefore, our shipmates, no matter whether they were waffoos, stewards – whatever. This in turn would be elevated to inter-squadron fights. This was then exceeded by inter-service spats. The only thing over that, was that we'd have even fought with or alongside the crabs and the pongos' against any other countries services. Which was what happened here with the 'Mo, although there was only us very proud sailors to represent the nation!! So we did.

To explain something else – all Pussers ships are put into squadrons. Each ship's captain would normally be a commander, but the deputy squadron leader, and squadron leader would be skippered by a full captain, although they might 'carry' a Vice-Admiral. There were many of these squadrons, and while we would all mostly act independently, we would occasionally muster as the squadron or part of. Then the squadron pecking order ran in terms of superiority of your skipper. It followed that the junior skipper therefore meant his ship was the gash-boat of the squadron, and had to 'pipe' first. The boss, known as 'Daddy-D', would have a large stripe painted round his funnel, so everyone knew he was more important than the other ships in his company. There would then be a mix of frigates – general purpose, anti-air, anti-sub, to form an effective mix of ships and skills.

And whenever we met Daddy-D, if he was showing the black ring, and flying the spotty flag, it meant only one thing. Rounds, and a pep-talk. Oh lucky us!!!

So back to Puerto Rico and Roosy Roads, where another night there, we reasoned that if we were on an island, then it couldn't be all that big. So we left the PX, and started walking to San Juan. Except that we quickly became lost in the vast sugar fields. The upside was that we swiftly acquired a taste for the canes, but got even more lost. After some time, we stumbled across a road, where we got a taxi back to the PX for last orders (free to us, after the earlier fight) – and the coach back to the ship. PR is a big, big island.

We left Puerto Rico, went back to mooching round the islands, looking for drug smugglers, gun-runners – whatever – and one day we stopped at Mustique where we were given permission to hold a banyan on the beach. We duly landed the whaler, full of sailors, beer, and barbecue gear/food – and held an impromptu party, at which several personalities attended. One in particular (I hope that one day he reads this and remembers it, I have always held two grudges against him) was sitting on the jetty reading a book. We went across to him, and started talking to quite the most unresponsive person I have ever met, even for a "major rock star". When he did manage to grunt in response to a question, we got bored, decided to buy our own beer, said 'No big ting', and started to walk off. He asked 'What was that?'. Again, we said 'No big ting – it doesn't really matter'. And continued to walk away. He refused to buy us a beer, first grudge, and then had the brass neck to release a record later, with a catchphrase that sounded suspiciously like our favourite saying – second grudge.

We were given the run of the beach, and met other equally famous people there, people who did talk to us. I went for a sailboard ride, fell off, and pierced my foot with sea-egg spines. You really, really know they're there when the sharp spines penetrate your skin to release poison that hurts like hell. One of the famous people – a model at that time, and a 'Lady', explained what to do to 'relieve' the pain, which I did behind a bush. The pain went almost immediately but the spines can still be seen in my toe.

When we went back to the ship, we asked whether we could go back that evening, as we had been invited to a barbecue the famous were holding for us, in return. We were held back – the wardroom took over that one...

During our West Indian travails, we used to have a large gang of up to fifteen or so, who'd always be ashore together. This would be handy when getting into trouble, better for looking after the fallers down. It guaranteed we'd all get back safely. However, when getting brown on the nearest beach, it meant we could organise sudden sports events. Like volleyball. We'd play that without warning, but with string stretched between trees. More than likely, we'd end up with tourists joining in, or playing against. These games could last hours/until we got too dry/until we got distracted by something else. If we decided to 'pose', we'd go into 'pyramid mode'. Eight or nine in an inward facing circle for the base, five or six for the next level, three for the next, with the drunkest climbing to the top. More often than not we'd collapse before we got anyone to the top. Occasionally we'd do it, which would spark bigger and larger pyramids from the beach competition. Of course, we'd have this well practiced, and could do it easily when we had to. We would also make pyramids with all the beer cans we drained, forcing anyone else to compete with us to make bigger ones.

We went to Martinique and looked at a volcano, we went to St Kitts where we drank our way through the 'Holiday Inn' drinks menu, including watery-eye-makers like Yellow Bird, Coco Punch, Zombie and Liamuiga Cocktail, brilliant colours, superb tastes, no effect whatsoever the first time round the menu. So, we went through it again, then tried to walk back to the ship through and round the many sugar cane fields. We forgot that the ship was moored in water so clear you could look over the side and see the bottom, and that we had to catch the whaler back. Unfortunately, bad weather struck during our run ashore, and the RatRat had sailed without us to lay off safely. Which meant we spent a night sleeping on the floor of a prison cell in the local police station, until we were roused the following morning by the ships' siren. Blearily – we climbed aboard the whaler and returned – then sailed

honour to actually physically serve our Monarch, and something I will always remember. We also bought some wonderful rabbits, mostly onyx, sombreros and ponchos.

Our six-month cruise was rounded off with several days in Florida, at Fort Lauderdale, where we ran trips to Disneyworld. These started at 0300, with a six-hour drive, and we spent the whole day there, queuing for rides, again and again (especially Space Mountain) before meeting Mr Michael Mouse and his mates. Of course – we went there in rig, so as to make sure we stood out (and grippo'ed). We had an absolutely brilliant day out there, buying all kinds of souvenirs – backscratchers, ear-hats, giant bears, small bears, sweatshirts, and insulated mugs with our own pictures in, which (some of us) kept for years, before climbing back, totally exhausted, into the coach for the return trip to Lauderdale. It was during this trip that we first discovered aftershave. Hai Karate from a vending machine on the wall of a service area on the way – we stank for days afterwards – that smell would not shower out!

We visited the local Sea World, and watched various nutters wrestle alligators by sticking their (the alligators) heads under their (the keepers) chins. Scary, and potentially painful, especially if the keeper hasn't shaved first. They weren't little alligators either! There was also the shark feeding, though we'd done that before on the Zulu! Other than that – we spent our time in a club/bar, called The Button On The Beach, where we also enjoyed ourselves.

One run I do remember, but I forget where we ended up, was where we could buy jugs of beer, which we genteelly poured out into our glasses, which we then drained before refilling the jug. We could finally stand it no longer, and the inevitable happened, and we finished up with our own jugs, which we drank from. Well, it saved all that pouring into glasses, so at least it saved on the bar-owners washing up.

We sailed from Lauderdale, called in at Bermuda once more to refuel, then legged it home with all our rabbits to dish out.

I recall that on the way back, after we finally left Bermuda, we conducted a 'Burial At Sea'. Apparently someone had died, and had always wanted to be buried at sea, so we sailed, and obliged. The coffins are weighted down so they sink immediately, instead of bobbing around taking in water. All very dignified as we stood on the quarterdeck in our (now even more gleaming after all those washes) white suits as an honour guard.

Slightly after that, we held a hula-hula competition. We spent hours stripping down lengths of manilla, tying them onto a waistband, then combing them out, until we had near as dammit authentic grass skirts which – coupled with our stuffed rapidly created bras, gave a good reproduction of the real thing. Except that we all had hairy chests. And we all sported a large set!! That was a good afternoon, especially the traditional banyan on the quarterdeck later on. We were very inventive – we could produce anything to create anything, especially if it was for a laugh, as the hula-hula was…

On returning to the UK, we had steamed 26,736 miles, spent 1908 hours under way, burning 4680 tonnes of fuel. We had eaten 70000 pounds of spuds, 4030 of sausages, enough to reach 2.5 miles, 60000 eggs, 7616 pounds of sugar, 7000 pounds of baked beans, drunk (!) 60000 tins of assorted beer, but only 36000 cans of soft drinks. One million and sixty five thousand cigarettes had been bought/issued, and 750,000 pounds of 'funny money' had been handled. We had also seen 91 films, and the lawnmower had flown 110.5 hours, making 284 landings, flying 9950 miles, with an estimated 2,685,900 rotor rotations.

Chapter 24

Off Fishing, but Not as You Know It

After a mini refit in Pompey, and some more well-earned leave, we sailed round to Chatham for Navy Days. Now there IS an experience, volunteering to be a guide to show the tourists round. We would offer, and sometimes succeed, in getting people to come with us to see the 'Golden Rivet' in the engine room. This rivet is (obviously) made of gold, and is always the last rivet to be placed into any warship. A very interesting sight. That and the place amidships on 'Tribals', where the whole ship used to flex as they went through the seas. I can still picture the 'flap' slightly in front of the for'r'd funnel, AND see it moving whilst traversing high seas at speed.

The Tartar sailed up into the North Sea, into exercises protecting North Sea gas fields and rigs, and during that time we went as far as Scapa Flow. We all knew what had happened, so when we had a 'first watch party' that night at anchor, we were most careful to NOT throw our empties overboard. We also visited Orkney. Enough said! We then traversed the North Sea – yet again – over to Velje in Denmark with a trip to Legoland, having worked out that we would need to pay the equivalent of two pounds for a beer. Even back in 1975! Legoland though, was enormous fun.

It was during this trip, that I took a very impressive photograph of an oilrig, with flames from the gases being burned off leaping from the top. It made a wonderful, stark photograph, which won me a competition. It was only the local WI from the village, where my Mum entered it, but it was nevertheless a terrifically composed (deliberately – honest!!) photograph.

At some point, it was announced via the notice board/list that we would be holding a wild dog shoot when we stopped in the Orkneys, and that volunteers should muster on the quarterdeck for training, after having drawn helves and gaiters from the gunners store, then collected their bagmeal from the galley. Bagmeals are like picnics – useful in all circumstances, usually comprising a hard boiled egg (or two) several rounds of sandwiches, and an apple or an orange. If anyone went to the Chief Supply Accountant (no point in merely going to the duty chef – it HAD to be the Chief SA) for a bagmeal, the buzz would fly round that something was afoot. Why else would you need a bagmeal at sea? And the stornophone (radio) from the wireless office. By the time the volunteers had mustered, we were there to watch, as the booties then read the rules. "Do NOT hit the dogs on the head with the helve – it makes them mad. Go for their legs. Marine Gardener will now hide, and pretend to be a dog, he is hiding somewhere on the quarter-deck, and will jump out on you. You have to subdue him." We stood on top of "Y" gun to watch, as a young, gormless sailor crept round, looking left and right for the "dog", fearlessly making threatening gestures with his tightly gripped helve. When Jock jumped out of a hatch at him., he reacted well, trying to down Jock, but as Jock was well over 6' 5" tall, and hideously ugly (but a brilliant geezer) – he stood no chance. Jock chased him round on all-fours, barking at him. Us? – we pissed ourselves enough to nearly fall off the gun-turret. By the time the first one caught on he was being seriously wound up, it was time for the next one, fortunately waiting in the wings, not allowed to see his predecessor. As the saying goes – we laughed until the tears ran down our trouser legs.

At one point, we also anchored off Rothesay, and had a terrific run ashore, when the pubs finally opened for the two hour lunchtime session – following which we ambled back to the libertyboat, returning fairly sober to the ship. You see – we walked that far trying to find an open pub, that by the time we sussed it was only the hotel that was open, we were too late to make as sensible go of it. We sailed down to Tobermorey for an evening, though I was duty, then eventually back to Pompey. That was all actually quite a nice few weeks, looking at all the scenery.

We also had a weekend in Le Havre, and we took the opportunity to get the train to Paris for the day, where we spent the day running between the best sights, up the Eiffel tower, up the Arc De Triumph etc, before getting the train back to the ship.

At one point, the ship sailed an apparent 'round the coast' jobby, we exercised off Cape Wrath (well named), crossed the top of Scotland, cruised through and stopped at several west coast islands including Tobermorey, then Douglas (Isle of Man) very, very briefly, before a weekend jolly in Liverpool. We were so impressed there, we all took short weekends. Straight home, on the first available train out.

While off that coast, we found Rockall, (which rhymes with what is...) a small, but high rock several hundred miles out into the Atlantic. We finally located it on radar, and landed the 'bee' on it with a flag, reclaiming our sovereignty over it. It is a well-named place, there is, literally, rock all there except waves, and more waves.

We discovered an instant and miraculous cure for acne one fine day – we had the G6 (gas turbine drive) on the Tartar, which had to be lit by hand allegedly, and was prone to flashbacks. One clanky got too close to the flashback, losing his eyebrows, and the front hair on his head, plus several layers of skin from his mush. We took great delight in winding him up about that for weeks afterwards – but it really did get rid of his acne. Temporarily at least, until his face grew back again.

At the end of September we were due to sail on Fishery Protection duties around the North coast of Norway. Before we sailed, I invested in a duvet and cover, which, in light of where we were going, proved to be a sound investment. Bearing in mind our mess beneath the quarterdeck was separated from the elements by some fractions of inches of steel, our after-mess used to boil in hot climes, but freeze in cold ones. My quilt kept me warm while my mates wrapped themselves in more and more blankets. It also took me seconds to make up my bed daily, rather than the minutes for my oppos. I could therefore lay in bed longer in the mornings, which was the true reason for my buying it.

We sailed, we went as far north as Spitzbergen (but didn't stop), and as far east as Murmansk. In-between, we stopped at Bergen and caught the funicular to the top of the mountain overlooking it, Tromso – with an amazing bridge, and Harstaad. We also called at Hammerfest – THE most northerly town you can get to. Norway was beautiful, but expensive. We toured round Bear Island and got our "Blue Nose" certificates, for crossing into the Arctic Circle. It got cold towards the end of the tour, but nothing extreme. We were though very fortunate one night, to see the extremely beautiful Aurora Borealis or Northern Lights. Something else I spent hours fascinated by.

I wasn't quite so fascinated by the storm we sailed in to as we left one of the ports. We were up a fjord, but as we hit the open sea, we were buffeted by severe storm force winds. I was on watch in the gloom room after we sailed, where we had a wind gauge and a tilt meter. The wind gauge went off the clock in one movement. Immediately, we tilted over, and most alarmingly, we kept going, and going. In the centre of the gloom room was a chair, a very comfortable one, and very high. Just high enough to be able to use the PPI radar, plus be able to reach various microphones, radar controls etc. Fit for a captain, when he was in the ops room. And fit for the i/c of the watch to sit in, with his feet on the display. So during steaming watches, the i/c of the watch would plant himself in the chair, and not leave it until relieved. Perks of the job. As the ship kept tilting, and I swear it went beyond the 45 degrees, there was a crack and a crash as the deckbolts holding the chair (and me) parted company, depositing me on the floor. Except that the deck was rapidly becoming the bulkhead as the opposite bulkhead became the deckhead!. There were all kinds of crashing noises from all over the ship, until suddenly, we started going upright again. There was untold damage, not to the ship, but to people in bunks who suddenly found themselves deposited on the deck.

That was a scary one. We thought we'd lost the top hamper (the air radar) that night – it was rumoured to detach itself if the ship tilted too far, but it didn't that night.

We continued past Murmansk, and were eventually overflown by a Russian 'Bear' aircraft, who continued to scan us and our movements for several hours. We were apparently further east then, than the Israel.

Talking of things going bump in the night – in extremely rough weather, the ship would occasionally meet 'milestones', which were larger than average waves, met every mile (or so hence, funnily enough, 'milestones'). These would literally shake the ship, and could cause storm damage (as per the Zulu on our way to Gib). The Tartar was a vicious cow in rough weather, but we found if you went right up in the bows, to the buffers store, if you connected with a milestone, you would actually go weightless for some seconds as the bows first shot up, then dropped leaving you several feet off the deck. Of course, she could corkscrew at the same time, making it difficult to walk the Burma Road (the main drag below decks on a ship) without ricocheting from bulkhead to deckhead. But when she hit milestones AND corkscrewed was where the fun would start. All top bunks had bars to stop the occupant from rolling over and out – hence the expression 'over and out…', and had straps to tie yourself in. And again, you could set the angle of the bed to form a wedge in which you would attempt to settle and sleep. There also had to be grab handles above the bed on which you would swing yourself upwards, then across to your pit. At least – that was the theory. During one such storm, the LMA was piped to my mess while I was on watch – it transpired that one chap during the corkscrewing, had swung himself up, and was in the middle of the 'over' bit. He let go of the bars, the arse end corkscrewed and dropped, meaning his bed was no longer below where he was heading for. As there was nothing there to break his fall, he dropped straight back to the deck, causing him not a painless landing. Hence the LMA's visit. Not that we took the piss, of course. It was a long time before he lived that escapade down.

It is strange, when you get out of 'roughers', where every other wave was a 'goffa' big enough to shake you to your steamers, you felt absolutely physically and mentally drained. While it was rough, you didn't know which way to walk, or which bulkhead to lean against – you just knew you'd get shaken off it. So you were therefore totally mentally alert trying to pre-empt which way to lean next. You were also performing physical exercises trying to keep balanced. When we therefore found flat sea, it took a long time to get used to having the ship permanently on an even keel. If we went straight from roughers to alongside it felt worse – the earth really did feel like it was moving.

We returned from that little trip. And I went on to a Leading Seamans' course, which I passed, and was promoted pretty well straight away. Fancy that now, me and Admiral Lord Nelson both reaching the absolute zenith of our naval careers. We'd even been to some of the same places!!

The course was held in Portsmouth, in a building in the civilian dockyard for whatever reason, and consisted of several weeks looking smarter than usual, performing various seamanlike evolutions, and creating extempore rigs with pieces of wood, and plenty of rope, plus drilling the proverbial 'awkward squad' for hours on end, whilst learning everything there was to know about RAS'ing etc. Oh yes, and Morse code, and the 'men, machinery, material' lecture, showing why the best asset the RN had, was its' men, but that without the machinery or material they were useless..., and every type of buoy, lighthouse, flashing light – you name it. I did come top of the board though after all that hard work, and gained a City and Guilds certificate for my troubles. Even though I had lived ashore in the Royal Sailors Rest Home in Portsmouth every day for the duration of the course, and being blue card for the duration, we'd managed to get ashore every night.

There used to be a proper pub over the road from the Seamanship School – while the school was not actually within the confines of the navy base, it was run from Whale Island, thus it had civvy sailors loading and unloading various cargoes from small coastal steamers scarcely bigger than the whalers we would charge round in to practice man-overboard drills. I don't recall the pub's name, but we went there every lunchtime, illegally in eights, drank two pints, ate thick ham with mustard, or cheese and onion sarnies all on extremely fresh bread – then returned for an afternoons lectures. It broke the day up.

It meant meeting more new mates, and learning more new expressions, especially from 'Tiddly' Rowe – a CPO there I knew from an incursion to Dryad, who's favourite insult was to call everyone a 'chimp'. We quickly picked up on that, and everyone we met ashore (and even up to today) was insultingly called 'chimp'. What with him and Mitch, our PO instructor, who genuinely taught me much more than I ever thought I'd learn in such a short period of time, I enjoyed that course very much.

One item all ships used to sell, was a Zippo lighter, with the ships crest engraved on it. My TARTAR one (like my watch) was treasured, and went everywhere with me. Until I went for my Leading Seamans' course to H.M.S. Excellent, and a thieving toe-rag stole it from me while I slept. While I could never prove anything, I remember his face even now. If I see him again, I'll have his fingers. With practice, you could squeeze the lighter, causing the lid to flip, and the wheel to turn igniting the wick, all in a split second. That looked impressive, unless you mistimed it, in which case the lighter could fly, flaming still, anywhere!. As Zippos' were not only guaranteed for life, but totally, totally reliable (you really could light a fag in the middle of a force eight gale), we'd hold contests to see who's lighter would ignite the largest number of consecutive times. This could run into dozens of 'lights' before it missed one.

Chapter 25
Cod Wars

Christmas 1975 was spent at home, after which the Icelanders got all arsey and protective about their fishery limits, and threw a wobbly, causing us to set sail to sort them out. The first trip wasn't too bad – the Icelandic gunboats kept their distance, and it was all fairly civilised. As control ship, each night we would 'call' all the trawlers, and plot their positions on a large chart. We would also build up a rapport with the skippers, and be able to have a chat and a laugh with them – remote from us as they were. It made a total change to talk to trawlermen, and to be able to curse and swear with them, as normally we'd have to say only correct, authorised words. Hull trawlermen were the best to talk to – as long as you remembered to prefix every other word with "F", just like they did. Nothing like the radio reporting I had learned at Dryad all that time ago.

Trawlers like the Farnella and her sisters, all ending with 'Ella' – wonder what happened to them. We got to know all the names, and would be concerned if one failed to answer. Normally, though, another trawler would come up and tell us where the missing boats were – that they'd gone to so and so to follow a shoal. If we got near, they (the trawlers) would call us on the close range radio, offering fresh fish, we'd then have to work out which trawler was offering, and where they were. We could, you see, see dozens of lights in all directions, and we had to be careful to not steam through their nets as we closed them. They would normally however, guide us easily straight to them. I was off watch one night, in the dining hall watching a movie when the hatch to the upper deck opened, followed by an enormous crash as something fell down the ladder into the dining hall. On investigation, it turned out to be the largest, freshest cod we ever set eyes on. We had that in the galley PDQ, gutted and chopped into large portions, with chips at a very good price. The money raised was sent to our adopted charity – Chailey Heritage at Littlehampton, which we often visited from Pompey, taking the handicapped kids there out for the day, to the fair or harbour or wherever, or back to the ship for a party. We loved doing it – they thought it was great too. I got my name in the Navy News one month, we had a sponsored slim during one Iceland trip, and I raised something over £100 – a lot of money back in those days – all of which went to the Heritage

By now, you may be thinking "What do booties do on board warships?". We frequently asked ourselves the same question. We know that even though we used to train as I.S. (Internal Security) platoon, we would know that if any pooh did head for the fans, that the booties would be landed first, with us as backup. They did, though do 'Boarding Party', that is, when we cruised the Windies we would frequently assist the US CoastGuard in their efforts to stop naughty minded people from smuggling illegal substances into the US of A. If we were up the Gulf, we'd be on the lookout for gold-runners. We actually found some one day. So, if we saw suspicious ships, yachts, boats – whatever, we would make them heave-to, then carry out a 'stop and search'. By that, I mean we'd throw the Marines over the side, hoping they'd hit the waiting Gemini semi-inflatable dinghy. They'd then bomb away to the stopped unit, board it, search it, find nothing, and come back to us. We'd then make them climb back up the jumping ladder, then hoist the Gemini back on its' davit. Then we'd steam off looking for someone else to stop.

During these operations, we were – allegedly – entitled to use whatever force we deemed necessary, in order to stop anyone. And if we were disobeyed, it was amazing what change of heart could be achieved by training the fo'r'r'd gun turret in the general direction of the target, even though it was unmanned and unloaded. We were assured we could quite easily plant a brick through a funnel (or a bow) if required.

The booties then did this. They also still held small arms firing off the blunt end, only occasionally allowing us to join in, we'd then all shoot the hell out of the empty oil drums until they vanished beneath the waves. They would clear off ashore to do 'exercises', or even do PT on the quarterdeck. Sometimes, they'd let us use their oil drums as targets (IS Platoon, remember?), and we'd muster with our SMG's, throwing out a whole mag in short order, trying to hold the barrel down so it didn't swing up showering lead everywhere but. Actually, those posers you see on the telly, holding their SMG by the mag, forget it – instant recipe for a jam. And the ones holding the barrel? Again – forget it. First round through makes the barrel hot, after several, the barrel goes extremely hot, and the skin on your hand then melts and sticks. After that it gets very painful. Also to be avoided, is holding the weapon by the end of the barrel. Not recommended, as guess where the barrel is now pointing…

There is a naval expression – Anchor Faced – which means the person you describe, is very pro-Navy, and who puts the RN first, and his mates second. It implies you should really have an anchor tattooed on your forehead or face, to warn everybody of your predilections. Another phrase with the same meaning we used was 'You fuckin' love it'. Bootnecks, however, are truly anchor faced, they truly 'fuckin love it…'!. Now, I'm all for everyone pulling in the same direction, but marines take this to new highs. The corps come first, second and last. They do everything they are told, and I MEAN everything. If you find a job you won't get anyone else to do – order up a bootie to do it. In the detachment we carried, there would be a first aider, a bugler, a cook, and a bunch of general purpose, and weapon specialists. The bugler would normally be the runt of the detachment, the rest would be – well lets say you wouldn't pick a fight with them. They would, though, be there to get you out of hot spots ashore. Not that we normally needed help, but if we did...

So, when a similar fish-crash-noise happened on the same dining-hall ladder some nights later, we ignored it. However, this time it was a marine who, having gone to collect some fish, had fallen out of the Gemini, and into the Arctic Ocean, precipitating extreme coldness. He survived it, being immediately thrown into a hot bath until he warmed up, but suffered exposure. We laughed at his misfortune, him being stupid enough to fall in, and all that, but we all knew how close to death he had come. We reckoned he had been obeying orders...

Almost nightly we were stopped and offered this great-tasting fish by the trawlermen, and were very grateful for it. Eating cod that isn't aware it is dead is different from that which you get in the local chippy. Half an hour ago it was swimming about with it's mates – now you are eating it. Wonderful.

We had several weeks back alongside, home, in Pompey, then went back to Icelandic waters. This time, the rules had changed – the Icelanders were getting more stressed and stroppy. One of their so-called gunboats (mostly converted trawlers with an Oerlikon fitted) had deliberately driven into the Lowestoft, removing most of the Lowestoft's forecastle. It actually removed the front twenty feet or so, above the waterline, and we sailed past her and saw her in this state, so we knew it to be true. That meant that after a considerable amount of Damage Control, she had to sail back to Rosyth at four knots. Astern – all the way. We Tartars weren't going to have any of that. Also, our skipper was the best ship handler I have ever seen, and here's why.

One morning (while we were closed up at defence stations), we came off at 0600 having tracked most of our trawlers and one of the 'gunboats'. (the "Baldur") for most of our watch, we breakfasted, and got our nuts down. At 0700, the action scraction alarms went, up we blearily rose, and we went straight away to "Riding off stations", where we had to position ourselves between the gunboat and the trawlers. It meant we had to get out of our pits, and all sit in the Burma Road, well away from the ships' side, and only one deck down.

It was then like chess – we would ride off the gunboats assault on our defenceless trawlers by getting between it and its target trawler. As I said –

our skipper was brilliant at this, and could make the gunboats look instantly and totally foolish. This occasion though, the "Baldur" (actually a converted stern trawler painted grey, with its popgun on the front) thought he'd get in the way. The Boss thought much differently. For around an hour we rode off its attacks, and we both sailed about gesturing and posturing – but we held the thing away, as ordered.

The Baldur finally got too close on one occasion, and we warned her by radio that we were rigged with stabilisers, stretching "two to three feet" out of both sides. It got closer and closer, and our Jimmy did a running commentary on the situation over the ships broadcast, tinged with pathos,. He reported the impending collision so precisely, that it was exactly on the third 'now' in "standby now, now now" that the actual impact was felt and heard by us below decks. This impact reeled us, but our port stabiliser unfortunately (!!) pierced the Baldurs' hull necessitating her extremely rapid return to Rekyavik. We laughed like mad buggers, especially when, while still closed up, we got a mention on the BBC world news. The stabilisers actually extended up to six feet out...

It was his fault – he started it!!

Another day, we were shipwatching round the south east corner of Iceland, and picked up a distress call from a trawler in the north, on the HF radio, that he was getting trouble from, I think, the "Tyr", another gunboat. We went flat out to get round there, banging our way through a very wet and snowy force eight gale. However, on the way, the 'on-task' Nimrod joined us for his twelve-hour routine patrol. We tasked it to go and see what was going on, and heard the Nimrod raising the Tyr on HF radio. The Nimrod pilot informed the gunboat that, as an RAF Nimrod on patrol, he was equipped with all kinds of things, including Mk46 torpedoes and depth charges, and that if he – the Tyr – didn't go away immediately and quickly, he – the Nimrod – would drop something on him to enforce the issue. The gunboat retreated : the Nimrod carried on with another of his allotted tasks – that of dropping bright yellow mail canisters to us. The pilot must have got confused about his payload that day – fancy confusing Mk46s' with letters to the Tartar!!! Silly old pilot...!

We had several more confrontations with the gunboats, but in general they kept away from us. It was still with great relief that the "Cod War" as it was known came to an end, though why did they do it hours before we would have qualified for active service medals?

And while we were up there, it was cold enough to grow icicles on the upper deck. We also swept off snow – it was so cold up there, I don't know how the trawlermen stick that out. We also sailed through fields of growlers,

but never saw any really big ones otherwise known as icebergs. Yes, we chipped ice off the four-fives whenever we got a good build-up, and yes we grew snow everywhere else. The bridge lookouts were actually allowed inside the bridge up there, and not – as they usually were – stationed outside on the wings.

When we first enlisted, we were – to remind you – issued with two seamen's jerseys. These were thick, and would keep out most draughts, but still itched like hell, even after dozens of washes, and through T-shirts. For this extremely cold weather, then, we would scrounge/nick/beg/borrow thick white polo neck jerseys, known as 'sub-sweaters', on account of their being standard bubble-head (submariners) issue. If you caught anyone else wearing your 'legally' acquired sweater – revenge was imminent. After several washes, the yellow colour would go, leaving a milky white sweater. They did not shrink or warp regardless of what you did to them. They were an impressive symbol – if you had one you gloated, if you aspired to one you schemed devious ways to get your hands on one. Sub-sweaters then were warm, extremely so, and when worn over several T-shirts and sets of eights, but under your foul-weather gear, you felt, at least, that you could survive any weather hardships, especially the oceans north of the Arctic Circle… …unless you fell in!

It was probably around this time, that The Admiralty decided we would all have two new woolly-pullies, this time not skin-scraping ones, but sensible wool ones, like they wear in the Army and Air Force, but ours were a deep, navy blue – of course. They had epaulettes on each shoulder, ready to put our new rank/rate badges on. We wore them self-consciously at first, but gradually got used to them, and threw away those bloody awful issue itchy things from all those sunrises away at Raleigh. We also were issued with berets, not that we knew how to wear them, we needed lessons for that. We wore these even more self-consciously than the woollies, as we all looked really ridiculous wearing these silly French inventions. They did, though, stay on our heads better in roughers, and could be jammed into the pockets of our foulies, along with all the rest of the crap we carried, so from that point of view they were an improvement. We still had to keep our two ice-cream hats, for divisions, for being on duty, and for being trooped and appearing before the skipper. The berets would also find a further use, as a quick shoe/boot cleaner, before then finding your own to actually stick on your head.

Officially, your 'length of service' was proportional to the number of 'badges' – otherwise known as long service and good conduct stripes. These badges, although officially l.s.g.c, were actually more accurately defined as four years undetected crime. You got another one of these to sew on then, every four years up to a maximum of three, but they could be taken off you as part of any punishment, along with stoppage of leave/a fine – something looked forward to, as it made you appear younger!! On the Tartar one day, we counted the number of badges apportioned to just a handful of ratings, and got a combined service record of (I think) in excess of 100 years. Badges made you look like a silly old git – you would called 'granddad' or worse if you had them. I ended up with two, but kept forgetting to sew the second on one.

A further indicator of length of service, was judged by the colour of your 'eights' or by your 'collar'. The more faded your eights were, clearly – the more times you had them dhobeyed, thus the longer you had served. You did, though, have to buy more eights during your service, mainly when they got too ragged to wear, and the sticky tape we used to repair holes with found nothing to grip!! Your collar then was the best giveaway, you would only wear it two or three times, then get it down to the dhobey wallah for cleaning. Thus, it would again fade. So, whilst your eights were the first indicator, your collar would always be the best barometer. Unless you were one of those people who never got dirty, never smelled, and therefore who would go for two whole days – or longer – without a shower, and only get your gear washed when absolutely necessary. Most people took exceptional pride in their appearance. However, berets just got filthier and filthier – to prove a point.

Tattoos were also a good barometer of service, though not as far as I was concerned. I could never see the point in sitting in a filthy room, with some scruffy, vicious bearded git sticking needles in you. For some, though, it was a tradition. One bloke had a "W" tattooed on each cheek of his bum, so when he bent over it (allegedly) said "WoW". There was no end to the designs we saw, from snakes, dragons, mothers, girlfriends, wives, ships – you name it, we saw it.

At some point during 'the Iceland troubles' we called in at Newcastle on Tyne for several days. We soon had 'ship open to visitors', and were then offered a tour of the local brewery. Bearing in mind that the previous evening we thought we'd drunk every bottle of 'brown' in the city, it isn't difficult to imagine the state we were in when we got on the coach. We reached the brewery though, and were taken round evil smelling tuns, full of fermenting ale. This did wonders for our hangovers. We saw every aspect of the process – the bottle washing, filling, labelling, then were shown 'the old boy at the end of the barrel line'. We were then told, yes – told, that under no circumstances were we to laugh. This chap sat there, with a hammer in his hand. Every barrel that went past him, he would hit, just one with the hammer, to ensure the cap on the end of the barrel was secure. That was his job. That was all he did. Ever. We controlled our laughter until we got away from him, then collapsed on the floor.

Then we got to the interesting bit. Lunch was plates and plates of sandwiches, washed down with as much 'newcy brown' as we could scupper. They left us to get on with it all afternoon. I have no idea what time we left, but it was late, and the staff there wanted to go home. George and I walked drunkenly back, and as we approached the ship, we saw TV crews on the gangway. They asked if we'd mind coming back around the corner while they filmed our return. "Not at all" said the obliging us. We had several 'takes' of us walking nonchalantly back along the gangway, before we decided to spice it up. The next take, then, was me and George, arms linked, legs kicking like Tiller Girls. The gangway staff, OOD, DPO and film crew just cracked up – we went below, sniggering wildly, for a siesta before that evening's 'run'.

We could only hope, though, that brown ale was not made from the 'water' flowing down the Tyne, as that was just an open sewer, with more dead dogs, body contents, tin cans and noddy hats per square inch than anywhere else I've ever seen.

George, being from Newcastle area, took several of us 'up-homers' one night for a feed, then out to his local club. Once more we left our wallets in our pockets – terrific hospitality that night. We awoke on the floor next morning, then attempted to get back to the ship, moored almost beneath the Railway Bridge. The trains were late or missing, and we ended up getting a fast-black (taxi) back, costing us a fortune. I know we were adrift, but didn't get 'in the shit' for it as we weren't the only ones affected by the trains' bad performance.

Newcastle then was a glorious week off from the stresses (!) of normal naval life.

Talking of Chinese (?!) we also had a Chinese laundry crew on here (and all the other ships I served on) who would wash and iron, beautifully, everything you sent in. Though they had some not very endearing habits. Like washing noisily – sometimes. They rarely took showers, preferring to take bird-baths in the sink, throwing water everywhere as they used their flannels. Or while we would eat our meals, they'd sit with us, noisily chomping noodles from bowls, usually with their fingers. They would also catch 'shitfish', so called because no matter which port you stopped in, shitfish would always gather at sewage outflows from the ship, i.e. from the 'heads', i.e. – shit. The laundry crew would then catch these, then cook them separately in the galley for their meals. We often pointed this shitfish matter out, they'd just laugh – and rebait their hooks for supper. Laundry crews were always conspicuous by their absence – occasionally they would go ashore, come back legless, and noisily play Mahjong for the rest of the night, locked up in their laundry room. No-one, but no-one was allowed in the laundry except them, not under any circumstances. They slept, ate, washed and ironed in there, apparently getting in and out through the top half of a door, which would be closed every evening, and at every action stations, at which time they'd continue dhobying, while we did whatever exercise we were supposed to.

A minor digression on the subject of sewage outfalls, concerns a trophy alleged to be held on the Royal Yacht, of a certain varnished, framed item, originally belonging to a certain person (NOT The Queen, but close – very, very close), which was extracted from one such outfall many middles ago. Subsequently, according to the sources, a 'smasher' was fitted to the outfall, preventing further such incidents. An excellent 'black cat' huh?!.

Therefore, the crew would always, but always have your gear delivered back to your mess by evening, except the days they would walk round bemoaning "No Stim, No Stim", indicating that they hadn't been able to do any washing that day!

This lack of stim would normally be caused by the clanks inability to do simple things like connect to a shore steam line, without making a mess of it. For most of the time they'd be able to do it, however, whenever it got near to going-ashore-time, they'd always manage to make it pack up. Normally halfway through a shower, so the water would suddenly go ice-cold. At that time, you'd scream and shout, telling everyone what an incompetent bunch of wankers stokers were. I was doing this happily one day, when the 'duty tiffy' stuck his gormless head round the bathroom door to see what was the matter. He got told in no uncertain terms, and ran off. The duty senior stoker then turned up to find out why his little chap was so upset about – we told him too. Pretty soon, miraculously, the water got hot again.

Showers, when the hot water was available to take them, were generally a time for bawdiness. This could take the form of 'measurement' or 'comparison', but that could get boring. Of course, cold water could mess up the arrangements temporarily. Or we would announce "I'm going to do basin trials", or "Four 'S's" – 'Shitshowershaveshampoo'. Anyone who didn't conform the naval standard of at least one shower per day, would immediately be labelled 'crab', and would thenceforth be pestered, daily, to ensure he brought himself up to scratch. Or shower. We had to live with him, you see, and nothing could be worse than being closed up on watch, or at action stations, or behind in the food queue, with someone the Lifebouy advert could have been written for. We, then, would self-discipline the offender, quickly, for there was always one you would hassle for living like a pig. Veiled references and politely dropped hints were never for us – we'd be right out there with "You crabby bastard – when are you going to get a shower?", or "Fuck off and dhobey – you smelly bastard". Niceties were never our strong suit – to be called anything less than "Wanker" was nearly a term of endearment, whereas anything harder was just a way of life.

It did sometimes get a bit difficult – there are few things more precarious than standing in a shower, covered in soap, trying to keep your balance while the ship has the wheel and rudder hard over, and is turning to port, at twenty knots plus. This tended to throw you against the side of the shower, or even out of it. As did attempting to stand on one leg to wash the other, whilst ploughing through a force eight gale. We got used to it though. To make life easier (or was it more difficult), we would always wear flip-flops while off watch. These could be dangerous at the best of times, due to the proliferation of ringbolts and other lumps of metal growing at various points from the deck, to catch the unwary. Normally, in shoes – you would merely curse and walk away. Flip-flops – you came to a grinding halt, swear roundly at the item, your flip-flops, perhaps collapse on the floor holding your foot, then, finally, limp back to the mess. You COULD break toes wearing them. Not that that ever stopped us. They made life more interesting in the shower, but stopped your feet becoming too pongy after wearing the steaming bats all day.

Of course, you could always suffer that most fatal of accidents – a flip-flop blowout. This occurs while trying to do something in flip-flops, which they are clearly not designed to do, i.e. walk in them on a slippery surface. The blowout is when the 'foot' part of the body makes the top of the flip-flop separate from the bottom, giving the 'toe' nothing to stop it from sliding forward. This in turn makes you lose your balance and fall. As warships are generally made from steel, the resulting fall usually hurts. At that stage, the rest of the messdeck collapses laughing…

Conversely, you could wear slippers, and have your messmates laugh at you anyway…

One of the associated dangers of warship design, is the hatches leading from one deck to another, or from one watertight compartment to the next. All hatches are surrounded by an edge, which can grow out of the deck by many inches. These have to be crossed, clearly, by lifting your leg over the rim. Normally not difficult, except after a night ashore, when those hatch rims grow extra height. This extra height causes you to not lift your leg high enough resulting in a rapid shin-to-metal contact on the surrounding hatch coaming. Now THIS hurts. And produces bruising and gashes which last for weeks, as well as leaving scarring for years. I still have mine.

A favorite game played by the jimmy, as mentioned, was 'throw the dummy over the side to see how long the lifebuoy spook takes to see it'. This was normally done at scran time by anyone not thinking straight, thus you'd be sitting 'enjoying' supper, having queued and rabbited for the best part of half an hour, to ensure the absolute best selection of food, and the finest table in the house, you would sit down, raise you knife and fork, then the tannoy would blare:

'MANOVERBOARDMANOVERBOARDMANOVERBOARDPORT SIDEAWAYSEABOATSCREW',

and you'd grab at your gobbling rods and plate before they joined the scrapyard at one side of the dining room. The OOW, you see, would immediately order the 'wheel' to be put right over, then back again to the other side, to swing the arse end away, then line up the ship to come back for the dummy. Totally 'forgetting' that 'the lads' were enjoying supper. You'd then be holding on hard to your tray full of food with one hand, the table with the other, whilst gripping the chairs or benches with your legs, hoping the bulkheads would go back to the proper place so you could continue eating. I have to point out that our trays had several compartments – one for a soup bowl, one for main meal, one for pudding. It was therefore in your own interests to keep the tray steady, or you'd end up with custard on your beef, or soup on your pudding.

A word about the aforementioned tiffys. Tiffys, after midshipmen, are a very elementary life form. Tiffys join the navy to see the world, but due to having attained higher educational qualifications at school, they assumed they were on a higher intellectual level than us mere sailors. Tiffys leave training, undoubtedly having worked hard at mending engines, and oiling lamps or whatever they claim to do, and are then promoted, rapidly, until suddenly they are 'chiefs' with lots of oiling and mending qualifications, but thick as pigshit, and with no concept of other peoples attitudes towards them, nor to how the navy really works. They then sit in the chiefs and POs' mess, with chiefs and PO's who have taken years of professional labour to attain their rates. All tiffs do, then, is piss people off, then occasionally get a complicated job to do, like mend a broken screw or nail, which tends to stretch their capabilities. It is rumoured, that when anyone electrically minded who wants to join the RN goes for their initial interview, they are handed a screwdriver side on. If they take it by the handle, they obviously recognise what it is, and how to use it, and can therefore be enlisted as an electrician. If they hesitate, or take it by the pointed bit, they are automatically enlisted as 'tiffies'.

Expanding this a bit, every night in the navy, especially on active warships, there is the duty watch. This comprises twenty five percent of the ratings – a quarter of all the sailors, then supposedly a quarter of the stokers and greenies, who, because they were not under any jurisdiction except that of their respective chiefs, would normally be able to slide off somewhere. There would also be a duty leading seaman, a duty PO (any branch), a duty CPO (any branch), and an officer of the day. If, then, anything went on, a situation would arise, and could then be escalated. However, guess who would be called out first, and guess where the problem would be resolved? I'll give you a clue, not the OOD, not the chief, not the PO. Corrrrrect. Anything happening – "Get the duty leading seaman". ...Which I now was. This did ensure though, that any seamanship evolution required could be carried out, even the ship was devoid of any more senior seaman ratings or officers.

Middys? Now middys absolutely were the lowest form of animal life. If you were fortunate enough to have a 'mid' on board, he would need to wear his shit-deflecting hat, and shitproof trousers all the time. If shit rolls downhill – guess where it stops. If the Duty LS had a spare job, he would try and convince the OOD that it would be a good bit of experience for 'the mid'. Generally the OOD would grin and agree, and the mid would be summoned in the middle of the night as well as me, to 'oversee' the slacking off (or tightening up) of the cable or wires. Of course, the duty watch of sailors would think that terrific, and play 'awkward bastards', to liven the mid up. Eventually, the mid would shout and lose his rag, at which point the duty leading sailor would get back in and resolve it all. Exit mid.

Of course, each chief had his own job to do, for example, the Chief GI, who would be the senior gunnery rating aboard, would be in charge of all the seamen, but also in charge of daily orders, and anything along those lines. There would be a chief greenie who did nothing, a chief stoker who perpetually had dirty hands and sweated a lot, the buffer, who was a chief of some seaman branch, a chief caterer – usually a lardarsed idiot, the jossman – chief cementhead, and other assorted good for nothing chiefs who we never did discover what they could do never mind actually did!

There would also be various numbers of POs', from all departments – the seaman ones would be in charge of their own 'parts of ship', traditionally the gunner would have the fo'c's'le, the RP 'top', and the TAS the quarterdeck. The greenies all stuck together, but either did radio, weapons or general (light bulbs). The stokers – well, I don't know, but they always had grubby rags hanging out of their overalls.

Next level was Leading Hands, and there were loads of them. They'd be the ones that actually ensured the work got done by the ABs' and below. The 'hookies' therefore caught the most grief, from above AND below. If it wasn't right, it wasn't the AB for not doing it, but the hookie for not making sure it was done. If there was extra work to be done, it was hookie who dragged the 'watch' out to get it done. More grief.

Then there were the workers...

Chapter 26

Once More into the Med

Eventually we got back to Pompey from the Ice War to a heroes welcome, from our families at least. We had a few more weeks refitting, and having taken some leave, we then sailed for Gibraltar, Biarritz, and Casablanca.

Not before we had a scare one day while alongside in Portsmouth. A fire was reported in a compartment, and the duty watch and ship's fire crews dived in to extinguish it. The Damage Control bods suddenly realised though that the compartment was adjacent to the deep Seacat magazines, which were fully loaded. It was decided to go to emergency stations even though we were alongside, and we spent many fractious if not frightened minutes trying to be the nearest ones to the ships side, just in case the anticipated explosion actually occurred. I think we'd have been over the side into the water as soon as we even FELT a 'bang', but if it had happened, we'd have made a large hole in the dockyard, Portsmouth, and part of Hampshire too, and thus would not have had time to jump anyway. The Pompey Fire Brigade eventually arrived, then quickly helped us put it out. That was far too close!

While we played in the Med, we came across the Ark Royal, only this time she was floating unaided, without scaffolding. She also had a full complement of aircraft, and it befell us to do Helicopter Guardship – sailing off the arse-end of the Ark as she went to flying stations. We were there just in case one of her pilots was dumb enough to make his multi-million pound jet fall into the water, in which case we were there to fish him out. Unlike the Yanks, who, if an aircraft went over the side they just waved (allegedly they had loads of spares, and weren't concerned about the odd one or two), we would have to drop dan-buoys and divers to remember where the aircraft went. In theory. Fortunately we didn't actually have to practice this particular evolution, and I like to think that was due to the greater capabilities of our RN flyboys...

When we did guardship, or when we ourselves went to 'flying stations', one of the things we'd do, would be to equip the seaboat with a crash-bag, and hang the boat over the side on the falls, engine running, just in case it was urgently required. Obviously, you had to sit in the boat while it was dangling apparently perilously above the ocean as you smashed along at 'flying speed'.

Our crash-bag contained various items of indispensable equipment, like maul, bolt-croppers, axe, flashlight, crowbar and strops to attempt to keep whatever had crashed afloat, so we had a good (!) chance of getting the pilot/crew out, should they feel the desire to ditch and swim. That assumed we got there before whatever it was sank, and that we could reach into it to extract the crew. Perhaps it made them feel better – knowing we were on full alert, but in actual fact we'd have been as useful as the proverbial tits on a fish – why would we risk our necks to rescue a sinking helicopter?

We would sail within a few hundred yards of the 'Ark', watching the aircraft taking off. At early dawn, this was THE most spectacular event – we'd see a shape trundle up to the cat, we'd hear the engines rev, then see the flames from the back of the aircraft. The roaring and flames would increase, then we'd see the flames shoot forward as the aircraft lunged towards the front of the flight deck. We'd then hear the extra roar, then see the flame shoot into the sky, watching the afterburners gradually tail off as the aircraft got away. We got to know the noise difference between the Phantom and my favourite – the Buccaneer. Then we'd track them round on radar, listening to their controllers. When they came back, we'd watch with bated breath as several tons of metal travelling at well over 100 knots hurtled towards the immovable rear of the carrier. If all went well, the aircraft would skim the rear, drop the last few feet, and be caught by the arrester wires. If not, a flare would soar into the sky (indicating too high/too far to the side), and the pilot would slam the engines back to reheat in a desperate attempt to give himself enough power to get himself airborne again, without smashing into the carriers deck or bridge!! We would laugh and make the obligatory rude gestures to those who got into this position!!

What with them and the Gannets which would not need seem to need the arresters – they'd creep up behind the ship, and seemingly drop directly onto the pitching deck!

While we were playing with the Ark, I got the notion that I might like to change branches to 'Photographer', having got on so well with my camera, so I applied. I recall having a long interview with my DO, who then sent me over to the Ark by boat (when we were moored somewhere), where I had another long interview with a waffoo photographer. That put me off, the likelihood of having to change branches to become one of the loathed waffoos'. As did the threat of spending two years ashore learning how to use a camera, though I already knew. I also knew all about exposures, speeds, and various lenses filters and effects, so I pretended great interest, impressed the interviewer who assured me I would easily qualify, got back to the RatRat, and told my DO to scrub round that idea.

It was shortly after this, that Rod Stewart released 'Sailing', a record forever and indelibly ingrained into my mind for two reasons. First – my future wife would watch the series about the Ark, and associate it with me, secondly we were with her while they filmed the series, and can remember all those brilliant shots of the 'Buccs' screaming off the flight deck under full throttle.

Biarritz was different, although we went to Monaco one day, and I think St Tropez for another, hoping to get a look at BB. When we went to Casablanca, we took the coach to Marrakesh – which is just like you'd imagine, down to and including the man with the sherbert water in the goatskin bottle. Whilst there, we rode more camels, and witnessed (right in the middle of nowhere) the locals racing on horseback, waving scimitars. We stayed out of the way, but were mightily impressed.

However, we weren't so impressed by the very large cockroaches (known as Bombay Runners – large enough to put your foot on, and watch it still move) and rats that would cruise the jetty at night. We demanded firearms whilst on gangway duty, but had to make do with the inevitable catapult. Eventually, we returned, once more to our home port.

In amongst our travels (a very busy ship was the Tartar), we'd also frequent several 'locals' in Portsmouth one of which we would play darts all evening, then sing along to the jukebox. We were the second people in the world (after 'Queen') to be word perfect on 'Bohemian Rhapsody', dancing around, all playing the 'air guitar' on the break, before singing the remainder – perfectly in tune (with the local population of crows). The only records we refused to play or pay for were Roxy Music or Brian Ferry, (reasons already mentioned!!), and we'd nudge the jukebox to get unwelcome records off. Our darts improved dramatically, specifically our ability to subtract any two or three digit number from any other two or three digit number, having first added up the three scores from the thrown darts. Our mate, Dago, had actually been a contestant in a major tournament some years before (before alcohol took charge of him), but he was nevertheless the best darts player I have ever seen. We never could beat him while he was sober, and even drunk he was still a formidable opponent. I watched him one night when he put three darts into the center of a polo mint. Darts was a way of life for us, but was eventually superseded by the advent of those peculiar table tennis TV games. They ruined it for us!! At least we knew we could challenge any team, any where to a darts match and know we'd either win or come second…

We still had such a good run-ashore gang on there, and still if one of us was skint, and didn't want to borrow from the beer fund, we'd go ashore anyway, on the understanding that you were broke, and all the rest of the gang would sub you all night knowing that you'd do the same for them at a later date. We all did it – it was well understood. We'd even get our chinky and taxi back paid for. We had a really brilliant inter-departmental drinking club (except the usual greenies who always skulked around together anyway) and would always be ashore together.

In actual fact, we didn't get rat-arsed EVERY night – if there was a new fairly decent film going, we'd go to see it. Then leg it back to the local for last orders, at which time we'd line up as many drinks as possible, and throw them down our necks as fast as we could before closing time. We'd see only good films, I remember going to see 'Tommy', but especially remember 'The Exorcist'. This one stands out in my 'list of runs ashore to never forget', due to George, who, getting bored during one of the quieter scenes, nudged me, giggled, leapt to his feet, and screamed "BOO", thus frightening to death the entire cinema audience. We then sat giggling through the rest of the film much to the annoyance of the audience!! Like I said – Me and George had some brilliant escapades. Like the one where I (and he) thought he had appendicitis, so we called for an ambulance. What actually turned up, was the crushers in their patrol 'tilly, who diagnosed George as having nothing more than too much scrumpy. At least we got a lift back to the dockyard, but promptly turned back round, back to the nosh shop for eats.

It was probably around this time that George decided to buy a guitar. What a bad day that was. Ninety nine percent of matelots cannot tolerate any kind of musical instrument, me included. It was bad enough that we had a bloke in our mess who thought he was good at playing the gob-iron (mouth organ), but whenever he got it out, we'd all give him such hard times, that he'd put it away, or go somewhere else to play it. We tried for years to find where he hid it, so that we could see if it floated, but we never did. Anyway, George started to play the guite, and started with 'House of the Rising Sun', much to our discomfort. He would sit for hours (which I suppose was one blessing…), tongue out, concentrating on the next chord. He improved ever so slightly, with the help of Dick Czarnecki (a committed D by P rating), but we'd still make him sit somewhere out of earshot to practice. Like the tiller flat. Guitars were at least an icebreaker – if we had a banyan somewhere, out would come the guite, and we'd break into song.

D by P, or discharge by purchase (buying yourself out) was a handy way of getting out. You applied for D by P, and if you were given it, you'd be a civvy again within months. If your job was pretty menial, you'd stand a better chance of getting it. Dick was a trained Seacat Aimer, so had no chance at all! Anyway, D by P ratings (as would we others) would walk round muttering phrases like R.O.M.F.T., but if they got their request, they'd immediately become RAMIT, as in 'Ram it (up your arse), I'm RDP' (and consequently not interested in the RN no more). They'd immediately also set up a calendar, and fastidiously tick off each day that passed, telling everyone at every opportunity exactly how many days (and hours) they had left. The nearer the end of the calendar – the more excited they visibly got. We felt for them.

Chapter 27

...But Windies Guardship Means You're Just on Standby – It Doesn't Mean You Actually Have to Go . . .

We were actually only 'standby' West Indies Guardship in the September, back in Portsmouth with just an outside chance of having to go, when we got the order to sail, so off we went again. Before we went, though, I had met the girl I had been writing to since the advert in the Melody Maker. We had spent a day in London, took lunch at the Tower Hotel, toured Madame Tussauds, gone to see the newest Pink Panther film, toured H.M.S. Belfast (I couldn't stay away in those days), walked across Tower Bridge, and had a meal in the West End, and finally, sadly, parted on Kings Cross station just in time for her to catch the very last train home. We subsequently saw each other every possible weekend after that, and had decided to get engaged that next Christmas. Except the Navy put paid to that. We were supposed to be back in time for Christmas, but things changed so quickly!!

One weekend, she asked me if we'd had a good run that afternoon we sat in the cement yard at Portland. That puzzled me – how in hell did she know about that? It was only when, eventually, I found out her then best mate was a splitarse, and based at Portland Naval Air Station at the time, and indeed in the same pub as us, that I caught on to that one. Lucky we behaved reasonably well that day. She also used to berate me about my still standard rig of Levis, sweatshirt (the one which proclaimed 'Disneyworld'), and desert wellies. Eventually I went for it – and bought a pair of proper shoes!

I lost count of the letters I sent and received, and would be extremely sad (now I knew how the married men felt on the Zulu) if the mail was delayed, late, or I just plain didn't get a letter. If you haven't been in that position – you don't know what a depressing feeling it is. You look forward so much to getting near land and getting mail, and if yours isn't there – the only consolation is to go and drink a bottle of Bacardi with a teeny drop of coke, and a few icebergs, and hope a letter will arrive tomorrow.

Before we sailed this time, we had taken a whip round, and all put a fiver or something in a kitty. I had taken it and purchased a stereo cassette with huge speakers that we wired in on my return. We would then all throw our cassettes in, playing them over and over. Those who were not allowed to use it (who hadn't paid) would on occasions play their tapes. But as soon as we rumbled them, we remove their tapes, giving them the float test. Unfortunately, tapes float, but there is no way they can be recovered. So the unfortunate losers quickly learned to NOT mess with it. As new members joined, they would be given the opportunity to buy a share in it, which we would have previously refunded to a mate who just left. We were always in equity with it, and it was always a source of amusement. Of course, we had to have rules, such as 'No playing it after lights out'. Unless nobody wanted to make a fuss about it. We would eventually draw lots to see who took this stereo away at the end of the commission, I think I won it, actually.

Once more to Bermuda, exercising all the way, so it took us just as long to get there. We moored, this time, on the town quay in Hamilton, where the liners normally would go. So this time, no need for hired mopys, just borrowed ones. We had all the floodlighting rigged along the side, so we looked extremely pretty!! We had tourists everywhere stomping up and down the jetty!

Trinidad, again, then to Jamaica, where we were told NOT to go anywhere unless authorised. We ended up getting coaches to the only place we were allowed to go, the Jamaica Pegasus – actually being jeered at en route – and having a civilised meal there, before returning sober to the ship. Except for the day we went on a coach tour, round a bauxite mine, ending at Oche Rios, and up THAT waterfall – the one in the '007' films. Dunns River Falls. Now there was an experience not to be missed. The tumbling water, after the air being in the '90s', was freezing cold, but better when you got used to it. I don't know how far up we climbed, but it was totally exhilarating.

We stopped at Norfolk, Virginia for a mini-refit, ironically on the day we should have been entering Pompey for Christmas. One of the first things we wanted repaired was our stabilisers, which had gone drastically wrong some time earlier, making every inch of the remaining journey extremely uncomfortable. I don't know what we expected (after the last yank base we stopped at on the last trip), but this one was different. We made our way through a snowstorm to the jetty, at which point a matey pronounced it to be the 'coldest day here for twenny yirs'. Boy, were we impressed!

I recall being duty that first night, and phoning the local 'Domino' pizza delivery service, deciding we'd have extra large please, each. I have never seen such enormous pizzas – we spent hours trying to eat them – they were gorgeous, then hours trying to get rid of what we clearly could not eat! The duty watch fed well that night.

Next day, we discovered we were at the end of the Tomcat landing strip, and that we would be constantly buzzed as they landed. Deafening. There was a PX there, which was massive. Probably bigger than most TESCO stores are nowadays. They sold everything and anything. We topped up with ten-ounce tins of tobacco, which cost us peanuts compared to our own baccy. And sweat shirts, real US Navy ones, which we insisted for years stood for unserviceable!! And small wind up toys (ducks, frogs) which swam, and ended up doing basin trials in our bathrooms...We eventually discovered that Norfolk was home to the USN Atlantic Fleet, boasting 200 ships and 77000 crew – larger than the Royal even then!

We then taxied out of the base, to a bar which was full of Hells Angels. Real ones. But they took an instant liking to us before spending all evening swapping booze. Eventually, well after closing time, the leader, 'Wine', offered to throw a party for us, and did I want to go with him to the 'all-nighter' to get some supplies. We left the bar, jumped into his open-topped limo, drove across the road, and bought bourbon, seven-up, and bourbon. Back to the car, 100 yards, round the corner to his place. By then, my mates, and his were waiting for us to begin. Now I am assured that the correct way to drink bourbon, is to drink a mouthful from the bottle, swallow, then take a small sip of seven-up. This, we found, was a cracking way to drink – even now I won't mix them! Wine also had a Harley D suspended from his ceiling!

We finally got back on board some minutes before seven in the morning – all ready for another day!!!!!

Every night thereafter we'd head for that place, they had the best bands we had ever heard live there, the company was great, the atmosphere was even better, although it usually smelled a bit – of strawberries usually. Ask me who was daft enough to ask why?

We were most sad to leave there, although we dropped just a few hundred miles down the coast to Savannah (Georgia) to spend Christmas. The one fact I remember about Savannah, is that it is where the composer of 'Jingle Bells' lays buried.

Now there we didn't expect what was to happen, even though one of the wardroom had arrived early to set up some surprises...

I was quartermaster when we arrived, and so was on duty on the gangway, where we had a shore phone connected. The idea of that was for locals to ring in, to arrange to take a sailor out for the night/day. This had been publicised locally, as 'Take a Sailor Home for Christmas'. Yeh Yeh – we thought! This family was hovering at the bottom of the gangway, so like a friendly ol' salt, I invited them onboard. One thing led to another, and I ended up feeding them beer whilst supposedly being on the gangway. I also got them lunch. Eventually, they asked if I wanted to go home with them, for Christmas. Bearing in mind this was the 23rd December, I was straight round to my DO (who was OOD), and asked if that would be all right. The OOD agreed, I arranged a hurried 'sub' for my Christmas duties, threw gear in my grip, and headed off the ship for the next four days. We started by going out for dinner, then back to their home for the night. Then up early, round to where the guy worked (as a computer operator in a bank) and a quick tour of there. Followed by a visit to the C130 base where he was a part-time aircraft loader (National Guard). I clambered all over and round that huge aircraft, very impressed I was.

Then we piled into his car, and set off for somewhere I still don't know to this day, but it is where his family lived. We arrived early evening, after stopping off mysteriously at a shopping mall, where I was wise enough to buy a few pressies for my host. We reached one of the small wooden bungalows shown in all the films of the deep south, and entered the main room, to be met by all his relatives. A whole table was filled with different food, a further one was filled with beer and wine. No glasses though, just jamjars! They were refilled as soon as they were emptied. The evening passed in a whirl of country music, wine, food, and more wine. Fairly late on, they decided it was present time, and we all sat round, and try as I might, I could think of only my girlfriend at home. Until the pressies started coming my way, and more, and more, until everyone had heaps, including me. To say I was overwhelmed was an understatement – I hadn't expected to be grippo'd while I was on watch, never mind travelling several hundred miles up-country, and then to be welcomed like a long lost relative, fed, watered, then given all this! I had an absolutely fantastic time. The kids in the family had been given one of those table-tennis on a TV games, which I could beat everyone at (having had lots of practice), although the more jamjars got emptied, the worse my performance got! At least they were pleased with the gizzits I had bought for them at the Mall, it seemed ungracious not to have bought them something, but I never dreamed I'd be given anything in return.

At the time, CB radios' were in vogue, and we then took it in turns to sit in the pickup, calling all kinds of people on the rig.

During the evening, we heard on the CB that a 'wreck' had taken place just a few miles from where we were. We boarded the pickups, and raced to where another wrecked pickup sat forlornly in the road. We were about to attempt to extract the driver, who seemed to be in an extremely bad way, when this terrified, wide eyed, drooling, snarling, barking dog reared up from the floor of the pickup, and tried to bite its' way out of the truck. We retreated rapidly. We never did find out if anyone ever got the man out – I was certainly not going near that dog.

Next morning, hangover permitting, the day started with more jamjars, and degenerated from there really – more delicious southern food and hospitality, with a dance later that day. By evening I was exhausted, but it was with great sorrow that we left the next day, and returned to Savannah. That was most definitely the best Christmas I ever spent abroad. I cannot describe adequately how friendly the people were. I did try to contact them later in my career, but never managed to re-trace them. I always wished I could somehow return the favour.

When I returned, I found out that there had been so many offers taken up – the ship virtually became a 'Marie Celeste', we actually had to turn the citizens of Savannah away – there were no sailors left!!!

I only had time for one run ashore, then, in Savannah, where we simply went into a bar where a man played Scott Joplin music – all night. We did the sights, though.

When we left there, we were just dropping the last line, when an adrift greenie hammered over the jetty, before launching himself across the growing gap, just managing to cling to the guardrails before being hauled inboard. This was accompanied by the jimmy (over the stornophone) demanding that person reported to the bridge NOW. This guy has also been in touch with me, and now lives in the USA.

We sailed, then, to St Petersburg, on the Gulf coast of Florida, for New Year. En route, we 'Ras'd' with RFA Retainer, who, in exchange for 130 pallets of stores, received 400 empty beer barrels from us. That one took hours and hours to complete.

After we had held the usual open day, where we apparently attracted over 8000 visitors, we made a further run to Disneyworld. Having got that out of our systems again (via Space Mountain etc), we toured St Pete's, finding the aquarium where we hand fed the porpoises, and climber the life-size model of the 'Bounty', moored in St Pete's, but built for the film 'Mutiny on the Bounty'. Then we got ourselves invited to the Scottish ex-pats festivities at their club. This is where they all assumed Scottish dress and drinking habits (we fortunately also favoured whisky), and did Scottish things all night, including country dancing and haggis piping. We left halfway through the festivities, and went to the local disco instead.

We had a brilliant range and mix of characters on the RatRat who always used to go ashore together, or in groups – then meet up later. One of the mainstays, was a brummie, known as 'Fart' (no explanation necessary, but he has been in touch with me recently – thanks Fart!) who, if not at the front, was never far back. We reached this disco, and he immediately invented a new dance. Called 'The Paint Shop Stomp', we only ever did it to 'Play That Funky Music White Boy', adapted from 'White' to 'Choir', as Choirboys were yet another name for 'them of different persuasion', or brown hatters. Anyway, the PSS was where you all lined up, much as you do for the Conga, only with alternate knees being thrown high into the air, whilst ducking the head. We emptied the place that night – EVERYONE in there joined us as we went outside, round the massive carpark, back in, out, upstairs – everywhere – with Fart at the front, and us giggling like maniacs!

The New Year came and went, so did we, but not without accidentally taking half the jetty with us when we sailed. Embarrassing!

Chapter 28

And Round the Windies We Go Again

First stop this year, was Belize (ex British Honduras) – now there's somewhere to avoid, from the open sewers to the mozzies, from the humidity to the warm rum. We anchored two miles off, and caught liberty boats to Belize City. We were happy to leave there. We went to Nassau again, only this time we found the beach – the previous time of course we escorted the Yacht out, and had to behave completely. Then to Barbados again, then to Freeport again, where this time we grippo'd a meal one night from someone with two enormous Dobermans, both of whom were left outside, both of whom barked incessantly, baring their teeth whenever we went near the windows. We didn't venture outside even though the owners assured us they wouldn't bite...

It must by now sound like all we ever did was eat, drink, and be merry, however, whilst alongside in Chaguaramus (Trinidad) one fine night, we left hurriedly in the direction of Barbados, where we spent several days scanning the ocean floor with our Sonar, looking for the remains of a Cuban DC8, which had blown up shortly after take off. We found both the big bits of it.

Whenever we were anywhere near Puerto Rico, we held either gunnery or aircraft exercises generally lasting several days or even weeks. We were deployed to Anguilla to land our 'booties' if the situation there deteriorated further, and landed a fifth of the crew in Dominica , to search for a lost Brit. He saw our Wasp before we found him though, so we considered that a success. A team of our guys climbed an extinct volcano on St Kitts, and we landed a work party on Grand Turk, for some 'community welfare' work. We searched for (but didn't find) a missing fisherman off Grand Turk, and laid buoys for other fishermen. We would also, always be on the lookout for smugglers, poachers, runners, and would often do a 'stop and search' whilst backing up the US Coast Guard. Even then, we would constantly be exercising the seaboat, the firecrews, the ops-room, the sonar – everything really. We did a live Seacat firing one day, against a PTA. They were always worth watching – it was a point of honour amongst the Seacat Aimers to totally take out the PTA. A near miss was good, but to totally wreck it – now that was something! Standing on the quarter-deck while one of those things blasted away from the launcher was a rare sight. Even rarer was when it burnt out on the launcher without actually launching. That would require a repainting job, as the burnout would normally take off all the paint in one go.

On virtually our final visit to Antigua, we revisited English Harbour – to find no trace of Ethel, nor anyone who remembered her. We did, however, go horse-riding up into the hills one drunken afternoon, while we should have known better and stopped on the beach. Bearing in mind I used to carry at least two cameras with me, everywhere, drunk, sober – whatever, it seemed like a good idea to ride it. The first problem was trying to get on the silly thing. Boarding a horse is difficult enough, but full of rum, carrying cameras, and with no steps to climb (to just jump on), it must be nigh on impossible. After much falling off and giggling, we cracked it, and got aboard our mounts, and spurred them into life with the usual horse-starting phrases. They stood still. We kicked our heels in – they stayed still. We swore at them – nothing worked. We were on the point of giving up, having shelled out good money, but hearing the bar calling us… …when the lead horse, with it's owner, decided to start off. When it went, the rest followed without further instruction, one behind the other – they'd done this before. No matter how much we kicked or swore, they all plodded along at the same pace, giving us ample opportunity to take photos as they ambled up the hill behind the beach, along the hill, over the streams, then started back towards the beach. We rejoined the beach probably a mile from where we left it, and were gaily meandering back towards the bar, when the lead horse started to run. I mean 'run', not 'trot'. The rest of the horses also started to run, with us saddled, drunkenly, vainly trying to hang on to horse, cameras and stomach contents. The headlong dash along the beach through the surf was exhilarating, but extremely hazardous, and it was with great relief that we got back to the bar, and refilled with Carib and Mount Gay.

My bum, at least, hurt for days afterwards, as did my shoulders and arms where I had been clutching my belongings and the crazy horse. Never since have I been on a horse.

I was QM for that last visit, and we were moored off St Johns, running the good old liberty boat. When anchored like that, we would have to check the bridge radar to check we weren't dragging the anchor, and the bridge wings were the ideal place to set up my fishing gear to while away the most boring hours. I did the 'first' one night, went off, then came back for the 'morning'. My opposite number told me that my rod had been almost dragged over the side by something during the night, but that he'd been smashed up by it. He also laughed whilst telling me this, and told me he'd changed the bait and the tactics. I reeled the gear in to find nothing on the end, so set it all up again, and rethrew it over the side. I didn't catch anything. It was only later that my opposite number told me that the returning libertyboat had actually got hooked by my rod, and that it was that which had smashed me. Not impressed was I .

We left the Windies in late February, refuelled in the Azores, got embroiled in Atlantic Winter Gales (bear in mind we had been stamping round in shorts and sandals 'till then, and it was always a great shock to change from bare knees to 'eights'), and came back into Pompey early March, 17,700 miles worse for wear.

Chapter 29

Back to Portland, Working this Time

I left the RatRat, very sadly, in the Spring, leaving behind a riot of memories.

I got engaged on my return from the Windies, and was therefore pleased to be drafted to H.M.S. Osprey, a Naval Air Station, but really the headquarters of Flag Officer Sea Training. Portland. Where all the exercises had been done so many times before.

Having struggled with all my kit from Weymouth station, and joining Osprey, I was immediately asked if I'd like to 'live out', as accommodation in the base was at a premium. On further asking, this meant living ashore in digs in Weymouth. This seemed like a good idea at the time. Further, I was allocated to 'models' up the hill from FOST, but part of the team. Ships companies ops room crews would come to us for shore based training – like Dryad, but smaller. It was my job, along with my colleagues, to ensure the smooth running of the models and the 'situations' we played out. Working there meant I was 'blue card', i.e. – no duties. Living in Weymouth AND blue card, all in the same day.

I remember doing 'Navy Days' there, and standing on the square in the base, having just watched the 'Red Arrows'. All the grockles were so busy waving bye-bye to them, that they failed to notice the Vulcan bomber sweeping towards them. As it approached, quickly and extremely quietly (due to its' altitude and speed), I slapped my hands over my ears just as it reached us. As it got in my overhead, the pilot pulled back the stick, and opened up the throttles. The deafening roar that emerged was, well – deafening. I was OK with my ears covered, but you should have heard the screaming from the general public!! That should have taught them to expect anything at Navy Days, especially at a Naval Air Station.

We would 'lunch' in Osprey dining hall, and as I may have mentioned before, I had a deep hate of Naval Airmen – believing them to be a waste of good oxygen. I have to point out this was a theory shared by all 'general service' naval personnel. The FAA only show up AFTER the hard work has been done, but just before any good runs. So general service ratings would develop ways to annoy the waffoos. One was to sneeze, loudly, and instead of 'atishoo', one would shout 'WAFFOOO', That used to hit the spot. Anyway, one lunchtime, me and Jonesy, my oppo there went for lunch, clearly not waffoo types, and commenced demolishing our food. Halfway through, I forgot myself, sneezed, simultaneously shouted 'WAFFOOO', then remembered where I was. Instead of backing down and apologising, we both cracked up laughing, much to the further anger of the airy fairys. We were still giggling when we left. If I ever needed a camcorder it was then.

As I said before, waffoos were also known as 'chockheads' as in having heads shaped like chocks, to put under aircraft wheels to stop them (the aircraft, not the chockheads) from falling overboard. In reciprocation, they would call us fishheads. Submariners were known as bubbleheads, or just 'dirty bastards', due to their habit of not bathing whilst at sea (not their fault, due purely to lack of freshwater). The one time we had a black pig moored against us, the occupants were straight on board us, down to our showers, removing layers of grime from their milky white bodies. We (fisheads) would always be brown, due to the sun at least. On submarines, they popularised the 'submariners bath'. Given that you have several minutes to get ashore (because you were too busy playing uckers, or whatever), instead of the nightly shower, you would empty most of the contents of a tin of talcum powder down your y-fronts, and in your hair (if necessary), and go ashore smelling sweetly. Subsplashers in their black pigs would do this more frequently, building up the layers of talc. No wonder they stank. Us 'skimmers' therefore had an easy life. Also, electricians were known as idle gits, or greenies, stokers as spannerwankers or clankys, radio operators as flagwaggers (always good for a wind up), and EW crew as gollies. Ops room crew were only called RPs' (but with a poofy accent). Chefs are discussed elsewhere! On the subject of 'greenies', it came to my attention one day, that no matter what piece of equipment the greenie was working on, they would usually operate one handed, with the unused hand tucked in their 'eights' trouser pocket. This, I discovered, was to prevent a bolt from live equipment arcing across your chest via your heart, stopping it instantly. The only way it could therefore go, was down. Not a bad piece of logic there, except that down meant via the wedding tackle... As I said, most greenies weren't too bright, or they'd have been doing a sensible job.

Our place of work was up the hill from Osprey, and as we were blue card, one reason was to work late nights training foreign warships. Now, the night the Nigerians crept in was the worst ever – we were there hours, attempting to make the Nigerians understand simple things, like holding chinagraphs. How they ever managed to organise and run a Navy, much less navigate accurately all the way into Portland, we never knew.

Most of the time though, we would be clearing/cleaning up the models, ready for the next ship visit, but that only happened infrequently. We would, therefore, fill the mornings with pratting about, car repairing (for those lucky enough to own one), then take it in turns to have make and mends in the afternoon. We would then scram back into Weymouth, or off home for the weekend if we timed it right.

After several days of getting a slow unreliable bus from Weymouth to Osprey, I acquired a ten-speed bike, and commuted on that, totally forgetting that where I worked was up a large hill. I eventually could climb it without running out of oxygen, but it took a while. The days it rained there though, I'd be very dejected after pedaling furiously across the causeway of Chesil Beach getting more drenched by the second. When it rains on Chesil – it really rains – there is NO shelter.

The digs were owned by a very nice chap and his very nice wife – I couldn't find it today, even if I searched all month. It was, though, very close to the beach, and also to the town. Strangely, although the digs was mostly populated by the airy-fairies, we would all go ashore together, or in my case (as I was by then saving to get married), watch telly, or find other, cheap things to do. The owners were brilliant – totally tuned in to sailors. We had cooked breakfasts, hangover cures, then back for a four course evening meal. Soup, main, pudding, then cheese and b's if you were still hungry. Sometimes, we'd go mackerel fishing, bring back the catch, and eat them either for that tea, or next night.

Interspersed with going to see my prospective wife each weekend (blue card remember – still no duties!!). This backfired one weekend though. After my Leading Seamans course, the navy invented a new rule stating all leading hands had to go on a two week leadership course, before being 'confirmed' as a leading hand. It was with reluctance then that I boarded a train at Weymouth, and caught a train to Yeovil, where we had to change lines, then catch another train from Yeovil to Plymouth. But not before imbibing of the local scrumpy while we waited for the connecting train at the second station. Thus relaxed, the remainder of the journey to Plymouth passed quickly.

We arrived at H.M.S. Raleigh – for me the first time since I'd left there in 1970 – and prepared ourselves for the first lecture of the course, the personal introductions (who am I, what do I like doing, what ship am I on, where have I been) and discovered that the following weekend would be taken up with an Exmoor yomp, plus we'd be doing PT etc every day, plus a gentle run every day, plus all the lectures, and in fifteen minutes you have to give a presentation on twelve uses for a dead dog. Or something. We thus learned the art of thinking on our feet, amongst other things. We had to stretch our man management, and while (on my leading Seamans course) I had learned how to march gangs of bods about, no other leading hand's courses prepared their particular branches leaders for that. They all worked from taskbooks, where as soon as their boss okayed it, they would be promoted. So there was me, standing at one end of the vast (even bigger than I remembered it from all those years ago), parade ground, marching men up and down the other end, shouting like a maniac to ensure they could hear me, and turn before they marched in to something (like a wall). Not to be outdone, all the other prospective leaders had to do this too.

Taskbooks, to explain, were books containing various tasks which had to be completed before the holder could go up to his next qualification or advancement. Taskbooks were the beginning of the end as far as seamanship was concerned. When I joined, you had to prove you could perform various evolutions, like rigging a jackstay, tying the ubiquitous monkey's fist, splicing nylon – whatever your PO told you to do. With a taskbook, you had to demonstrate a 'working knowledge' of the jackstay, and tie some bowlines/reef knots etc. As you did each one, you got it signed off by your immediate boss, and once you had all the necessary signatures, and you were old enough – you were promoted. So we had the laughable scenario where alleged able seamen were having to be told what to provide in order to set up for stern refuelling, or towing. Me? I would have HAD to have known that, or it would quite literally have been knocked into me. Just an aside – by this time, we had a new bunch of 'juniors' on board, who lived in their own mess. We would either teach, or torment them depending on our frame of mind at the time. Most of them were quite switched on, but one, who came from Kettering (!), was a bit different. Don't get me wrong – he was a nice lad (even though his musical taste never extended past Gilbert O'Sullivan (YEEEEUGH!!)), just that he had trouble with the old grey matter. If you taught him anything, you could guarantee he'd forget it, or have be re-told an indefinite number of times. We often used to threaten to stick our dick in his ear to fuck some sense into him. I often wonder where he ended up!!

As a matter of fact, naval tradition has unwritten rules that say if your juniors get on well with you, enough to be accepted, then you would go out of your way to, for instance, teach them how to make bell ropes, or how to splice wire or nylon properly, or how to make beermats – whatever. It follows then that these skills were only selectively passed down through the 'generations' of matelots. You had to be taught how to do it – there was no possibility you could learn these skills from any books! If you knew how to do these ornate things, you could make a small fortune ashore, in various hostelries. Or onboard, where the clankies and other branches would buy them to sell for themselves.

We did the lectures daily, we also had to give lectures, frequently, plus contribute to debates (of our own choosing), with officers etc being drafted in to answer our 'questions'. Not that they were phrased to wind anyone up, of course., especially not when we got the sky pilots in, and gave them grief. Also known as "godbotherers", or "sin-bo's'n's", the padres' would be met with mixed interest on ships. Ostensibly there to keep up morale, they would glide around the messdecks drinking beer, and talk crap. They were never addressed as 'Sir', having no rank, but we always felt uneasy with them around.

Bearing in mind there were Waffoos, stokers, greenies – all sorts, with two seamen on this course, we (collectively), on a daily basis, were given 'tasks' to resolve. The old chestnut about given planks of wood, rope etc – how do you get across this chasm populated by crocodiles. Piece of cake to us sailors – we had done it all on our leading seaman courses, but the rest had to think hard about it. We seamen were, then, usually barred from contributing, but would be there more in consulting roles, i.e. tying the knots, checking any rigging. Just my luck – the hardest one was allocated to me, where we all had to get down from the top of an old fort, and across a moat without leaving any equipment behind – not even the rope we used as a slide. I confess it took a while for me to work that out, but we did it. The scariest bit was convincing the first person down the slide that it was safe!

We also had the old conundrum about the aircraft crashing in the desert – what do you take, what do you leave, do you stay or do you go. I had to do this again some years later on a course when I left the RN, and the course organisers gave me top marks for convincing everyone to 'go'. They also had to revamp their answer – they'd always advocated the 'stay' solution, but after I'd explained my reasoning, based on sound knowledge and fact – they changed it!

The middle weekend, then, was led up to by the daily exercise, and we set off for Exmoor for two days of eating 'compo' and yomping between various Tors and checkpoints, each attended by the umpires in Landrovers, just in case of emergencies. I recall it rained that weekend (but when doesn't it up there), and again it was with relief that we finally crossed off the last of the checkpoints, and dragged our gear back to the trucks to get back to Raleigh. Things didn't change – we were still expected to have all our gear in A1 condition ready for the first lecture on the following morning.

Apparently I did all right on the course, because as soon as I got back to Osprey, I was 'confirmed' as a leading seaman, having only been 'acting' up until then.

The problem with being shore based then, was that we had to pay towards our accommodation. That got expensive for me, so I volunteered (stupid thing to do, really) to go back to sea early, specifying that I wanted a ship staying around the UK, based in Pompey or Chatham. I didn't think this was entirely unreasonable, after all, I was saving the Navy money, going back to sea with my expertise.

Chapter 30

The Plymouth? *This is the Worst Ship I've Ever Been On.*

I was therefore drafted to the Chatham based H.M.S. Plymouth at the end of the year. I had never been to Chatham for more than three days before, and that was just for 'Navy Days', so – gullibly – I looked forward to being based nearer my home.

However, if there was one ship that came as a surprise to me – that was the Plymouth. Let me say that on the first page of this history, I pointed out that if you couldn't take a joke, you shouldn't have joined. I admit it – I couldn't take this particular joke. The Plymouth was the worst ship (to paraphrase the Beach Boys) I've ever been on.

After having two nice shiny, clean, fairly modern 'Tribals', this was a run down, smelly, grubby, rusty, ancient 'Type 12' frigate, which, when I joined it, was languishing alongside a dark part of the dockyard. It didn't look impressive, though to be fair, it was where the Argentine surrender was eventually signed after they were kicked off the Falklands some years after, so it is now classed as 'historic'. Hysteric may be nearer to my memory.

First night aboard, I slept on somebody else's unmade bed in the after sailors mess, constantly aware of the smell of fuel oil and sweat. After the cleanliness I had become accustomed to on the Tartar – this one was disgusting. Next morning, after I had been greeted by 'Bert' Clisby (another Leading Sailor, always giggling or laughing about something), who made me feel very welcome, I went through my joining routine, whilst we sailed for Portland for a week, before then sailing for the Med for three months. Was I impressed with this so far.

The only thing I found different on here, was that in our 'mess' (literally) we had an old colour TV. This had been commandeered from somewhere, and bore pride of place above our mess 'bar'. It had an aerial attached, which had to be positioned on the upper deck through the partially opened hatch leading to the quarterdeck, and most of the fun was setting it up well enough to get a clear(ish) picture. Eventually though we would be able to distinguish images, and through trial and error, and a lot of shouting through the chain of people from viewer to adjuster, we would finally be able to understand. Peculiarly, the mess members would all come to a standstill at 'Crossroads' time, and watch intently as Amy Turtle went through her nauseating paces. I could never, ever stand watching crap like that, though it seemed to be a religion on the 'Gob. I must admit I gladly watched Kenny Everett, and Magic Roundabout. We would laugh like loons at these two. It transpired that it didn't matter where we tied up, we could usually get a picture on that ancient telly, even in the States.

We were trialling IRBs' then, rigid hulled, inflatable sides (like the RNLI still use), powered by extremely powerful 40HP engines. I was now happy-ish, 'cos I was 'boat party'. We trialled against regular seaboats from other ships doing 'man-overboard' exercises, and found we could be dropped, pick up the 'body', get recovered and be out of the water and secured while any opposition was still chugging towards their 'body'. This was because we could drop this beauty whilst doing up to twenty knots. We would start the outboards, drop ourselves onto a convenient wave, bang it into ahead, and scream off into the distance. We would recover, and hurtle back alongside the ship, still shifting rapidly, secure to the crane/hoist, and be back on board ready for the next one.

I found this thing was jack-proof. Whatever you did it was forgiving, like spinning the wheel right round whilst touching 35 knots had no effect on the boat, but you got whiplash injuries. It would skip all waves, and bounce any sea state. In effect – this was fun!!

Except for the one day when we anchored off Penzance, and the skipper decided he'd go ashore for some reason. I drove the IRB into the tiny, walled harbour, with him scowling at me in the back. We went alongside, and 'waited there' for him, only after an hour, we got bored, and went separately to find him, via a couple of bars and pints. We got back before him, and he decided he'd drive the boat back. He revved the engine, slapped it into 'forward', and drove straight on to a mudbank in the harbour. He immediately vented his fury on me, asking if I'd checked the tides etc before we left. 'Of course I did, I checked the chart with the Navigator, and he also reckoned plenty of water in the harbour' I replied, 'But we didn't know we'd be this long'. I carefully extracted it from the mudflat, got off the driving seat, and sat down at the front. He got the message, and drove the boat sedately back to the ship. The subject was never raised again, but he frequently tried to get his own back on me.

More fun with it which should clear up a long standing mystery of what kept me – we had to go to get rid of the remains of the Eleni V, which was doing a good job of sinking out in the North Sea. I recall we were in Lerwick at the time, either that or we had called in for fuel. Whatever, I was detailed (as boat driver) to slip the Plymouth from the jetty with my boats crew. I was then to drive the boat out, play catch-up, and be recovered. We stood on the jetty, slipped the ship, and watched her sail off, quickly. We stayed near the boat, but not exactly making any hurry to return. The reason, you see, was that the locals, who had come to see us off, were brandishing bottles of whisky in our direction, and giggling. In view of prying binoculars from the bridge, we dropped into the boat, and made 'engine starting movements'. Despite our apparent best efforts, the engine would not start, and it required several large slugs out of the proffered bottles to help us. As the ship disappeared round the headland, we began to get 'What is the problem?' messages on our radio, to which we replied 'Engine won't start – think it's flooded. We will try again shortly'. The only thing we flooded was our mouths with the mostly single malt whisky. After some time, we started slurring into the radio, and decided we'd better go now before we got into real trouble. We had one (or two) last mouthfuls', kicked up the outboard with the first actual turn of the key, shouted our thanks, and took off at the maximum speed (as I said, around 35 knots), posing really, after the Plygob. We very quickly caught it up, and having told them we were on the way, she was already doing 15 knots or so. I got the boat alongside right away, hooked up to the winch, and was back onboard before you could say 'whisky'. I got rocks for that too, but steadfastly blamed the engine. Since no-one could prove anything different except my bowman, and he was also pissed…

The Eleni V was eventually sunk by us planting PE all round the visible front end. We blew the bows off it, and watched it sink, to join all the other hulks at the bottom of the North Sea. We had stopped in Rosyth to load the PE, and had actually sailed with several tons of it stacked on the flight deck. No smoking, or what!!

More risky business related to the earlier described 'Dog Hunts' – we were due to exercise with Hunters, or Phantoms or something who were to strafe and bomb splash targets towed by us at high speed, These targets were wood and metal rafts, towed well behind us, and were configured to throw a large plume of water high into the air. We asked for, and got a volunteer to be splash target cox'n. This person, as I remember, had an unhealthy preoccupation with his bits, and was always to be found with his hand round them. He also had abnormal ears, thus the nickname 'Wingnut'. He also had the brain of, and was as useful as that after which he was named. However, he temporarily let go of his own tackle, collected his bagmeal, radio, boots, gaiters (standard gear), and mustered on the quarterdeck ready for his training. The buzz had gone round well on this one – we lined the AX, and the flight deck, wardroom were there too. The MUPPET listened attentively as the gunners told him how he was expected to report the fall of shot from the strafing back to the ship, who would then relay it to the attacking aircraft.

He was shown how to use a rake marker, and sat on the splashtarget at the arse end, as people ran towards him simulating shot. They would hit the deck in front, behind, and to the side of him, he then reported back as 'left 100', or 'over 200' etcetera. We got bored after half an hour or so – this kiddy was particularly obtuse. We rigged two (hidden to him) fire hoses. We told him that if he got hit on the head, he was to shout "Direct Hit", but that clearly if it was a direct hit – he would get wet. Now what kind of a moron do you think would sit through this? Would anyone in his right mind actually volunteer to sit on three pieces of wood being towed at twenty knots or more , as Hunters shot live ammunition at it? Armed only with a bagmeal and a radio? So as one chap ran down and smacked him on the head, he screamed "Direct Hit", we opened the nozzles of the previously charged hoses to simulate the hit, and nearly knocked him overboard. Straighfaced he was asked – "OK, that was excellent – do you need another practice" – the dipshit replied that he would. Once more our trousers became extremely wet. It was a long time before he lived that down, it still brings a smile to my face.

On the subject of names, all Smiths' were 'Smudge', and Browns were 'Buster'. On here we had a Hardwick – known as 'Softjob', but otherwise people were given names to match their profile, i.e., Wingnut above, Alligator, because of his twitch that made him appear to be biting things, whatever they reminded us of. Continuing this vein, everyone from 'the west country' was called Jan (from Janner), it was assumed everyone from anywhere near Sunderland was in fact a 'monkey hanger' (guaranteed to get an instant fight), and that all Yorkshiremen were considered to be 'a cross between a Scotsman and a Pig' (also followed by a punchup).

We eventually got to Gib, where we were to be Gib Guardship over Christmas. Lucky me – I got to be crew on the MFV which was to prowl the straits while the ship sat alongside. We were 24 about for that, and guess who was even lucky enough to be 'on' on Christmas Day? We'd sleep on the 'Gob, then walk through the yard to the MFV. We'd then spend 24 hours catnapping and prowling, cooking our own food, before going back on board, by which time we'd be ready to go ashore. It seemed it was a much-coveted duty, but I could be wrong. The rest of the crew were all good, as was the officer in charge. So the day we all strolled down towards the MFV, and found a yacht crew clearly in distress, we had to assist didn't we? Fortunately, we had the bottle opener the chap needed, then tasted both his beer and the scotch. We finally got on the MFV slightly the worse for wear, and it was still only 0800!! I don't remember what his problem was, but he was alongside at the time...

As I said, then we'd take it for a little look round the yard and the straits, then come back, eat, sleep, sail, sleep, eat – whatever order. Then go ashore properly, to have our ears battered (everywhere we went) by 'Mull of Kintyre...'.

On Christmas Eve we were 'off', and got totally legless along the strip, before going to 'The Hole In The Wall' (is that still there) down by the border. When we got back in the early hours, we slept until shaken, then blearily made our way to the fishing boat. I think we all virtually collapsed when we got there, I certainly missed most of the day.

All too soon, we were back on the 'Gob, and sailed for Toulon for New Year. We celebrated twice, once for French time, then for UK time.

We then sailed to Haifa, which has to rate alongside Norway as 'The Most Unfriendly Place I Have Ever Been'. We were rejected, ejected, and couldn't wait to get to our next stop. We did, though, get a trip in to Jerusalem and Bethlehem, very poignant considering the time of year, and Jerusalem has so many beautiful sights and things to see. We were only there overnight though. We returned to Haifa, then sailed immediately, overnight to Port Said. Having just had a bad experience, we weren't looking forward to this, but found to our astonishment that Port Said was brilliant. We started by inviting aboard the 'Gully Gully' man. A magician, who had entertained passing ships for years. We all mustered on the flight deck, having all paid a couple of quid each for his performance. To my further amazement, I was dragged by his assistant from the audience, to help him. I suddenly found live chicks being extracted from all over my body, plus playing cards – I really enjoyed that. Plus the bumboats alongside (lessons learned by me from Freetown all those years before) where we bought copious amounts of oranges, and ate them all – turning our skin yellow in some cases. Then we found the ships caterer had bought loads too, which we were then expected to eat AFTER our own. That was another good point about navy food – wherever you went, you'd get local bread, local fizzy drinks, sometimes local veg, but always we'd get fresh local fruit. If we got wind there was watermelon or strawberries – a queue would form at the galley door. We also had a fridge in our mess, where we'd put our tins of drink, and God help you if you were caught drinking someone else's freezing cold savings. This is also where we'd stash our nutty, in the fridge, to keep it cool, or in the ice section, to make Mars Bars chewier!!

A trip was arranged to Cairo, which I immediately put my name down for. We left, driving down the Nile to Cairo – the most heavily populated place I have ever seen. We ate 'al fresco', devouring grilled chicken, and meat in olive leaves. Absolutely gorgeous. We went out to the Pyramids, which I had never noticed were actually stepped, not smooth sided. We rode camels down to the

Sphinx and back, then climbed up and into the Great Pyramid which held the tomb. That was easily the spookiest, eeriest, and most impressive thing I had ever seen or done, before or since. The atmosphere inside that pyramid was indescribable. We ascended a 45 degree tunnel to the sarcophagus chamber, and gazed round in the creepy silence. It was difficult to imagine you were so far inside that ancient structure. So, so impressive. It makes the hairs stand on the back of my neck even thinking about it now.

We returned, and fed, again, then went back to the plateau later, for the 'Son et Lumiere', which entailed sitting far enough away to see Pyramids and Sphinx, alternately lit in different colours, while a running commentary was given relating to 'What May Have Happened' all those thousands of years ago. Followed by the floor show in a huge tent, with local dancing, including the belly dancer. Guess who she dragged out of the audience to dance with her?

We got back to the ship next day, totally elated from what we had seen.

At some point, Malta was a port of call, again – I always liked it there. This time we arranged the legendary Malta Dog Hunt, watching with incredulity as the latest batch of baby sailors volunteered to march up and down the jetty with gas masks and bag meals. Strangely, the midshipmen were always volunteered for this. They always got the biggest laughs. The 'dog' hunt rates alongside getting people to volunteer for MUFF diving (Marine Underwater Fire Fighting) courses as a constant source of wind-ups.

A couple of us organised a (genuine) fishing trip one afternoon, and cadged a boat which took us round the coast to a small bay. We disembarked, and fished, waiting for the boat to come back. Only it didn't. We waited longer – still no boat. In semi-desperation, we went walkabouts, only to find a village just around the headland, with several bars – and no sailors, apart from the six or so of us. We then discovered that not only was the beer very cheap, being well off the beaten track, but that the local wine delicacy (Marzavin) was only ten pence per bottle, and that when mixed (as the locals were doing) with Seven-up or lemonade, it tasted great, and had no effect until you attempted to get vertical. Then you had problems. I remember the locals getting us a taxi to get back, but forget the actual journey.

Sliema harbour on Malta is a wonderful sight, all walled with fantastic buildings etc, and a trip into the town, steeped with history for many centuries going back to knights and Moors was always high on the list of things to do in Malta. Oh yes, and going down to the world famous 'Gut' was always worth an evening. The Gut is an area of the town, just connecting alleys and streets, mostly full of bars believe it or not, where it is possible to drink all night, and to not find the bar you were in last night the following day. Compare it to a rabbit warren! We returned from the Gut one night to find the lift which took passengers from the top of the harbour wall to the bottom had stopped, so it was with trepidation that we descended the wall and lift slowly by ourselves, climbing carefully through all kinds of prohibited areas to get back to the base of the lift. From there, on customs jetty, you would then hail a passing harbour boat, pronounced 'Dyso', for the trip back to the ship, which would normally be moored near H.M.S. St Angelo. On no account, though were you allowed to fall overboard from the boat to escape paying the boatman – the harbour was literally filthy, we were told. These boats would always be painted in garish colours, with large eyes to scare off evil spirits, and each boatman spoke enough English to try to charge you extra, or sell you something you didn't need.

Returning to Chatham, we stopped via Bayonne in France, and got well acquainted with the local wine, beer and Ricard. However, we were scorned for putting Ricard and red wine in the same glass. It goes a funny purple colour, but tastes reasonable.

Whilst there, and QM'ing one day, with a severe hangover, it was decided to sail in the afternoon. I was therefore the driver, sailing the ship out (at Special Sea Dutymen), obeying the orders relayed from the bridge. As I was not yet sober, I could anticipate severe problems, the biggest two of which were a) I was going to be sick – SOON, b) I couldn't see straight. Nevertheless, I signed on in the wheelhouse. I recall the wheelhouse had a porthole out onto the forecastle, and remember my so-called mates grinning at me through the closed window, and I don't know how I survived – but I did. When I was finally fallen out, I carried my bucket to the heads, and cleaned it out, before collapsing on my pit, fully clothed, for a well-earned rest. I was fortunate to get away with that – it was a very narrow river, where any error on my part could have parked us in Bayonne town centre.

Chapter 31

Married Life Lasts Several Weeks, Then Off to Canada and North America

We reached Chatham in one piece, and I finally got married to my pen-pal, enjoying several weekends of being together before we once more sailed, this time for Canada and the US.

We exercised all the way out, with me made to now operate on the anti-submarine side. This ship didn't have air radar – my speciality, but we could turn our hands to anything. So there we were calculating probable submarine positions from their last known, so we could at least make a best guess as to where they'd pop up. We therefore had to be spot on with our calculations, or we'd be miles out. If, however, we resumed contact, we'd be heartily congratulated on our REL-VEL (relative velocity) skills, and earn the praise of the PWO and captain. However...

We had light moments, me and Ben Cartwright. We would be the chief sodder-abouters, and we would therefore find new ways to wind people up. One way was to award ourselves decorations made from paper, which we taped to our shirts. We then crossed swords with this lieutenant from Scotland – a really foul, bad tempered, nasty bastard he was, promoted 'from the ranks', and out to make his mark by shouting to impress his superiors... He would want information from you 'immediately', and, even though we were both capable of very quickly assessing and calculating what he wanted, and giving him the answer 'immediately', there was no way he was going to get it 'immediately', for two reasons. A) we only just got the info to work out the answer, I'll have that in two minutes, sir (spelt C.U.R.), B) say please you Scots git. We could play him brilliantly. One day, we stuffed cotton wool into our ears and feigned ear infections, meaning if he wanted something from us, he first had to attract out attention by getting in our line of sight. We would then raise a warning finger and point to our headsets then at him to indicate we were getting a message over our ship-to-ship radio, then we'd take off our headset, and say 'WHAT?. Sorry, What SIR?'. At which point he'd be on the verge of apoplexy. His rantings would possibly impress the captain, but cut no ice with me or Ben. When this 'officer' started raving at me one day, I took it all, then calmly announced that I had this ear infection, and that whilst it appeared I could hear him, I was actually listening to other ships radio traffic, and that I couldn't hear him then, due to the cotton wool in my other ear –

look at it. I have a painful ear, caused by having to wear manky headsets with unwashed covers. Also, just because I was looking in his direction while he shouted at me, it didn't automatically follow that I was looking at him, but at the callsign board behind him so I could work out the other ship in our group, who was attempting to relay vital information to me about their new submarine contact. He ranted more, I tried to keep a straight face, put the headset back on, turned my back on him and started talking back into the radio. As 'PWO', he was more concerned about keeping 'the battle' going (therefore had to rely on me and Ben to give him all that very relevant information), than he was about calling our bluff there and then. That would have made him look even sillier in front of the captain, and the rest of the ops room crew.

So, hours later while I was off-watch, I was summoned to his cabin (cabin nine), along with the Ops room PO, where this alleged officer, otherwise known as a total arsehole, attempted to give me a dressing down. I stood and accepted all he had to say, queried whether I was supposed to ask him who was in front of me to wait, or to hold off the person on the other end of the radio, in another ship, miles away from us, who was giving us valuable data about the submarine contact which we were chasing, and whether he would prefer I was to miss that and give him another reason to shout at me. He accused me of being subversive, of undermining his authority. ME??!! I was then threatened and finally ejected from the cabin. Next time I went on watch I had a new decoration – CTC9 (called to cabin nine). Ben and I fell about after that, as did everyone else who knew about it. Pompous bastard. Like I said, I always got my own back.

I wonder what happened to him, nothing too nice I would hope.

I always liked the surface side, as I said before, I know I was extremely good at my job, at playing with radar, and could work out the course, speed, closest point of approach, course to intercept – any relative velocity problem, either by eye, or shortly afterwards. It was therefore decided in someone's extreme wisdom to take me off ops-room duties, except for exercises, and dedicate my skills to upper deck duties, starting with being quartermaster for a while. That suited me just fine!

This as previously described, included standing on the gangway checking the crew on and off, ensuring the ships' security, and standing on the gangway. This happened day on, day off. It was the days off that were best.

We stopped at St Johns, Newfoundland, (closed the day we were there), and Summerside, Prince Edward Island, happily coinciding the visit with their lobster carnival. Everywhere sold lobsters, and I've never eaten so many. Apart from that, we were invited to the Canadian Forces base for the evenings. These started out with indoor games – darts, pool etc. Then we progressed to 'chug-a-lug', or what we'd call boat-races. This entailed sitting like a rowing eight, each with a glass of beer. On the command, the first would scupper his, and put the (nearly) empty glass upside down on his head, which was the cue for the next in line, and so forth, until the last glass was empty, therefore the winner. This happened several times, with us winning each race. Soon, we got bored, but the Canooks wanted to raise the stakes. We then started boat-racing with 'Swamp Water'. This, we discovered afterwards, was made up from cherry brandy, gin, vodka, lemonade, orange squash, and lemon squash. Which gave it it's title – a muddy drink. The kick from this came later – drinking it was the easy part. We had several more races then, until the poor Canadians' legs started to malfunction, at which point we proclaimed ourselves the winners, permanently. I don't remember how we got back that night…

Halifax, Nova Scotia – scene of many historic convoys gathering – came and went, before we then found ourselves in Bridgeport in Connecticut. As quartermaster, still, I drove my first car, a loaned, left hand drive automatic, and came very, very close to parking it in the sea.

By now, a small gang had been established by four or five of us Leading Seamen, called 'The Crunch', one of whom – Mitch (who I am still in touch with and who won the pools whilst still in service), had several endearing habits when drunk. One was to eat beer glasses. This would happen AFTER he'd stuck his thumb in his mouth and blown down it, inflating his chest as he did so. Each time he did this, his shirt would rip. Funnily, just like the 'Incredible Hulk'. This was a terrific party trick of his. Mitch was my best mate, and he'd often pull these tricks to impress, or to annoy. One night, he went ashore while I was QM, and we later got a call from the Bridgeport Police, saying they had Mitch in hospital. Allegedly, they had tried to remove him from somewhere, he hadn't wanted to go, and he stuck his thumb… The police panicked, and hit him with a nightstick, which only enraged Mitch. They continued to hit him until he went down, at which point they wrapped him up and took him to hospital. He was back next day, very sheepish, with several bandaged lumps round his head. For our part, we swapped badges, hats all sorts of things with the police. Also, Kev Hexley, (who would call everyone either a Growbag, or a Bucket (of shit)), plus Mac the Gunner, and THELMA (The LMA – the rating doctor on board). We got to be a tight group before getting split up yet again. When in our cups, we would sing the 'Rambling Club' song :-

"We are the Plymouth Rambling Club
We ramble on from club to club
All dressed up in our rambling suits
You'll always find us pissed as newts.
So raise your glasses way up high
We've found a pub that's never dry
We are the Plymouth rambling club
We ramble on from pub to pub to pub to pub to pub... "

...to the tune of 'Oh Christmas Tree'.

While we were there, we hired a car, six of us got in it at 04 dubs one morning (just after I came off the hey-diddle-diddle), and we drove to Niagara Falls, just for the day. Another very impressive, not to mention unforgettable sight (we did get around), although we had trouble at the border. We saw the falls from the US side, but wanted to see from the Canadian side. We asked the border police if we could, they said no. We pointed out we'd been in Canada just three days earlier, and that we had passports, and that we were English sailors. The guard agreed, and over we went. On returning several hours later, the guard had gone 'off' – his mate knew nothing about us. They had to make some urgent, panicky calls to several places before they finally acknowledged we were who we said we were, and let us back in to the US. We hightailed it back towards Bridgeport, got lost, fell asleep, got stopped for speeding – fortunately, as we were going in totally the wrong direction – and finally got back to the ship minutes before we were due to be back on watch. We were totally exhausted, and slept dressed as soon as we next came off watch, and had to be shaken roundly to get up for the next one!

The Sunday we were there, we got the AMTRAK down to New York, New York, and spent a memorable day walking Fifth Avenue, trying to get to the Statue of Liberty from the Empire State Building. I'll rephrase that, we came out of the station, eventually, and immediately found the Empire State Building, which we entered, caught the lift to the top, and exhausted our camera films on everything there was to see. Then came the death drop lift back to the ground floor. One of our gang, Kev, assured us he'd been here before, and therefore knew the way to the ferry. Not only that, it wasn't that far. Accepting this, we set off, but by the time we'd been waylaid by record stores, bought an LP called 'Bat Out Of Hell' by a chap called 'Meat Loaf' a long time before it got popular, and whatever else was open (not much on a Sunday morning), we found we were still heading the right way, but were still miles away. We got a taxi in the end. We crossed on the ferry to the Statue, queued for hours, got the lift halfway, walked the rest, and eventually reached the top of the head, where we marvelled again at the view. Then we descended, dashed back to the station, and caught the train back to Bridgeport. Amazingly, when we sailed, we actually drove round the bay and Island before returning to the UK.

I forget where we were at the time, but it was Easter Sunday, and we were at sea, so we held an impromptu 'Easter Bonnet' competition. We all turned to, creating our variously themed masterpieces, but as we were at sea, and I didn't feel like celebrating – being away from my wife – my creation was a black top hat, combined with my navy burberry, with a black sash round the hat, like undertakers wear. I than drew up a placard saying 'Easter Is Dead', and won first prize. I guess everybody else was not too happy about being at sea, on Easter Sunday, on the 'Gob.

One (or two) things about returning to the UK after time away, is that of sailing up the (English) Channel. This isn't yer ordinary sailing up the channel. This is sailing up the channel flat out, overtaking everything on the basis that if you're going past it, it can't come back up your stern. What it does require is an excellent radar lookout, reporting all contacts that may come within a mile of you ONLY. Normally, you see – you'd report everything, inside ten miles, inside five – whatever the 'orders' were. Channel – forget it – one mile circle only. We'd be responsible for the avoiding action, especially trying to miss the ferries travelling across the bows rather than towards/away from you. Bearing in mind we'd probably be kicking better than twenty-five knots, you can imagine how on the ball we'd need to be.

So it was a peculiar thing that we'd always have channel night on the approach (I'm not just talking about the Plygob here), where we'd all get totally shitfaced, if possible, on all those crates of beer we had stored up over the preceding months. Channel night, then, consisted of probably a 'Sods Opera', or just sitting on the arse-end throwing beer cans into the towering wake off the back, as they became empty.

Sods' Operas' were impromptu evenings of entertainment, shall we say, which would have been practised for days or weeks beforehand, and would be skits or sketches taking off whatever we felt like. These ranged from 'Chelsea Pensioners' to Mr Men, to songs, comedy acts, impersonations, magic shows, all done very much tongue in cheek. Chelsea Pensioners was several people in a line, slouching on chairs. At the command 'Chelsea Pensioners – AteeeenSHUN', they would sit up straight, eventually, groaning. It would then go to 'Quick March', when the 'pensioners' would pretend to propel the (wheel)chairs with their hands. It would then go to 'Double March', at which point their little (old) arms would propel them at top speed. But it was the order 'HALT' which would collapse us – the 'pensioners' would be trying to slow down the 'chairs' with their hands, but as they were at speed, they would be burning their hands from the friction of the turning wheels, and cursing, and spitting on their hands. You need to see it!!!

Mr Men is 'bellies', with giant hats worn covering the arms, upper body and head. The 'belly' then has a face painted on it. The belly gyrates, the hat wobbles – again, hilarious.

Another – 'Three Shits', is a demonstration of the three services toilet habits. First, Percy Pongo, 'eft 'ight 'eft 'ight HALT About FACE, two three, trousers off two three sit two three strain two three grunt two three, wipe bum two three etcetera. Next RAF – mince in, wipe toilet seat, delicately sit down, contort face, daintily wipe bum, apply talc, dress, mince off. Finally, Jack (pissed), stagger in, throw up, take dump, remove trousers and perform 'grand-slam (puking whilst dumping), clean self up, grumbling all the time…

My favourite was – Rating goes into sick-bay, says "Doc, I have a sore throat". Doc says "Have a gargle from this beaker". Rating does so, and leaves, feeling much better. Next Rating goes into sick-bay, says "Doc, I have a stomach ache". Doc says "Have a good drink from this beaker". Rating does so, and leaves, feeling much better. Next rating goes into sick-bay, says "Doc – I'm having trouble passing water". Doc says "Hmmmm – you probably have a 'dose', I'll need to test you – piss into this beaker". Again – you have to be there.

Or we would 'skit' the captain or the officers, or an event which pissed everyone off on the trip, knowing that there was nothing 'they' or anyone else could do about it. We would let off all the steam we had built up over the previous months at sea in just a couple of hilarious hours.

So that was Channel night, always a good evening, unless you had 'the middle' on the way through, but always something to look forward to.

We got back to Chatham, into that terrific dockyard where even though you were tied up alongside, you still had to use the 'shore heads', and night buckets which some poor devils needed to empty each day (by taking what was left to the shore heads, from below decks, up the ladders, over the gangway, off the other end, over the road…). Several buckets full of drunk sailors urine was always guaranteed to provoke retching by the carriers. No wonder most of it either got poured into the showers, or straight over the side. Not many people were stupid enough to carry it all that way.

One bloke onboard, Chats, was the son of a London policeman, and he arranged for a run one night to his Dad's local, with all his Dad's mates – all coppers. Actually, after catching the train to London, then taxi'ing to wherever, we had a good night. Until we came to get back to Chatham. One of the idiots we took with us decided to 'perform' on the train, before we left Victoria. For my part, I was talking to some French people, swapping the ability to swear in each others native tongue. The moron, slightly less capable of holding his ale than most of us, performed, and allegedly smashed a window, at which point the transport police were called out, and we were all dragged off the train. Except the PO in charge of the party, and his good friends. Which left me to carry the can. Eventually, the Cementheads (Naval Shore Patrol) got off their backsides and arrived, at which point we were passed from the transport police to the navy robots, then actually individually interrogated (no other words for it) until they thought they'd got to the bottom of it. We were after some time allowed into the back of the paddy-wagons, and taken to Victoria, where we were unceremoniously put on the train. We all, by now, knew who was to blame, but no-one had said anything to the cements. We arrived back at Chatham, were rounded up again by the 'cements', and ferried back to the Gob. More or less right away, I was forced into my best suit, to attend 'Captains Table', facing charges of whatever the on board Police could dream up. While the Captain went red-faced and ranted at me, I confirmed that I was talking to French people and was unaware of what the clown was up to. I was eventually sent away from his table. My D.O. told me later that the Captain wanted my blood for that, but that even he could see I was not to blame. Funnily, nothing ever happened to the PO in charge – maybe because he was a 'field gunner'. I exacted my revenge on the clown who caused me all the grief though – every time after that I was Duty Leading Seaman, (and he was in my watch) guess who got detailed to be shithouse cleaner for rounds? ...And had to empty the piss-buckets every time I got the chance to enforce it?

Another 'run' I remember, was when several of us went to the 'Monarch' not far from the dockyard gates. This was a dive in all the traditional sense. It had stools at the bar, it sold scrumpy, and you could buy T-shirts and badges proclaiming you were a 'Monarch Marauder'. Except for the night I remember falling backwards, unaided, off one of the stools, laying in a heap on the deck. Why – I don't know. If I can remember doing it – I couldn't have been that far gone. They also had several TV/computer games in there, which, after some practice we got quite good at.

Another gang on the Gob, was made up from ex field-gunners, and their acolytes. The field gun looks great on the TV, and is very exciting live, but once the volunteers are accepted, something happens to them – following the brain removal, charisma bypass and deliberately induced psychotic personality disorder, they become incapable of rational discussion. I'll rephrase that – they become incapable of talking about anything EXCEPT field gunning. Day, night, ashore, onboard – fieldgunfieldgunfieldgun. It tends to become boring after several seconds – the ex gunners don't notice you falling asleep though, and assume your head is nodding in agreement. The hangers-on are no better, and there were several of them on the 'Gob, much to us sensible peoples' disgust. Field Gunners were the worst at attempting to 'black cat', however it must be said that they would say anything to get other peoples attention, and make total fabrications up, just so someone will listen to them. There is always someone stupid enough to believe what Field Gunners drone and drivel on about. The phrase 'Strong of arm, thick of head' describes them accurately. To finish this bit – most people who volunteer for anything do it for the skive, for the crack, and for the chance to meet interesting people. Ask yourself – does this sound like field gunners to you?

We would liken them to Domestos – Thick and Strong, or wonder, loudly, how anyone could be so big, so strong, but so FUCKING USELESS!!!!!!

On the other hand, as all matelots were in a 'command'. I was Portsmouth Command, and proud of it, then there was Devonport Command, and finally, were the waffoos, in the Fleet Air Arm (Command). You were put into a command when you signed on, and that is why my official number started with a 'P', and Guz ratings were all 'D'. Until the Admiralty made us all 'D'. I digress, whenever the Royal Tournament was on, and the Field Gun Runs proper took place, we would have the latest times and placings displayed on the Ships Company Notice Board, and we would groan loudly when our 'team' lost, and take the piss, noisily, when they won. To remind you, we all still loathed the FAA.

One chap on there who was always good for a laugh, was 'Bud' Abbott. He was a waffoo, with a predilection for the falling down water. He could snore for England when pissed. He could also fill peoples wellies up during the night, actually thinking he was in the heads. Other people would struggle into lockers and waz in there, or find quiet corners, but they WOULD be asleep, and WOULD think they were in the right place. The one night Bud slashed in my 'bats' I immediately emptied them out over him again while he slept. I didn't put them back near him though. He was warned thereafter (as were others I really did take a dislike to) to 'sleep with one eye open from now on...'.

On the subject of trouble, on most navy ships, there is a 'Bosuns' dinghy, occasionally thrown into the sea for (normally) the wardroom to play with. On the Tartar and the Zulu I had launched it on numerous occasions, recovered it as often, and had known that you would put the thing on a 'shot mat' to drag it to awkward places. The 'shot mat' is normally put by the guns to soften the impact of discharged shells hitting the metal deck, though they have other uses. So when I was asked to move the dinghy, I got all my lads together, lifted it onto the shotmat, and we manhandled it to where it needed to go. Somewhere in transit, a ringbolt went through the mat, and made a small hole in the side of the dinghy. This was not a major disaster – it would (on a sensible ship, with sensible shipwrights and sensible officers) have taken perhaps three minutes to mix up some fibreglass resin, and apply it. Not that the Plymouth contained any of the above. Within minutes of me telling the shipwright of the accidental damage, which I fully expected him to either repair, or give me the makings to do it myself, I found myself once more in front of the OOD, then the Captain, on a charge of negligence. I pointed out that in all my previous years, that was how I had achieved moving dinghies, and once more was sent away, with the captain once more red-faced from his shoutings. They were definitely out to get me on that ship.

Chapter 32
Dryad, *again…*

Very happily, and finally, I left the Plymouth well behind me in Chatham, and started a short spell at Dryad, while waiting to get my real draft, to H.M.S. Londonderry.

Many years later, I discovered the Plymouth moored at Plymouth as a tourist attraction, and while I tried to convince the then civilian crew that I could find my way round it blindfolded, he still wouldn't let me on for free. Perhaps he had heard it all before. I didn't feel too sad, I had a bellyful of that ship over the time I was on it.

I arrived at Dryad one weekday, and was told I was to be Quartermaster there. I asked when my first watch was, and was told 'Sunday, Afternoon'. What am I supposed to do 'til then?'. 'Go home if you want' came the reply. I did. I came back Sunday lunchtime, started my 'afternoon' watch, and within hours of me being there, a fire alarm lit up in an accommodation block. I 'piped' for the duty watch, rang the fire brigade, and watched the action. Within minutes, the fire was out, the fire brigade arrived, walked round – and went home again. I finished my duty, and went sleepy-byes. Shortly after I finished the 'morning' on the Monday, and only moments after my tired eyes closed, I was ordered to report to the (retired) martinet, sorry – Lieutenant, who allegedly ran Dryad, who demanded to know who I was, and what I was doing, more – how had I known what to do when the fire was reported. I responded that I had tried to find what to do, but had been told to go home, that when I had reported there the previous week, no-one was at all interested, and that it didn't take a moron to work out the alarms, nor what to do, nor how to do it. We never saw eye to eye after that.

Having spent many hours patrolling Dryad on previous visits, it was now my turn to direct the patrols, and woe betide them if I didn't get my coffee – frequently. One day, whilst we were at a high state of alertness, an officer entering the base got stroppy with the main gate sentry (controlled by me), demanding to be given admittance. I think he had forgotten his ID card, or something. Whatever, he got stroppier, and the main gate sentry then radio'd me to ask what should he do. We clearly had our orders to not give entrance to anyone without an ID card. I suggested the sentry make the officer get out of his car, while the sentry examined it, minutely, including using the provided mirror-on-a-stick to check beneath the car body, plus the boot which had to be emptied, and the bonnet which meant searching the engine compartment, and making the officer explain each wire in it. After nearly twenty minutes, the officer was really, really fuming, at which point we finally let him in. I got a further bollocking from the martinet over that one, but us ratings thought it put us ahead – at least the officer didn't try that one on again – he remembered his ID card the next time.

As QM, we also used to haul the ensign up during divisions every weekday morning, under the watchful eye of the aforementioned lieutenant, just in case we weren't capable of doing it by ourselves, without his assistance. We'd then hurtle back into the lobby as all the classes marched off, before leaning out of the window going

'Schloop Schloop Schloop' in time with the WRENS as they marched off. (Think about it).

Mitchell was drafted to Dryad at the same time, so we continued our friendship, also teaming up with another man – Hall. Eventually, all three of us would end up on the 'Derry, and we grew as thick as the proverbial thieves while waiting ashore. Hall was married, so we'd go to his house on occasions, to play with his Scalextric (Honest!). We would, though, divert past his local to fill up, then take some 'carry-outs' back with us.

Chapter 33
H.M.S. Londonderry

I was eventually taken off QM, after months of weeks on, days off, which really did wonders for my married life to date, and assigned to 'models' at Dryad, with the standard blue card. Now I could get home at weekends, if only I could afford to.

Models there were fun, we learned all about the shiny, brand new, very expensive computer assisted radar installed on the Derry, and how to use it. It was nearly as good as me at working out courses and speeds... We were assigned to 'staff', which meant listening on the radio between models, recording it all, highlighting idiot bits, then picking holes in whoever it was at the post exercise debrief.

This visit, time passed quickly, and we left Portsmouth for Rosyth once more, but not before the whole of the Derry ops-room crew plus the officers had been to Dryad for a week training. We left for Rosyth en masse, but split up for weekends on the way. This first weekend, Mitch, Hall, me and a couple of others had arranged to get the overnight train from Kings Cross, which called at Stevenage, where I got on. The lads had the compartments organised, and the beer, but when we stopped at Peterborough, Mitch and I ran to the nearest hotel for refills. At around midnight, then, we decided to try to get some sleep, and crashed out one on each seat, one in each luggage rack. This was our norm for the overnighter to Edinburgh. However, wise to what happens throughout the night – the continual stopping, the continual door opening/slamming/'Move over please', we set our 'anti-disturb' traps. This took the form of two tins of vegetable soup, tipped one outside the compartment, one inside. I don't need to describe what it looked like – needless to say, we were NEVER disturbed.

The Derry was of the same class and therefore the same age as the Plymouth, but without armament – she was now a trial ship, testing a new propulsion system (different shaped propellers), and trialling new radar, which explained the after mast, much higher than the foremast. And the hutch beneath it, with computers and boffins ensconced inside.

For my part, I was detailed for upper deck duties, leading hand of the watch on deck and i/c of the fo'c's'le, both jobs I thoroughly enjoyed.

Also LHWOD's were Mitch, Hally and Shiner. We would have boat drills every time we went to sea, and as LHWOD, it was our job to drive the boat. The first time I took it away, I got back alongside, where Shiner, Hall and

Mitch were lining the flight deck, arms behind their backs. To my question 'What the fuck are you doing', came a display of score-cards, like they do with ice-skaters, giving me my 'score' (up to a maximum of '5' each) for performing the recovery. I nearly fell out of the whaler laughing. We carried on that tradition, no matter who took the boat away after that. It was deemed that all leading hands should do it, so stewards, cooks, stokers – whatever, all lined up to take the boat away (remember, you dropped the boat into the sea onto a wave, then had to rebuild the disengaging gear before being hoisted again), and getting their score afterwards. Terrific fun, lots of laughs on a very relaxed ship.

We also did upper deck duties – I was i/c of the fo'c's'le as I said, Shiner was Quarter-deck. One day, both watches (of seamen) had to put up the awnings, to make sure they fitted, and went up ok. Foolishly, the Jimmy announced they didn't look right without the wind to billow them out. Solemnly, Shiner lined every sailor up with his respective nose inches away from the awning, and commanded 'On the count of three – blow. One, Two, Three – BLOW'. We did, we fell on the floor laughing – even the Jimmy saw the funny side of that one. Not that the Jimmy needed any effort to wind anyone up.

We were still in the cold war then, and while we were stamping round the North Sea one day, we were approached by an AGI – a Russian 'trawler' bristling with EW gear, determined to take a good snoop. As I said – we were unarmed, unless you counted the 'spud locker', but looked very impressive, with large masts. With great presence of mind, the Jimmy instructed us to drape canvas over the seaboat oar stowage (all in full view of the AGI remember), then put the 'DANGER, LAUNCHER MAY TRAIN WITHOUT WARNING' signs (left over from when we had teeth) on the stowages. The AGI obviously felt it had a scoop here, and made several passes with cameras going at full steam while we sat still for them. I wonder what they made of it? Or whether they knew we were winding them up? Or that we had a new and secret propulsion system.

It was nice to get back to Rosyth, to recall old runs and old stamping grounds, though at the drop of a hat, we'd volunteer for all sorts of courses in the south, just to get the weekends at each end of it. I went on one to maintain the ships' onboard liferafts with their automatic pressure releases, plus the ships stock of lifejackets. It also meant learning how to board rafts and repair them – extremely useful for me, and especially useful for the RN, who by then knew I was nearing the end of my twelve year contract, which I was not likely to renew. It did, though guarantee two weekends at home – one at each end of the course.

One morning we woke up to find an enormous lampshade in the mess. One of those voluminous paper things, many feet in diameter. I have no idea how it got there, but remember seeing several of them hanging from a ceiling in one of the bars we stopped in. How the hell did anyone manage to get that off the ceiling of a packed bar without anyone noticing, and how did it get back from Dumfs to Rosyth without being spotted? And how did it get past the gangway crew, down two flights of stairs, and into our mess? Five of life's' little mysteries...

In my duties as LH of the fo'c's'le, I was in charge of it, but second to the officer, whose name I forget. One of the highlights of my job was that I was allowed to work the cable without anyone standing behind me saying 'not like that', or 'you're not allowed to do that – you're only a rating'. This came about one day when the officer was late getting there, and I had to get the anchors (hooks) ready to drop, as all ships did at special sea duty stations, just in case of emergencies. I requested permission to work the cable, and was told yes. I got the anchors ready to go, capstans steaming – the lot. I was greatly pleased with myself. The officer (therefore 'the bridge') would subsequently allow me to do it without interference. A further job was, when getting alongside, we'd pass heaving lines, and attach mooring ropes to them, which were dragged ashore. We'd then tighten these up before securing them. The trick was in knowing when to pay out – when to take in. Assuming that the wire cables (springs) would take the strain of a two and a half thousand ton warship stretching it, it was then my job to gauge the strain by attempting to depress the spring with my foot, listening for it singing, assessing how much more strain it could take before parting and killing most of the handlers. I got good at that, and never damaged anybody. Also, the headropes, made from nylon, would crack alarmingly as pressure came on, worrying the hell out of anyone nearby. I'd nonchalantly kick the rope again, deciding when to give and when to take in on the capstan, winching and inching the ship nearer to the jetty, to allow securing as directed by the bridge. I used to love doing that. I also was greatly elated by being allowed and trusted to do it.

We also used to set up for all evolutions like RASing – on a normal ship, it needed at least a chief petty officer, the Derry had four extremely capable leading seamen – any of whom could at the drop of a hat do any of the jobs normally only done by the aforementioned chiefs. We had a 'buffer', a petty officer, but he knew he could let us get on with it, and did. It ran extremely well, we always did it professionally, and correctly, and we never, ever fouled up or took advantage.

Plus all the other bits, like the constant painting and repainting, cleaning, washing, deck scrubbing, and the hosing down contests between 'parts of ship'. We would hand out make and mends like sweets, which, it seemed to us only encouraged our juniors to work harder, and we wondered why it had never been tried before. It made sense to us – put the time in, get the time off, at home, because they were 'RA's.

We actually had a banyan one Sunday at Rosyth – a gang of us took the seaboat away, with some crates of ale we 'found', plus a couple of loaves, and two cooked legs of lamb nicked from the galley while the chefs backs were turned. We motored to just past the Rail Bridge, got near to the shore, threw the anchor over the side, and sat in the sun all afternoon, fishing, yarning and emptying tins until just before we were too drunk to drive it back. Very restful.

Apart from the sudden training courses we used to volunteer for, we discovered that the RN was holding a fleet-wide tug-of-war contest. Several of us put a team together, and commenced training. This involved many things, amongst them running daily from the ship to the Gym at Cochrane, being dive-bombed by a rogue shite-hawk that lived on a building, and which hated humans. We got him, though it took us a while. We'd then exercise vigorously for some while, and run back to the ship... We'd also pit our strength against many more people than the eight of us, always winning (well, nearly). Just to ensure more weight 'redistribution', we scrounged NBCD suits made from clear polythene, and found that whilst wearing them, we would sweat heavily, therefore – lose weight. More properly 'redistribute' our surplus bits of relaxed muscle (fat) into proper muscle. That was the theory at least... Then we'd get changed, go ashore, and drink copious amounts of 'heavy', then eat haggis suppers or Chinese takeaways'. Eventually, when the big day came, the Scottish Command teams all met at Cochrane, were we pulled every bit of competition right away. We were therefore Scottish Command Champions, with the medals to prove it. As the PTI was in our mess, and all the other leading hands, he convinced the powers that be to feed us special diets on top of all the above mentioned. We'd therefore get steaks on demand, instead of the other excellent food already there. That was great, while it lasted!

As Champions there, we were then able to compete at the next level, i.e., the whole of the navy. With great anticipation we set off for Portsmouth again on the train, with the obvious weekend en route. We then reached the playing fields at Dryad, where the events were to be held. We got through the first round, then went ashore to celebrate that. We went to Sid's place, and imbibed of the old wine mixture, then found our way back, via Dots', then to bed. When we crawled out the following morning, Mitchell and me were summoned to the Regulating Office, where we were interrogated about an alleged incident the previous evening. Apparently, a Reliant Robin, innocently parked within the base gave the owner a surprise when he inspected it – it had miraculously overturned itself during the night. Imagine that – trying to blame me and Mitch for it. We knew nothing...

Whatever, it must have affected our performance in the tugawug, as we were knocked out in the second round. The week's jolly in Pompey therefore got cut short, and we returned to Rosyth, with our tails between our legs. Well, until we got on the train, and all mustered at the buffet.

I mentioned daily orders before – these tell you of the next days events, 'both watches of the hands' (time to get up and go to work), lunch (for RPs, dinner for everyone else), duty watch, duty PO, rig of the day, etc. We used to do the orders on an old typewriter, then print them out on an old Gestetner, before distributing them around all messes, offices etc. We had a strange habit, though, of slipping naughty bits into the orders, vertically. For instance, a separator line might be all FFFFFF across the page, which looked quite attractive, but if the next line was UUUU and the next was CCC, then KKK, then OOOOOO, followed by two lines of FFFF – you begin to see what I mean. On a Friday, the lines would spell POETS (Piss Off Early Tomorrow's Saturday), or FOREST (Fuck Off Reasonably Early Saturday Tomorrow), or FUFUFFFH (Fed Up, Fucked Up, Far From Fucking Home). Funnily, while most of the junior ratings saw through it – no-one else ever did., or if they did – they never told us.

Eventually again, we sailed from Rosyth back down south, back to Pompey at last, but via Hull where we had a quick weekend. During this weekend, we, as usual, challenged local teams to play us at Rugby, so it was with hangovers that we turned up to play, I think, a local Police team. Mitchell and me used to play 4 and 5. We changed, groggily, then mooched out on to the pitch, almost ready to play. Mitchell still had one up his sleeve. He waited until both teams were gathered for the 'riot act', walked over to the ref, indicated a hideous Neanderthal throwback on second row of the opposing side, and in full earshot of everyone, including the caveman, said 'Before I play against that – I want to hear it talking first'. We collapsed laughing, the caveman got stroppy, and we ended up playing 'dodge the fist' in all the scrums. That was a dirty game. By full time, though, we were all best of friends, and celebrated as only rugby playing matelots know how! At least, we didn't get nicked whilst we were there.

On the way, we exercised with an ageing Hunter, who was trying out our new radar, and who was being controlled from our gloom room. As I said, I was i/c of the fo'c's'le, and nothing to do with it, however each time he flew inbound, he just happened to roar over the fo'c's'le at virtually no altitude and made me and Shiner jump. It wasn't the kind of thing we were expecting, so he caught us out two or three times. We – of course – gave him the two-fingered salute, which clearly made him want to do it again, and again. So we started to keep an eyeball watch for him, and the next time he did it, we were ready for him, and started slinging brooms, deck scrubbers etc at him. We had not a chance in hell of hitting him, but next time he came back in, he kept a respectful distance and height while we again saluted him... ...I swear he was grinning at us that last time!!

We recommissioned in Portsmouth, and entertained our wives and families in our cramped quarters. One thing about recommissioning, or any other major event in the ships calendar, was that the food was outstanding. Especially when all the leading hands were billeted together on the Derry, including the cooks and stewards. We fed well that day, were waited on, and got the best food (after the wardroom). WE knew who ran that ships' routines...

My last few months were taken up with my EVT (extra vocational training) course, which everyone leaving the forces gets. I had expressed a desire to get involved with computers, having seen how powerful they were, and applied for a six week course in Wandsworth, which I knew I had no chance of getting. There had been a cancellation shortly before I applied, and I found to my amazement that I was getting placed on it. Unfortunately, this meant that I had to live at home for six weeks (with my wife – remember her?), and commute from Hitchin to Wandsworth daily, ...while the navy paid for my travel, oh and they also paid me much, much extra to live at home. I couldn't believe my luck. I even met an old mate from the Tartar on the course, so we spent six weeks doing lectures and site visits, with the obligatory pub visit each and every lunchtime, with a special one on the Friday, prior to sliding off home early. I will point out, that when I left for the course, my regulation haircut was longer than normal, due to having avoided the on-board cementhead. After the course, I deliberately went back to the 'Derry with my hair even longer, solely to wind up that same cementhead. My hair survived slightly longer than it took the top of his head to blow off.

ROMFT is a word every tar will be familiar with – it is the word that appears on the guitar of one of the members of, I think, 'The Spinners'. I wonder if he is aware what it means – I guess he does. ROMFT is the expression used by disgruntled jacks, after – for instance -he has had to get up at four in the morning to check the mooring ropes, after some panicky, junior officer of the day has decided, wrongly, that the wires need slacking off. This evolution usually takes place three hours after he last got you out to tighten them...Or when he is roused for 'action stations' minutes after he has finally got his head down. Or – the list is endless. ROMFT stands for 'Roll On My Fucking Time'. It has been quoted for years, and obviously means 'please let me out of the navy, soon'. ROMFT ratings are created as soon as they see an end to their naval career, say after their D-By-P (discharge by purchase) had been granted, (or worse, if it has previously been refused) or when they are within months (or even years) of the end of their contracted service. ROMFT ratings usually begin to suffer from chronically severe RDP (run down period), and run down, quickly. You get no sense out of them from the last few months/weeks/days, as they cross off another day from the obligatory countdown calendar. ...And mine was a very large calendar!!! I always maintained that WHEN (no, not 'IF', but, categorically 'WHEN') I went outside, I would sweep roads rather than re-enlist. "You'll be back", or "You'll sign on again within a year" was the favorite wind up for those too far away from their own discharge, and yes – more than a little jealous. I swore vehemently they'd never see me again. Sorry fellas, I miss you all, some more than others, but I was right, I had the last laugh – you didn't.

Chapter 34
My Final Farewell to Arms

Again, it is not possible to describe my feelings over my last few naval days, apart from a growing elation, but summing up this previous large part of my life, career and personal development would cover attributes like pride in oneself and the Royal Navy : absolute professionalism – being able to do anything with any equipment at the drop of a hat under any conditions or circumstances : the ability and eventually the willingness to do anything for ones mates, but not necessarily for anyone else : and the comradeship which totally ignored anyone else from any other walk of life, ship, or organisation. These qualities would apply through thick and thin, hell and high water. And the dedication we all had to see a job through, whether we had volunteered, or been volunteered. We used to say "the quicker you stop fuckin' well moanin', and get it done, the faster you get back to fuckin' bed". How true. How very, very true.

Finally, you would always know that although your best oppo had just called you all the bastards under the sun, and a few more choice names besides, and had then threatened you either with physical violence or a chair, all because you'd just given him a whitewash at uckers, and then accused him of not being able to take a joke, but you'd know that minutes later he'd be crying like a baby on your shoulder because he'd just got a 'Dear John' , or worse – no mail at all, and that ten minutes after that, you'd be poncing a tenner off him to go ashore, finally asking him to 'stand in' for you, while you went ashore and pissed his money against some far flung wall, ensuring you always had enough to bring him some big-eats back, even if it was by then cold, and that, while now totally shiters, you shook him at three in the morning, unable to comprehend why he was now telling you to "Fuck off'n getcher head down, yer pissed". Now THAT is comradeship, that is what mates are for, that is what the Navy is all about.

However, my day finally came, and I left the Derry and my mates, who all fell in, piped me over the side and saluted me as I left for the short fast-black journey from the dockyard to the dispersal section of H.M.S. Nelson. I handed in all my gear (over a three day period), gave back my ID card, (but renewed my passport, just in case I needed it in the future), had an exit medical, assured them I didn't need the dentist, and left the base with just my grip filled with my remaining personal possessions and civvies, thinking about not having to shepherd pissed matelots any more, not staying awake half the night on a cold gangway, not having to get up at oh-five-dubs to weigh anchor then RAS, – actually to a life full of 'nots'. Now I was going into a normal job I organised during my final few months – programming computers – and here I was, heading home to a normal life with my wife who I had hardly seen since we married, looking forward to getting up at sensible times. Funny, the hardest thing I had to adapt to, was getting out of the habit of going into a pub, and getting as pissed as I could as cheaply as possible in the shortest space of time. It took years to break out of the habit of knocking a pint back in two or three hits!

I strode – no not marched – strode out of the gates of Nelson, turned left, ambled in a very leisurely manner up the road, past all my old haunts, takeaways and food stalls, en route for the last time to Portsmouth Town Station, and without looking back, I boarded the train, with my final, free, Navy issue one way ticket to Hitchin. While I was on that final free train ride, I left behind all those memories, all those escapades, all those mates, all those experiences, all those runs ashore, all those buzzes, all those…

…however, although I was JACK, and really didn't give a flying fuck about anyone or anything at the time, I get the shivers down my back every time I hear that Naval hymn ('For Those In Peril On The Sea'), and even now (even as I write this) the tears roll copiously down my face whenever I hear the Last Post, or see the Poppy Day, or even think about either of them…

You see, although I was safely installed in 'civvy street' by then, I lost mates on the Sheffield and Coventry and Amazon – I'll never forget, nor will I forgive Argentina for that, but I'll always remember my mates. The peace treaty was signed on the 'Plymouth', if you remember, and a bomb actually went right through where I used to sleep. Last black cat was that!

Two final things. First, the answer was pennant numbers, and the ships' nameplate. There you are, naval expert, and you didn't know that!.

And the second thing – a final sea story. You know when you and your kids scream "OGGY OGGY OGGY" whenever Devonport do their field gun run at the Royal Tournament? Well, I have to tell you, that phrase comes at the end of THE filthiest (lyric wise) song we ever used to sing, containing subject matter ranging from camels orifices' to tramps, paint to people from Cornwall, and Aladdin and his famous magic lamp to Indian currency. I leave it to your imagination. And if you don't believe THAT particular final sea-story, you can always ask your mates' Uncle… and if he doesn't know, then you KNOW he really was making it up all that time, don't you…

Glossary

(for those who really do not know!)

Aggie Westons	The Royal Sailor's Rest. Originally created by Dame Agnes Weston as a temperance hostel for ratings, and usually abbreviated to 'Aggies'.
AX	The quarterdeck (QD). If the fo'c's'le (sharp end) is the FX then the quarterdeck at the opposite (blunt) end – and known in Tudor times as the Aftercastle – is the AX.
Bends	Knots!!
Bins	Binoculars. Very much prized rabbits, if you could manage to get away with it.
Black Cat	Sea Story.
Black Pig	Stinking, sinking thing which sails underwater, a sludgemarine (submarine).
Booties	Royal Marines, Bootnecks, who I actually have a lot of respect for no matter how much I took the piss.
Budgie	Smelly paraffin drinking thing, Parrot, Helicopter. 'No smoking on the upper deck abaft the after funnel – helo ranged' was a pipe on the Tartar which used to strike hatred and more loathing (toward waffoos) in our hearts. 'Hands to flying stations, no smoking on the upper deck' was worse. Every time it took off and landed our after-mess used to stink of AVCAT. Deeply uncomfortable during night flying, something else that used to keep us awake.
Buffer	The Chief Bosun's Mate, a senior Petty Officer/CPO in charge of all seamanship operations on the upper deck. 'Buffer' is THE buffer between 'the jimmy' and the lads.
Burbs	Burberry, any kind of raincoat. A Wanchai Burb is, though, an umbrella.
BWH	Both Watches of the Hands. 'Start Time' for real sailors, 0805, five minutes after 'Colours'!!
Carry-On	After piping (see below) The Still (see below) then you would pipe the 'Carry on'.
CDF	Common Sense (work it out yourself, but it involves dogs)

Clanky	Any marine engineer, more specifically a former stoker who has allegedly trained to be a 'mechanician' – a half-price tiffy. See 'tiffy'
Closed-up	'Closed up' (at Action Scractions) means all on board are ready to defend the ship from any assault.
Cockies	Cockroaches. Bombay Runners are frighteningly large cockies, and will continue to move even while you put your foot on them.
Compo	Ration Pack, mix everything together (except the toilet paper, fuel blocks and matches) and trough it! (see Trough).
Cooks	(1) Cooks of the mess, your turn to clean up everybody else's crap, normally after everyone else has gone to 'both watches' to turn to. (2) Navy 'cooks' like to think of themselves as chefs, but as we frequently pointed out, chefs have to be trained...
Crabfats	Members of the 'junior service' – the RAF. The colour of their uniform, introduced in 1918, is similar in colour to the ointment (known as crabfat) issued to the troops in the trenches, which was applied to deal with body-lice. CRABS!! Whenever we noticed RAF people, we'd click our fingers (like crabs claws) and start to walk sideways. Unsurprisingly, they would react badly to that.
Crash Out	(1) Sleep (2) wash (nix & sox) by hand.
Daddy-D	Captain D, the Captain commanding a Destroyer (or Frigate) squadron, when they used to exist. When I was around, as well as the ships serving away from home, there were normally a dozen or more destroyers AND frigates (plus the sweepers and pigs over in Gosport and 'up the Creek') in Pompey or Guzz any day, and more at weekends. Portland used to be full every night, with more 'anchored out'. Rosyth used to hold several more, and those figures did NOT include those in refits. What happened?
Desert Wellies	Suede ankle-boots as worn by the Eighth Amy in WW2. My favourite shoes. Could be used from slippers to flippers, at a push.
DF	(1) Duty Free, as in booze, ciggies or rabbits from abroad, or (2) Direction Finding as in HFDF (huffduff).

	'Duff' also means defective.
DI	Drill Instructor.
Divisions	(Diversions), a parade with all the ship's company mustered by divisions. Each bunch of sailors ie RPs, TAS, Gunners, Clankies, Greenies, Sparkies etc, is a 'division, and no matter what 'rate' you are, you are in that division. For example, from the PO(PRI) to the Junior Seaman (RP), they would ALL be in the RP Division.
Dogs	(1) Dog Watches – 1600-1800 was the first dog, 1800-200 was the last dog. (2) Dogs, doggo, ugly. Another favoured word was Gronk, as in 'going gronking' or having 'gronk trapping contests' at the local hops. Ashore in Pompey, that sometimes backfired, as YOU could be the gronk captured by one of the local ladies, especially if the hop was at Vernon or Nelson. Also 'wolverines' as in 'rather chew your own arm off than wake it up to say goodbye'. (3) A severe dose of the shits generally after a bad beer (or few), or even worse, local big-eats. (4) a 'dog hunt', usually in Malta, but could be anywhere, looking for fictitious dogs, when really it meant 'the shits'.
Double	Run, at double-quick time.
DQs	Butlins, Detention Quarters – the RN's own prison, until recently in Portsmouth Dockyard, attached to what was HMS Victory, now HMS Nelson.
Dubs	as in '04 dubs', 0400, 04double-oh.
Fanny	Large mess utensil, the derivation is from 'Fanny Adams', but it is a long way round!!
Fast Black	Taxi. It is NOT recommended to ask, drunkenly, 'where can I find a fast black' in the Windies…
FES/Fez	Far East Station.
Fo'c'sle	Sharp/pointed end, the bit that hits gophers first.
FFB	Fast Patrol Boat.
G6	Gas Turbine Power Plant.
Gemini	Semi-rigid rubber boats, coveted by booties, sailors were not allowed to mess with them nor the matt-green

	'Johnson 40' engines used to propel them. Booties, if not found anywhere else on board, would always be otherwise found flushing and cleaning those engines in large freshwater tanks in the 'waists'. (Waists were decks that ran either side of the ships, normally covered in wooden decking).
Gizzit	Give us it.
Gloom Room	The Operations Room, where RPs live, in the dark but warm, with only (warm) radar/displays and (warm) UV lights for company. Also a drop-in coffee shop for a privileged few with something to swap.
Gopher	(1) A soft drink. (2) A bloody big wave you just ploughed through, which temporarily hid everything for'rd of the bridge screen
Greeny	Anything holding something resembling a screwdriver, but not necessarily holding it at the correct end. Generally found slouching by a junction box, with one hand in it's pocket.
Grippo	A generous person who pays for your entertainment, usually a 'local' or a 'navy fan'.
Guzz	Plymouth – there are as many different explanations for this as there are pubs in the city!!!
Hey-Diddle-Diddle	I've got the 'middle' watch – 2359-0400.
Hitches	More knots, slightly harder to tie.
'Ho'	The Navy's executive order to 'stand to attention'. From being 'A-tten-SHUN', the 'shun' rising to a squeak (which would carry), it then became A-tten-hun, then 'hun', then 'Ho'.
Hooly	(1) A messdeck party, usually an illegal one. (2) A storm at sea or otherwise, known as 'blowin a fuckin hooly'
IS	Internal Security (riot control).
Jack-proof	Trust me – NOTHING is totally 'jack-proof, but if it nearly is, then it must be good.
Jackstay	The line sent across between two ships alongside at sea, RAS'ing. (see RAS), across which men and equipment can be transferred.
Jimmy	Second-in-charge of a ship, the First Lieutenant, Jimmy-

	The-One.
Joss	Jossman/Master-at-Arms, or one of the regulating petty officers, the ship's police, and normally the most unpleasant and unpopular person aboard...
Liberty Boat	Used to get you from ship to shore, and (sometimes) back again. Normally the ships seaboat/whaler, but sometimes a civvy boat. NB – the difference between a ship and a boat is that ships carry boats... Black Pigs are also 'boats'.
Libertymen	Anyone legally allowed ashore for leave.
Make and Break	Make and Mend, originally meaning a tar's free time to make new and mend, and now any free time. You get a M&M if you did the middle last night.
MFV	Motor Fishing Vessel.
Mod Plod	MOD Police, who used to provide security for dockyards. Also unpopular, especially if they caught you with too many DFs in your bag, causing you to be sent back to your ship for immediate 'stoppage of leave' (and trooping).
NBCD	Nuclear, Biological, Chemical Defence.
Nutty	Any kind of chocolate, from 'fruit and nut'.
Oggy	Tiddy Oggy, Cornish Pasty
Oppo	A particular friend, from 'oppo-site number', the chap in the opposite watch who had the same duties as you.
Ovies	Overalls.
P7R	Temporarily medically unfit to go to sea.
Parrot	The Wasp: that bloody paraffin drinker again.
PE	Plastic Explosive.
Pipe	(1) A broadcast, providing information over the ship's tannoy system. (2) a Bosun's Call. (3) 'Pipe(ing) the side', 'officially' getting the skipper or any visiting dignitary aboard with the maximum amount of fuss and bother. Normally, a 'piping party' would be fallen in to do this, but usually, only one or two of them (the best ones) would actually 'pipe', the others would inflate their cheeks, put their tongue over the hole, and waggle their fingers. The only thing better than 'piping' from a bullshit position, was to get the marines booted and

	spurred and doing 'the present' with SLRs.
POS	Part Of Ship, where you work. Also 'not my part of ship' when trying to wriggle or skive out of something.
PTA	Pilotless Target Aircraft, operated by waffoos, fantastic when the Seacat aimers shot them down: poor waffoos had to – grumblingly – build a new one for us.
Pusser	The Andrew, The Navy
PWO	Principal Warfare Officer – the officer running 'the battle' in the gloom room, in the absence of (or supporting) the Captain. Very very easy officers to wind up.
RA	Ration Allowance – if you were RA, it meant that you were living at home (while alongside), and in receipt of 'RA', rather than living on board. This didn't stop 'RAs' from thieving more rations on board, nor from scrounging mine, nor from illegally taking meals. Who'd drop them in it? What would they gain? RAs traveled from miles away to be aboard before leave expired at 0745, but were also the first ashore at 1615. Many a mad panic occurred as RAs ran up gangway seconds before their leave expired. More so when they noticed their civvies had been hidden just before secure...
Rabbit	Formerly a piece of dockyard material unlawfully 'borrowed permanently' for one's own purposes, and by extension, a rabbit-job came to mean a semi-official job done by the dockyard for ones greater comfort/efficiency on board. In turn, this was extended to mean any present taken home for one's family or friends. Also used as a verb – to 'go rabbiting' means to go shopping for presents, or to 'go on the scrounge'.
RAS	(1) Replenishment at Sea. (2) to not really steal, but to acquire permanently what wasn't yours in the first place.
RatRat	Endearing term for H.M.S. Tartar.
RDP	Run Down Period – the period towards the end of a commission, or near the end of one's 'naval engagement', when a 'couldn't care less' attitude prevailed. See ROMFT
RFA	Royal Fleet Auxiliary

ROMFT	Roll On My Fucking Time – a cry frequently heard when one had 'had the Andrew up to here…'. Originally Roll On My Flippin' Twelve, once the normal length of service in the mob.
RP	Radar Plotter, the most intelligent, always in the warm, first for lunch, first for everything!
R&R	Rest and recreation.
Scratcher	Backscratcher. Your rack, your 'pit', your bed.
Scribes	A writer rating – 'masters' of clerical and accounting procedures, unless they got your pay wrong on payday, in which case they were as verminous as the rest of the 'S&S' (supply and secretariat) division.
SNLR	Services No Longer Required – busted, thrown out of the mob ignominiously.
Splice	(1) Splice the mainbrace, give everyone a tot of rum. (2) Splice a rope/wire – put an 'eye' in, or secure the end of a length of rope/wire/nylon. If you could splice well, your services were in demand. If you couldn't splice, then you were treated like an idiot. Fortunately, I spliced well, and still can. A favourite 'challenge' was 'Reckon you're clever? – then put a backsplice in this' – while holding out a single hair…
Still, the	The 'alert' made on a Bosun's Call.
Tea-Boat	Nothing that floated – the tea-boat was the contents of a corner of the Ops Room, or mess, or wherever tea, coffee, kye, or 'makings' were kept on the brew. Akin to currency, if another POS or department ran out, you could call in a favour and ponce off someone else, or owe a favour for the future.
Tiffies	Artificers, allegedly the Navy's skilled technicians, either greenies or clankies.
Trooped	Caught in a misdeed, and charged with it. Served you right for getting caught in the first place. Long Service/Good Conduct Badges were issued in the knowledge that they showed a number of years of undetected crimes.
Troughing	Eating greedily, as in 'troughing nutty' during the dogs, before supper.

Turn To	Get to work. After BWH, your captain of your part of ship would say 'right, let's get turned to'.
Waffoos	Fleet Air Arm, originally WAFU (wet and fucking useless). Loathed by all 'General Service' ratings, and always treated like the scum they certainly were.
Weekly War	A pretend war – generally off Portland and anywhere in the Channel, in which many (remember when we had 'many' ships and aircraft?) ships and aircraft operated together over a period of days, to 'fight' hostile forces from other (RN) units. Actually good fun for the most part, except for the Wednesday morning 'weigh anchor' at 0400, just as the Buccaneers rocketed overhead.
Windies, The	The West Indies, everybody's dream commish (cruise).
Windy Burbs	Short windproof jacket.
WOD	Watch On Deck.